DATE DUE

			PRINTED IN U.S.A.

TWAYNE'S
ORAL HISTORY SERIES

Donald A. Ritchie, Series Editor

DONALD A. RITCHIE

DOING ORAL HISTORY

TWAYNE PUBLISHERS
An Imprint of Simon & Schuster Macmillan
New York

PRENTICE HALL INTERNATIONAL
London   Mexico City   New Delhi   Singapore   Sydney   Toronto

Twayne's Oral History Series No. 15

Doing Oral History
Donald A. Ritchie

Copyright © 1995 by Twayne Publishers

Twayne Publishers
An Imprint of Simon & Schuster Macmillan
1633 Broadway
New York, NY 10019

Library of Congress Cataloging-in-Publication Data

Ritchie, Donald A., 1945–
    Doing oral history / by Donald A. Ritchie.
        p.   cm. — (Twayne's oral history series ; no. 15)
    Includes bibliographical references and index.
    ISBN 0-8057-9124-8. — ISBN 0-8057-9128-0 (pbk.)
    1. Oral history.   I. Title.   II. Series.
    D16.14.R57   1994
    907'.2—dc20   94-20304
                                                              CIP

The paper used in this publication meets the minimum requirements of American
National Standard for Information Sciences—Permanence of Paper for Printed
Library Materials ANSI Z3948–1984.♾™

10 9 8 7 6 5 4 3 2 1 (hc)
10 9 8 7 6 5 4 3   (pb)

Printed in the United States of America

To Anne Ritchie

Contents

Most human affairs happen without leaving vestiges or records of any kind behind them. The past, having happened, has perished with only occasional traces. To begin with, although the absolute number of historical writings is staggering, only a small part of what happened in the past was ever observed. . . . And only a part of what was observed in the past was remembered by those who observed it; only a part of what was remembered was recorded; only a part of what was recorded has survived; only a part of what has survived has come to historians' attention; only a part of what has come to their attention is credible; only a part of what is credible has been grasped; and only a part of what has been grasped can be expounded or narrated by the historian.

Louis Gottschalk, *Understanding History* (1969)

Introduction and Acknowledgments

"Oh, you do that *vocal* history," someone once said, trying to fathom oral history. That identification was half right, since oral history thrives on talking, largely by the interviewee. The interviewer's job is to do thorough research beforehand, then ask meaningful questions, suppressing the urge to talk and listening instead. Yet it always seems amusing that oral historians, who have disciplined themselves to be silent during interviews, behave so loquaciously when they gather at professional conferences. The truth is that oral historians love to talk. As the only historians who deal exclusively with the living, they have to be convivial enough to establish rapport with interviewees, to put them at ease and encourage candor. Practitioners of the craft of posing questions, oral historians also find themselves constantly questioning their own concepts, methods, and applications of new technology. Those who collect the voices of history make their own voices heard on how to do and use oral history.

It is impossible to pinpoint a place on the globe where people are not now doing oral history. Since the appearance of the first recording devices, from wax cylinder to wire recorder to reel-to-reel, cassette, and videocassette tape, interviewers have questioned politicians and protestors, indigenous peoples and immigrants, artists and artisans, soldiers and civilians, the sacred and the secular. Oral historians have recorded the reminiscences of survivors of the Nazi Holocaust, the Japanese-American internment, and the Soviet gulags. Interviews have also captured the everyday experiences of families and communities, whether in inner cities, satellite suburbs, or remote villages. When historians came to realize that women and racial and ethnic minorities were missing from the pages of most history texts, oral historians recorded their voices to construct a more diverse and accurate portrait of the past.

Archives of oral history interviews exist throughout the world and in every state and territory of the United States, ranging from a few tapes housed in the local history collection of a neighborhood public library to thousands of transcripts preserved at major university libraries. Inside the federal government, oral historians have collected testimony about national parks and historical sites, diplomatic maneuverings, military strategies, intelligence activities, space flights, and social security and welfare programs. Over time, this information has been returned to the public in countless books and articles, museum exhibits, folklife festivals, radio programs, and documentary films.

The real impact of the oral history movement may not be fully realized until the next century. Although the earliest recorded memories date back well into the nineteenth century—one transcript at the Columbia Oral History Research Office contains firsthand recollections of the bloody New York City draft riots of 1863—most of the collected interviews have been with contemporary figures discussing more recent events. Individual researchers do not always need to wait for archival oral history collections to release interviews; armed with their own tape recorders, they can go forth themselves to question whoever is willing to answer. But as generations pass and participants in historic events are no longer living, future researchers will have to depend on what earlier interviewers collected, processed, and deposited in archives. How will these future researchers judge our work? How much of today's oral history will be considered an important supplement to the written documentation of this century, or dismissed as superficial and superfluous? How much of what we do will be preserved, and how much will be lost? Oral historians need to look beyond their own immediate needs to consider the corpus of work they will leave for the future.

Doing Oral History raises many questions and provides answers that address the range of current practices and considerations. Its question-and-answer format is intended not as a catechism of the true faith but as a dialogue between the reader and author, similar to that of an oral history interview. Questions ranging from the open-ended ("What is oral history?") to the specific ("Should transcripts reproduce accents and dialects?") are intended for those conducting group projects, working as individual researchers, establishing oral history archives, videotaping, teaching, and seeking to make use of oral histories in various forms of public presentation. These questions have repeatedly been asked at oral history workshops, particularly by those just entering into oral history. The answers offer realistic and practical advice while maintaining the standards that oral historians have collectively devised and promoted. Some questions come from more established practitioners who are reevaluating their methods and missions midway through their projects. The answers seek to be as serviceable to veterans as to novices.

Early in the oral history movement, the director of Columbia University's Oral History Research Office, Louis Starr, lamented the absence of manuals for interviewers but wondered how useful any single book would be, since every interviewer would have a different personality and style and every subject would have its distinctive requirements. Subsequently, manuals and fieldwork guides have appeared in profusion, reflecting the many disciplines that employ the interview technique and differing according to the standards, practices, and technology at the time they were written and the backgrounds and interests of their authors. Historians, archivists, librarians, folklorists, anthropologists, educators, journalists, linguists, and gerontologists have contributed to the burgeoning literature. This book draws from that body of scholarship as well as from my personal experience: as a historian, I use interviews as part of my research, and I conduct an archival oral history program for the U.S. Senate Historical Office. Although my work has been largely in political and public history, my service as editor of the Twayne Oral History Series and my contacts with the many state, regional, national, and international oral history associations have given me opportunities to view the far reaches and creative diversity of the field.

From 1988 to 1991, I coordinated the efforts of the Oral History Association (OHA) to revise and improve its professional code of principles and standards and its evaluation guidelines. In such a fluid and dynamic field, these fundamentals plainly needed reexamination after a generation in use. Several appointed committees addressed interviewing, processing, videotaping, teaching oral history, the roles of independent researchers, and ethical issues. The committees discussed and debated every conceivable aspect of oral history and presented their findings at the OHA's annual meetings, first in Galveston, Texas, in 1989, and the next year in Cambridge, Massachusetts, where the membership further debated, amended, and eventually adopted the new guidelines. Numerous disagreements occurred during this process, raising eyebrows and voices over this or that practice, because oral historians represent many fields that often have different objectives. But a consensus finally emerged from this process, the findings of which are incorporated throughout this book (and are reprinted in appendix 1).

Not every oral historian will agree with every point made here, since there is no uniform way of doing oral history, and unconventional approaches may sometimes work well. The principles and standards were established for good reasons, but for every rule there has been an exception that works. Oral historians welcome innovation and imagination. Rather than seek to make all interviewers march like soldiers in cadence, this book aims to help them first think carefully about what they are doing and to be aware of potential consequences.

The questions and answers that follow deal with so many principles and potential pitfalls that they may intimidate and overwhelm some beginning oral historians. But awareness of the issues should not paralyze the process. Oral history interviewing may not be easy, but it can be enormously satisfying and rewarding to meet and engage in dialogue with memorable individuals and to make sure that otherwise neglected aspects of the past will be preserved for the future.

Most oral historians learn by doing, and our understanding of the theories of interviewing and our interpretation have more often followed than preceded our interviewing. *Doing Oral History* seeks to provide practical advice and reasonable explanations for those planning to conduct and collect oral history interviews. Its emphasis is on doing; planning is essential for the success of an oral history project, but I have seen project directors fret for years without actually conducting any interviews. They worried about raising money, about what types of questions would be legitimate, about whom to interview, and additional problems that other projects were capable of solving. My recommendation is always to stop worrying and actually do some interviews. Projects can begin small and grow as funds become available and personnel gain experience. Finishing just one interview gives a project something tangible to show for its efforts, something to present to funders and to use as a model for volunteer interviewers. Even a poor interview offers mistakes from which a project can learn. Lengthy deliberations and delays run the risk that desired interviewees will die before they can be interviewed, for oral historians are in a perpetual contest with the actuarial realities.

Because the costs of doing oral history vary widely and the technology associated with it changes rapidly, this book does not give estimates for operating budgets, such as the cost per hour for interviewing or transcribing, nor does it endorse particular equipment. Anything so specific would become out-of-date almost upon publication. Readers planning to launch an oral history project would be better advised to contact other projects in their locality for cost estimates and equipment recommendations. There are also no mechanical descriptions here of how tape recorders or videocameras work, since the author boasts no mechanical skill other than being able to turn on a tape recorder and check periodically to make sure it is functioning properly. Nor should this book be taken for a cookbook of recipes that specify the precise measurements of ingredients and instructions to guarantee satisfying results. Instead, it offers a wide-ranging discussion of the methods of oral history, with notes and a bibliography that can lead those with specific queries to more specialized sources.

Each chapter presents a different role related to oral history: starting a project, doing interviews, processing interviews, using interviews in independent research, videotaping, preserving interviews in libraries and archives, teaching, and presenting the material to the various publics. Few oral historians are involved in all of these phases, and most will specialize only in a few aspects. But rather than confine themselves to a single niche, readers should examine the complexity of oral history. Interviewers need to understand thoroughly what archivists want from the process, and vice versa. Teachers and students should consider aspects of public presentation, and audio interviewers should have at least some curiosity about videotaping. The various chapters offer glimpses of each area and suggest further reading.

More useful than any written sources, however, were the many oral historians with whom I have talked and compared experiences over the years. I owe special thanks to Terry Birdwhistell, who prompted me to write this book and whose advice and editorial judgment I depended on throughout its writing. Martha Ross introduced me to oral history as a research tool and to the network of oral history associations. Richard Baker gave me the opportunity to create an oral history project at the U.S. Senate and the exceptional experience of uncovering the Senate's history through the observations of senators and career staff.

Oral History Association presidents Ronald Marcello and Lila Goff commissioned and supported the revisions of the OHA's principles and standards and evaluations guidelines. In coordinating those efforts, I received extraordinary assistance from the committee chairs, Sherna Gluck, Linda Shopes, Pamela Henson, Barry Lanman, George Mehaffy, and Terry Birdwhistell, and from all the other committee members. The exchange of memoranda, draft reports, and conference calls and the face-to-face meetings that went into that project constituted my complete reeducation as an oral historian.

Many colleagues and friends have generously read and wisely commented on various portions of this book, among them, Frank Clearfield, Maygene Daniels, Barry Lanman, David Mould, John Neuenschwander, Mary Kay Quinlan, Terri Schorzman, and Brien Williams. Charles T. Morrissey, a prolific writer on oral history methods and proficient trainer of interviewers, submitted his helpful editorial impressions appropriately on tape. Cullom Davis, Michael Devine, Ronald Marcello, John Neuenschwander, and Gary Hoag provided welcome breaks during several spring training baseball seasons, where oral history was discussed between innings. I especially want to thank Anne Jones for launching, and Mark Zadrozny for continuing so adeptly, the Twayne Oral History Series. Each of the many authors with whom I have worked on Twayne books has added to my appreciation of what can be done with oral history. This book is dedicated to my wife, Anne Ritchie, who does oral history interviewing for the National Gallery of Art in Washington, D.C., and whose companionship, advice, and keen memory I rely upon daily.

I

AN ORAL HISTORY OF OUR TIME

What is oral history?

Simply put, oral history collects spoken memories and personal commentaries of historical significance through recorded interviews. An oral history interview generally consists of a well-prepared interviewer questioning an interviewee and recording their exchange on audio or videotape. Tapes of the interview are transcribed, summarized, or indexed and then placed in a library or archives. These interviews may be used for research or excerpted in a publication, radio or video documentary, museum exhibition, dramatization, or other form of public presentation. Oral history does not include random taping, such as President Richard Nixon's surreptitious recording of his White House conversations, nor does it refer to recorded speeches, wiretapping, personal diaries on tape, or other sound recordings that lack the dialogue between interviewer and interviewee.[1]

To avoid repeating common mistakes, oral historians have established standards for doing interviews and principles for dealing ethically with interviewees. But oral history is too dynamic and creative a field to be entirely captured by any single definition. For every rule, an exception has worked. Imaginative interviewers are constantly developing and sharing new methods and uses of oral history. Any definition of the oral history process, or any method of interviewing, must reflect the goals of the specific project, the resources available, and other practical considerations.[2]

When did people begin collecting oral history?

As distinct from oral traditions—stories that societies have passed along in spoken form from generation to generation—oral history *interviewing* has been occurring since history was first recorded. Three thousand years ago, scribes of the Zhou dynasty in China collected the sayings of the people for the use of court historians, and several centuries later, Thucydides interviewed

1

participants in the Peloponnesian Wars. Skepticism of oral testimony dates back equally as far. Thucydides complained that "different eye-witnesses give different accounts of the same events, speaking out of partiality for one side or the other or else from imperfect memories."[3]

In 1773, when Samuel Johnson argued against the proposition that an impartial history could not be written in the lifetime of those who had experienced the events, he reasoned that "a man, by talking with those of different sides, who were actors in it and putting down all that he hears, may in time collect the materials of a good narrative." Johnson admonished that "all history was at first oral" and noted that this was how Voltaire had prepared his histories of the French kings. Indeed, Voltaire wrote that he had questioned "old courtiers, servants, great lords, and others" and recorded only "those facts about which they agree." Jules Michelet studied the French Revolution, a half-century after it took place, by contrasting the official documents with the recollections of "peasants, townsfolk, old men, women, even children; which you can hear if you enter an evening into a village tavern." In the 1870s the California publisher Hubert Howe Bancroft began to compile his seven-volume *History of California* (1884–1890) by sending students out to collect the papers and reminiscences of nineteenth-century Mexican military governors and *alcaldes* (civilian officials) and of the first American settlers.[4]

It seemed reasonable to consult oral as well as written sources until the late nineteenth century, when the German school of scientific history promoted documentary research to the exclusion of other, less "objective" sources. Leopold von Ranke asserted that documents created at the time historical events occurred are the most reliable form of historical evidence; Ranke's followers helped transform history from a literary form into an academic discipline dependent on the rigorous use of evidence. They trained historians to scrutinize documents in their search for truth and dismissed oral sources as folklore and myth, prized only by well-meaning but naive amateurs and antiquarians. They deemed oral evidence too subjective—shoddy memories told from a biased point of view.[5]

Ironically, historians turned away from oral sources just as other professions and disciplines were embracing the interview. Journalists made interviewing a mainstay of their craft about the time of the American Civil War. In 1859, when the *New York Tribune* editor Horace Greeley went west to conduct a highly publicized interview of the Mormon patriarch Brigham Young in Salt Lake City, he launched a trend in newspaper interviews. By 1868 President Andrew Johnson, facing impeachment by Congress, sought to present his side to the public by giving the first presidential interviews for attribution. "I want to give those fellows hell," Johnson told the reporter who was interviewing him, as he gestured toward the Capitol, "and I think I can do it better through your paper than through a message, because the people read the papers more than they do messages." Interviews became so popular that clever politicians took to preparing their own question-and-answer dialogues, which obliging journalists published as news.[6]

In the 1890s the U.S. Bureau of Ethnography dispatched researchers to record on wax cylinders the songs and stories of Native Americans. During the Depression of the 1930s, the Works Progress Administration (WPA) hired unemployed writers to chronicle the lives of ordinary citizens. Especially valuable were the WPA's interviews with former slaves; decades later, when historians finally accepted them, these records helped to alter fundamentally the historical interpretation of American slavery.[7]

When the United States entered World War II, President Franklin D. Roosevelt ordered all military branches and civilian agencies of the government to prepare records of their wartime experiences. Planning not only a postwar history but a series of morale-boosting "American Forces in Action" booklets, the U.S. Army dispatched historians into battlefields, armed with heavy wire recorders. Directed by Lt. Col. S. L. A. Marshall, a World War I veteran and journalist turned army historian, they pioneered in the postcombat interview, debriefing soldiers immediately after battles to reconstruct events of the day. Sgt. Forrest Pogue spent D-Day interviewing wounded soldiers who had been evacuated to a hospital ship anchored off Normandy Beach. Recalling concerns that his bulky wire recorder might attract sniper fire, Pogue noted that the army wanted live history—"and live historians."[8]

Although the term had been used earlier, not until the 1940s did "oral history" attach itself to interviewing. A Harvard-educated Greenwich Village bohemian and flophouse denizen, Joseph Gould, otherwise known as "Professor Sea Gull," wandered around Manhattan collecting what he called "An Oral History of Our Time." A profile of Gould that appeared in the *New Yorker* in 1942 drew attention to his crusade to record the stories of average people. "What people say is history," Gould insisted. "What we used to think was history—kings and queens, treaties, inventions, big battles, beheadings, Caesar, Napoleon, Pontius Pilate, Columbus, William Jennings Bryan—is only formal history and largely false. I'll put down the informal history of the shirt-sleeved multitude—what they had to say about their jobs, love affairs, vittles, sprees, scrapes, and sorrows—or I'll perish in the attempt." The quest garnered many a free meal for Gould, but his oral history proved to be a figment of his imagination. When Gould died, he left nothing behind but the name.[9]

Another journalist-turned-historian, Allan Nevins, established the first modern oral history archives at Columbia University in 1948. A decade earlier, in his book *The Gateway to History*, Nevins had proposed to reinvigorate historical study in America by making "a systematic attempt to obtain,

3

from the lips and papers of living Americans who had led significant lives, a fuller record of their participation in the political, economic, and cultural life of the last sixty years." Recognizing that modern communication and transportation were making letter writing and diary keeping obsolete, Nevins founded the Columbia Oral History Research Office. This new effort raised complaints from those who considered "Oral History" either too imprecise or too Freudian. But by the 1960s Nevins's successor, Louis Starr, could point out that the term had so worked its way into the language that newspapers were referring to it in the lower case. "Oral history, like it or not, is here to stay," Starr declared. "It's gone generic."[10]

The University of California at Berkeley launched a similar oral history archives in 1953, as did UCLA in 1958. The Harry S. Truman Library inaugurated the first presidential library oral history program in 1960. The John F. Kennedy Library began interviewing shortly after Kennedy's assassination, before the library was even constructed. Oral history soon became standard practice for building presidential collections. By 1967 the Oral History Association was founded, gaining membership throughout the United States and abroad. Oral history projects developed on every continent, and national oral history organizations formed around the globe, from Canada to New Zealand. A 1987 meeting in Oxford, England established the International Oral History Association, which meets periodically throughout Europe. When the Soviet Union dissolved, Russian and Eastern European oral historians began immediately to reexamine and rewrite that region's discredited official history by collecting personal testimony long suppressed under Communist regimes.[11]

Who is being interviewed?

In the United States the first oral history archives studiously avoided Joe Gould's "shirt-sleeved multitude." Allan Nevins was a political historian who interviewed the major players in government, business, and society. Long after Nevins's retirement, Columbia continued to interview people of the stature of judges, cabinet members, senators, publishers, business executives, and civic leaders. By contrast, European oral history projects from the start were the domain of social historians who sought to record the lives and experiences of working-class people exclusively.

Not until the 1970s did a new generation of American historians begin writing history "from the bottom up." Lacking the abundant manuscript resources and formal documentation available on the elites, they turned to oral sources. Encouraging these efforts were the best-selling books of Studs Terkel, a Chicago radio talk-show host and former WPA interviewer whose books, such as *Hard Times* (1970), *Working* (1974), and *"The Good War"*

(1984), captured the voices of everyday people in a compelling manner. Alex Haley's *Roots* (1976) similarly inspired people, especially African-Americans, to collect their own family histories through interviews. The availability of convenient and relatively inexpensive cassette tape recorders and video recorders further helped to popularize oral history.[12]

For years oral historians argued the respective merits of "elite" versus "nonelite" interviewing. By the 1980s that debate had tapered off and oral history projects had grown more all-inclusive. The more interviewers studied their practice, the more they realized that no one group had an exclusive understanding of the past and that the best projects were those that cast their nets wide, recording as many different participants in events or members of a community as possible. Once a military historian was questioned about the possibility of using oral histories to study the social acculturation of barracks life. He responded coolly, "I only interview generals." Since then, oral history has changed, even in the military, where historians now conduct interviews with all ranks of enlisted personnel and officers, in garrison and in combat, to build important research collections.

When journalists interview, are they doing oral history?

Journalists usually interview subjects for very specific purposes having to do with the newspaper story, magazine article, or evening news broadcast they are preparing. Working on short deadlines, reporters depend heavily on oral rather than written sources. They may corner someone in a corridor or phone them to ask highly focused questions; often they have no time to elicit or listen to lengthy elaborations. Only a few short quotations may appear in their articles or as "sound bites" in their broadcasts. Journalists frequently interview without attribution, collecting "off-the-record" responses simply for background information with no intention of revealing these sources in their stories. Sometimes their interviews are recorded—especially if intended for broadcast—but after the story appears, journalists do not retain the original interviews and notes for long. The record that journalists leave for the future consists primarily of their published articles or tapes of their broadcasts. Journalists rarely expect to deposit their interview tapes or notes in a library or archives where other researchers might examine them.

In this regard, journalists are not unlike many scholarly researchers who conduct interviews to provide documentation for their articles or books without plannning to open the interviews for general research. Usually they only excerpt the interviews in their books, rather than reproduce their full notes or transcripts. After the book is published, these documents most often languish in the author's files, packed away in a basement or attic.

An interview becomes an oral history only when it has been recorded,

5

processed in some way, made available in an archives, library, or other repository, or reproduced in relatively verbatim form as a publication. Availability
for general research, reinterpretation, and verification defines oral history. By
preserving the tapes and transcripts of their interviews, oral historians seek
to leave as complete, candid, and reliable a record as possible.[13]

What does it take to become an oral historian?

Oral history has always been multidisciplinary. Although many professional
historians conduct oral history, a degree in history has never been a prerequi-
site for entering the field. Well-established scholars sometimes make poor
interviewers, and those who are part of the community or profession being
interviewed, if properly trained in conducting oral history, have advantages in
establishing rapport and in prior knowledge. Law students have interviewed
judges, women coal miners have successfully interviewed other women coal
miners, and members of a community have conducted oral histories with
their neighbors.[14]

Saying that a Ph.D. in history is no requirement for doing oral history
does not mean that anything anyone tape-records is oral history. The Oral
History Association has developed principles, standards, and guidelines to
raise the consciousness and professional standards of all oral historians. There
are interviewing skills to be learned. There are right and wrong ways to
conduct an oral history. There are great differences between usable oral
histories and useless ones, and there are far too many of the latter.

Oral history welcomes both the academic and the layperson. With reasonable training, through oral history courses, workshops, or manuals, anyone
can conduct a usable oral history. Oral history conferences are notable for
the variety of participants, among them, radio and video documentary makers,
museum curators, archivists, journalists, gerontologists, anthropologists, and
folklorists. Regardless of their diverse objectives, they share many common
methods.

How reliable is the information gathered by oral history?

"The most naive policeman knows that a witness should not always be taken
at his word," wrote the French historian Marc Bloch. "Similarly, it has been
many a day since men first took it into their heads not to accept all historical
evidence blindly." Oral history is as reliable or unreliable as other research
sources. No single piece of data of any sort should be trusted completely, and
all sources need to be tested against other evidence. The historian James
MacGregor Burns, who was trained under S. L. A. Marshall to interview

American soldiers during World War II, found that the interviews generated some spurious information (about how frequently infantrymen fired their rifles in combat) and also some startling insights (about how many troops were killed by friendly fire). Burns concluded that "such interviews were a most valuable contribution to military history, but only if used in careful conjunction with more conventional sources, like documents and enemy records."[15]

Although archival documents have the advantage of not being influenced by later events or otherwise changing over time, as an interviewee might, documents are sometimes incomplete, inaccurate, and deceiving. For instance, researchers have found more than one occasion of a local newspaper ignoring an entire event, such as a strike against one of its major advertisers. Until the 1960s most general-circulation newspapers omitted most news from black communities. As a result of such blind spots, oral history can develop information that might not have appeared in print. The novelist Gore Vidal has commented: "Since I have been written about perhaps a bit more than most historians, I am not as impressed as they are by what I see in print, no matter how old and yellow the cutting."[16]

Scholars have accepted correspondence, diaries, and autobiographies as legitimate documentation, although their authors may be biased or incorrect. Politicians have kept diaries with publication in mind, designing them to present themselves in the best possible light. Oral history interviews are often conducted years after the event, when memories have grown imprecise, but they have the advantage of being conducted by a trained interviewer who can raise questions and challenge dubious answers. As any researcher can attest, letter writers and diary keepers do not always address all the issues that scholars are researching. Autobiographers are often unaware of all the issues that interest researchers. Well-trained interviewers can coax interviewees into areas of concern to researchers that interviewees might never have thought of discussing otherwise.

Then why are some historians still skeptical about oral history?

The skeptics distrust eyewitness accounts as too subjective. When historians describe evidence as "objective," they mean not only unbiased but also unchanging, such as documents that remain the same over time even if interpretations of them shift. "Subjective" suggests a partial and partisan point of view, less reliable because it is subject to alteration over time. When the oral historian Alessandro Portelli wrote of the need for broad-based interviewing that would "tell us not what people did, but what they wanted to do, what they believed they were doing, what they now think they did," he was criticized for passivity and "unsystematic" reasoning. Some social historians have accused oral historians of swallowing whole the stories that informants tell them. They argue that a truer "people's history" must be based on statistical analysis and other objective data rather than on subjective individual testimony. The correlated assumption is that the historian, with hindsight and thorough research, perceives past events more clearly than those who lived through them. Or, as David Lodge asserted in his autobiographical novel *Out of the Shelter* (1989), history is the verdict "of those who weren't there on those who were."[17]

Should the interviewer be an objective—or neutral—participant?

Oral historians have debated how much an interviewer should intervene in the interview. Initially, some argued that independent researchers—those doing interviews for their own publications—are too biased to conduct oral histories, and that archival oral historians would be better interviewers because they have no vested interest in any interpretation. In the type of oral history Allan Nevins pioneered at Columbia, the interviewer was envisioned as a neutral, objective collector of other people's reminiscences; this concept was carried to such extremes that the questions were eliminated entirely in Columbia's early transcripts. The interviewee's responses were rendered as an uninterrupted narrative. Although Columbia soon adopted the question-and-answer format for its transcripts, many books featuring oral history testimony continue to expunge the interviewer. Studs Terkel, for example, has disclosed only a few of the questions that elicited such compelling replies from his interviewees.[18]

Other oral historians rejected the image of the neutral questioner and saw their role as that of an active agent in the process. The codirector of the Duke University Oral History Program, Lawrence Goodwyn, insisted that interviewers who remain passive surrender too much of their professional capacity. Goodwyn acknowledged, however, that more active interviewers risk distortion of their interviews by intruding their own cultural assumptions and political perspectives. Accepting subjectivity as inherent in the process and impossible to avoid, the advocates of a more active and scholarly interviewer believed that the interviewer's questioning actually involves "a first interpretation" of the interviewee's narrative. Influenced by trends in anthropology, literary criticism, and social history, they examined not only what was said but what was left unsaid, and they speculated about the lapses in historical memory. The more methodologically oriented oral historians criticized the uncritical acceptance of oral testimony, called for more thorough research and higher standards in conducting interviews, and lamented that the lack of scholarly analysis, by both interviewers and interview users, had turned oral history into "movement without aim."[19]

Since the 1970s a proliferation of methodological studies has added not only "aim" but increasing depth and sophistication to oral history. Still, a difference remains between analyzing oral evidence *after* it has been collected and suggesting that theorizing *precede* the interview. An interviewer must always be prepared to abandon carefully prepared questions and follow the interviewee down unexpected paths, always helping the interviewee by questioning, guiding, coaxing, and challenging. Michael Frisch has explained the process in his book *A Shared Authority* (1990), whose clever title promotes the notion that both participants in an interview are responsible for its creation and share its authorship. Interviewers may believe that they are a more than equal partner in this shared authority, since their questions shape the responses and they are extracting the raw material of memory for use in scholarship. But interviewers are actually less than an equal partner in the sense that the ultimate value of an oral history lies in the substance of the interviewee's story. Nor does the interpretation of the interview rest exclusively on the interviewer's side of the microphone, for interviewees are constantly interpreting and analyzing their own motives and actions as they recall and describe them.[20]

Discussions of oral history practices have been enriched by new applications of communications theory, feminist interviewing, and psychological studies of memories. Beginning oral historians should not be discouraged by the complexity of hermeneutics (the principles of interpretation), discourse analysis (language in use), or deconstruction (hidden and unspoken information in a narrative). Rather than start by trying to put a particular theory into practice, a new oral historian would be better advised to adopt the more pragmatic approach of "putting practice into theory." First gain some experience in conducting interviews before plunging too deeply into theoretical issues. Doing interviews actually raises curiosity about methodological debates, since it soon becomes apparent that the interviewer is doing more than collecting "just the facts."[21]

These debates over theory and methodology were already under way at the first oral history colloquium in 1966. In a review of the proceedings of that meeting, Herman Kahn noted that the participants spent much time worrying about the nature and validity of oral history. All their self-questioning reminded him of an adolescent peering into a mirror and wondering, "What am I?" and, "Why am I not better known and more popular?" Introspection will and should continue, but Kahn urged oral historians to get on with their job of interviewing: "They will need to cultivate patience, acquire self-assurance, and be content to leave the proof of their pudding to the scholars who are its ultimate consumers."[22]

9

If doing an oral history is a shared responsibility between the interviewer and the interviewee, which one is the oral historian?

Both participate in the oral history, and neither one's role should be minimized, but for all practical purposes the oral historian is the one who schedules, prepares for, conducts, processes, and interprets the interview. The interviewer participates in the give-and-take of an interview by questioning and following up on the interviewee's responses and by providing names, dates, and other commonly forgotten information. But interviewers—especially when doing life histories—should never forget whose story is being told.

What's in a name? Some oral historians dislike "interviewee" for its passive sound and have searched for a more active designation, like "informant," "respondent," "oral author," and "narrator," the last term often being used by folklorists and social scientists. The weight assigned to the two terms is reflected in the index to a recent collection of essays on oral history whose various authors used both "interviewee" and "narrator." The index listing for "interviewee" is divided into "abandonment of," "apparent contradiction of," "deception of," "manipulation of," and "misinformation by." The index terms for "narrator" include "free expression and," "power of," and "in negotiation with researcher." The role of both is the same; only the nomenclature differs. Such vocabulary concerns aim to make oral historians more aware of how inequalities in the interviewer-interviewee relationship can influence the interview. In drafting its evaluation guidelines, the Oral History Association chose to retain the familiar triangular relationship of interviewer and interviewee producing the interview. Whatever the terms employed, keep in mind that an oral history is a joint product, shaped by both parties.[23]

MEMORY AND ORAL HISTORY

Isn't oral history limited by the fallibility of human memory?

Dealing with memory is risky business, and it is inescapably the interviewer's business. Every interviewer has a story about someone interviewed too late, when memory had lost its sharpness, begun to dim, or faded almost entirely. Such disappointments are balanced by experiences with interviewees who possess remarkable recall, who remember individuals and incidents clearly, and whose accounts can be corroborated in other evidence. As one of the interviewers who collected oral histories with immigrants for the Ellis Island museum noted, elderly interviewees "might not remember their daughter's phone number. But they do remember what it was like when they got off the boat."[24]

The study of memory by psychologists has concentrated largely on short-term memory rather than on the long-term recall of a life span. Short-term memory studies that evaluate the accuracy of an individual's perception of events are of little help in explaining the uncanny preciseness with which some interviewees recall events that took place decades ago, or in understanding how interviewees who have reached obvious senility—forgetting even that they have scheduled the interview—can still speak authentically about events far in the past. Long-term memory has been less thoroughly explored, although the phenomenon has often been commented upon. The Confederate leader Jefferson Davis, for instance, on his deathbed began recalling scenes from his youth as a West Point cadet. "I seem to remember more every day," Davis marveled.[25]

The gerontologist Robert Butler has postulated that all people, as they grow older and perceive that they are approaching death, undergo a mental process of life review—accounting for depression and despair in some and for candor, serenity, and wisdom in others. The past "marches in review," permitting the elderly to survey it and to reflect especially on moments of unresolved conflict. Older people will review their lives whether anyone asks them about their memories or not, either mulling over their thoughts silently or regaling family, neighbors, and visitors. In this process, the elderly may reveal details of their lives, and characteristics about themselves, previously unknown to their families and friends. Butler concluded that memory "serves the sense of self and its continuity; it entertains us; it shames us; it pains us. Memory can tell our origins; it can be explanatory; and it can deceive."[26]

Oral history is an active process in which interviewers seek out, record, and preserve such memories. Knowing that with age most people find it difficult to recall names and dates, oral historians conduct preliminary research to assist interviewees, give some context and structure to the dialogue through their questions, and mutually address any seeming misstatements and contradictions in the testimony.[27]

What should interviewers take into consideration about memory?

People remember what *they* think is important, not necessarily what the interviewer considers most consequential. An oral historian studying Texas teachers who made the transition from the one-room schoolhouse to modern consolidated schools found that white teachers said almost nothing about racial segregation or the details of the integration process. Blacks, Hispanic-Americans, and handicapped students remained largely "invisible" in their memories. Black teachers, by comparison, recalled the days of integration vividly because it affected their own lives so personally.[28]

Regardless of a project's objectives, a good oral history will always leave room for interviewees to speak their own minds and will not try to shoehorn their responses into a prepared questionnaire or mind-set. Since people remember best what was most exciting and important to them, their most vivid memories are often of the earliest days of their careers, when events were fresh and invigorating, even if their status at the time was relatively insignificant. By the time they rose in stature and assumed more important positions, daily events had often become more routine, making details of later life harder to isolate and identify during an interview. One interviewee summed up three decades on the U.S. Senate staff by observing that when she began work, she was young and the senators were old; when she retired, she was old and the senators were young. As is often the pattern, her descriptions of her youthful experiences were lengthier and richer in detail than her recollections of more recent events.[29]

After the Second World War, when Congress investigated the Japanese bombing of Pearl Harbor, the chief of naval operations, Adm. Harold Stark, could not recall where he had been the night before the Japanese attack on 7 December 1941. By contrast, Stark's flag lieutenant, H. D. Kirk, remembered precisely that they and their wives had gone to see a performance of *The Student Prince* and then returned to the admiral's home, where Stark received a telephone call from President Roosevelt. One of the investigating senators asked Kirk how he could remember the occasion so well, considering that Stark could recall nothing. "Because I was a small fish, and great things were transpiring," Kirk replied, "and you don't forget that sort of thing."[30]

People regularly reevaluate and reexplain their past decisions and actions. Just as historians rewrite history to incorporate new evidence and fit different theories, individuals use the insights gained from current events to help them make new sense out of past experiences. There is nothing invalidating about this reflectivity, so long as interviewers and researchers understand what is occurring and take it into account.[31]

Memories start with the initial perception. Interviewees speak from their own points of view, and no two will tell a story exactly alike. Not everyone had a clear picture of what happened, understood what it meant, or felt self-assured enough to accept responsibility. The contradictory tales told in the classic film *Rashomon* (1951) represent the tellers' differing impressions, self-images, and self-delusions, but not poor memories. In combat, generals in the rear may see the broad sweep of the battle, and battlefield troops will have a more microscopic view of the action. As LTJG John F. Kennedy wrote from the Solomon Islands during World War II: "Frankly I don't know a god-damned thing, as my copy of the Washington Times Herald arrives two months late, due to logistical difficulties, and it is pretty hard to get the total picture of a global war unless you are sitting in New York or Washington, or even Casablanca. I understand we are winning it, which is cheering, albeit hard to see, but I guess the view improves with distance. I know mine would."[32]

Those at the center of events can well recount their own accomplishments, but those on the periphery are often better able to make comparisons between the principal actors. Perceptions that were originally flawed will produce distorted memories. Distant and secondhand information is more susceptible to distortion. By contrast, direct, dramatic, and emotional situations tend to produce more fixed and lasting memories. For these reasons, oral history projects attempt to collect a wide range of interviews, to piece the puzzle together from various points of view.[33]

Not every perceived event is retained in memory. When the broadcast journalist David Brinkley wrote *Washington Goes to War* (1988), about the years when he first came to the capital as a young broadcaster during the Second World War, he was surprised to find so much in the old newspaper files that had faded from his memory. "I've always thought I had a good memory. Now I know I don't," Brinkley commented. "Things I knew very well and in fact stood and watched and interviewed people about, I'd totally forgotten. That was the startling thing—how much I'd forgotten." Once-meaningful information can become irrelevant or insignificant by comparison with later events. Since Brinkley continued to absorb current news as a journalist, the more events grew distant from the latest headlines, the less likely he was to think about or retain them.[34]

The passage of time enables people to make sense out of earlier events in their lives. Actions take on new significance depending on their later consequences. Certain players grow more important in the story, and others diminish over time. People's later memories may take on a more mature, mellow, or disillusioned cast according to their mood and condition at the time of the interview. Community members who share a common experience, such as the trauma of a flood or tornado, will talk about it among themselves for years, reinforcing the memories vividly. By the necessity of availability, oral historians interview "survivors," those who lived through it, stuck to it, stayed behind, or otherwise succeeded—all factors that shape how and what they remember.[35]

Interviewers have to consider how creditable their interviewees are as witnesses. Were they in a position to experience events firsthand or are they simply passing along secondhand information? What biases may have shaped their original perceptions? Have interviewees forgotten much of their past because it was no longer important to them or because the events were so routine that they were simply not memorable? How differently do interviewees feel now about the events they are recalling? What subsequent incidents may have caused them to rethink and reinterpret their past? How closely does their testimony agree with other documentary evidence from the period, and how do they explain the discrepancies? None of these considerations would disqualify an interviewee from giving testimony, but answering these questions as completely as possible helps the interviewer and future researchers to assess the value of the information recorded.

The memories of direct participants are sources far too rich for historical researchers to ignore. Interviewers must be aware of the peculiarities of memory, adept in their methods of dealing with it, conscious of its limitations, and open to its treasures.

Don't memories tend to grow nostalgic?

In his typically tart manner, President Calvin Coolidge once observed that the folks of his hometown in Vermont "remember some of the most interesting things that never happened."[36] Coolidge was referring to how history can be inflated by retrospective associations. It is similarly common to encounter rosy reminiscences about "the good old days," considering that oral historians interview older people about their youth; people whose dissatisfaction with present conditions makes the past look far better; and people whose very survival has convinced them that the hard times were not so bad after all. Many interviewees will talk about the pain and suffering in their lives, about humiliation, harassment, and discrimination, about disappointments and losses, but others have blocked out the most negative aspects of the past or rewritten their own histories, consciously or subconsciously. It is the oral historian's task to move the interviewee away from nostalgia to confront the past candidly and critically. If things were different in the past, what were they like? When did they change? How did they change? Why did they change?[37]

In reaction against the elitist practice of interviewing only famous people, many oral historians changed their focus to community-based "people's history." But after letting the people speak, historians examining community history projects soon realized "that 'the people' weren't speaking unadulterated truth." Linda Shopes, who interviewed for the Baltimore Neighborhood Heritage Project, has argued that "so many people want to do oral histories in well-intentioned but extremely naive ways: to get interesting stories, to get the anecdotes, to get the colorful stories, to get the cute things. People don't want to confront the fact that history is . . . not a happy little story of days gone by." Quite often people do not want to talk about difficult issues, such as the changing ethnic and racial composition of a community or one generation's rejection of another generation's values. Interviewers must be prepared to ask questions about painful and embarrassing subjects and should not be satisfied with superficial responses.[38]

Nostalgia is hardly limited to social history. Political historians have observed that the longer politicians are out of office, the more highly people rate them, a phenomenon that has been characterized as the "law of rising recollections."[39] Presidents still in office are compared with their predecessors; out of office, they are measured against their successors. The uncertainty of today's headlines sometimes turns past anxiety and turbulence into images of happy days. It becomes more challenging for interviewers recording the reminiscences among members of a presidential administration, or associates of any other retired or deceased high-ranking official, to keep them from mentioning only the most positive aspects of their former leader—the side they too often assume is all that the interviewer wants to hear about.

Whole groups may blank out unpleasant memories. When the Southern Oral History Project interviewed the men and women who worked in southern cotton mills during the 1930s, they encountered mostly silence about the General Strike of 1934, "a kind of social amnesia, born of defeat and of the failure of trade unionism to take root in a living tradition." One mill worker explained: "You see, after we come back and got out of the union and got back to work, why that was a thing of the past. . . . You forget about things in the past, 'cause you don't think about them, you don't talk about them, and that leaves your mind." The lack of oral testimony sent the researchers back into the documentary record, where they found ample evidence of these events, even if the participants' memories had suppressed them.[40]

Oral historians documenting traumatic events of the past have found that many survivors will refrain from talking about those events, even to their own children. But as they grow older, and as others who shared the experience die, the survivors will grant interviews as a way of reconciling a haunting record, and also of ensuring that future generations do not forget. Researchers studying the Holocaust have heard the victims' refrain: "I kept quiet for many years, but soon I will be gone and now I must tell my children."[41]

What is the relationship between oral history and folklore?

Oral historians and folklorists both use interviews to collect information, but not necessarily the same type of information. The two practices have been described as opposite ends of a continuum: oral historians concentrate on recording the personal experiences of the interviewee, and folklorists collect the traditional stories, songs, and other expressions of the community, fact or fiction. An oral historian would most likely interview a husband and wife separately, seeking to identify the unique perspective of each spouse. A folklorist, being as interested in the way a story is told as in its substance, would interview the couple together to observe the interplay as one begins a story and the other finishes it. The folklorist Barbara Allen has observed that oral historians for the most part are historians, and as such they see oral historical sources as "mines of raw data" from which they can extract historical interpretations; folklorists are more concerned with "recognizing identifiable patterns" in the ways people shape their narratives.[42]

What distinguishes a "life history" from other interviews?

Gerontologists refer to the "life review" process of the elderly, and oral historians speak of conducting "life histories," by which they mean full-scale autobiographical accounts that allow interviewees to recount their entire lives, from childhood to the present. Social scientists may concentrate on a series of shorter interviews with members of a group in a particular community or environment, such as workers on a shop floor. Oral historians call these "episodic" interviews. Conducting life histories usually means selecting fewer interviewees and devoting more time, and multiple interview sessions, to each one. Life histories give the interviewee enough time to relate what both the interviewer seeks and the interviewee wants to tell. The oral historian conducting even a subject-oriented project should seriously consider expanding the scope of the questions to record as much as possible about each interviewee's life. Broader questioning establishes links that neither interviewer nor interviewee may have considered in a more narrowly focused interview session.[43]

When the Oregon Historical Society launched an oral history of the federal court system in that state, it focused on the people who conducted the court rather than on the institution of the court itself. Following a full biographical approach proved especially useful when dealing with the appointment of judges. An institutional approach might also have included questions about a judge's appointment, but interviewers found that the meaning and significance of the responses were enhanced when told within the context of the judge's full life history.[44]

The first presidential library oral history projects concentrated almost exclusively on the interviewees' relationships with the president or roles in the administration. This approach produced a large number of relatively short interviews. In later years some of the libraries returned to reinterview the key players in greater depth. In this second round of interviewing, the oral historian at the Lyndon B. Johnson Library conducted 36 hours of interviews with Lawrence O'Brien (who served as congressional liaison and postmaster general), and 64 interview sessions with Joseph Califano (who was special assistant to the president for domestic affairs). Although this level of in-depth interviewing lies beyond the budget of most oral historians, projects should aim, however selectively, to do fuller life histories. Even individual researchers need to look beyond their immediate interests when interviewing. The American Historical Association has advised that, "to the extent practicable, interviewers should extend the inquiry beyond their immediate needs to make each interview as complete as possible for the benefit of others."[45]

PUBLIC HISTORY AND ORAL HISTORY

What is the role of oral history in "public history"?

Public history was once defined exclusively in terms of historians' activities in public agencies and as private consultants outside of the university. But the definition has expanded beyond place of employment to include the audiences that historians try to reach. Public historians aim for an out-of-school public audience, which might be officials in the government agency, corporation, union, philanthropic organization, or professional association that employs the historian or the library-using, documentary-viewing, museum-going general public. Other professional historians, for whom the bulk of historical literature is intended, account for only a small portion of the public historian's audience.[46]

Public history is an organized effort to bring accurate, meaningful history to a public audience, and oral history is a natural tool for reaching that goal. The oral history and public history movements share a natural affinity, both having attracted practitioners and audiences different from those for more traditional history writing. Both oral and public history have experimented with videotape, slide-tape, and even interactive videos, in museum exhibits, dramatic performances, and other applications outside of the classroom and in publications.[47]

How have oral historians marketed their services?

The public presentation of oral history has generated a number of independent enterprises. Oral historians have set up businesses to conduct family interviews, and they work as freelance interviewers for corporations, charitable trusts, scientific organizations, and various other government and private agencies. Charles Morrissey, who since 1975 has worked as a freelance oral historian in fields ranging from politics to biomedical research, commented, "To my total amazement, once my availability evidenced itself to others, the number of clients seeking help from me as an oral historian became formidable."[48]

Independent interviewers work on both specific projects and long-term contractual arrangements. Joel Gardner, as head of Gardner Associates, specializes in conducting oral histories for corporations and other organizations, and his clients include the Robert Wood Johnson Foundation, the Philadelphia Fire Museum, the Union League of Philadelphia, and the Pew Charitable

Trusts. One of Gardner's projects resulted in a book, *Seventy-Five Years of Good Taste: A History of the Tasty Baking Company* (1990), based on interviews with 35 employees. Noting that corporate executives were increasingly attuned to the value of preserving their historical records, Gardner helps create corporate archives and libraries. When doing oral histories, he seeks unlimited access to records, documents, and employees. Gardner urges his corporate sponsors to make the oral histories available to the public, but he notes that some of his clients turn to him because they feel uncomfortable with university-based oral history programs and prefer to keep the interviews within their own archives. In Rockville, Maryland, near Washington, D.C., Philip Cantelon founded History Associates, which has done oral histories for the federal government, for MCI, and for the American Furniture Hall of Fame. Such independent projects have been remarkably successful, but as one independent interviewer noted, "When your funding depends on grants, as mine does, I spend more time writing reports and applying for grants than I do interviewing."[49]

When the president of Atlantic Richfield Company (ARCO) concluded that the corporation was losing the knowledge of its "epochal events" because employees and managers with firsthand knowledge of those events were dying, he commissioned Enid Douglas to conduct oral histories that would produce both an oral history archival collection and a written history of the company. The book was intended to make the company "more human and real" to the public, as well as to help ARCO employees better understand and thereby identify with the company so that they would become "more loyal and dedicated employees." Management used the oral histories to develop case studies on decision-making process and for workshops to train potential corporate executives.[50]

In contrast to these corporate activities, oral history has also been used for public-interest projects. In the Southwest, anthropologists, historians, legal scholars, lawyers, folklorists, and oral historians worked together to assist citizens in the fight for land and water rights. The New Mexico-based Center for Land Grant Studies was particularly concerned with protecting the rights of Native Americans and Mexican-Americans who lacked the traditional types of ownership documentation to their lands. Representatives of the center used oral history as part of their courtroom testimony—a use that required proper techniques for gathering oral evidence and a greater need to assess the reliability of the oral testimony.[51]

What are the potential drawbacks of doing corporate oral history?

Oral historians hired for corporate projects report that many corporate executives and policymakers do not understand how historians work or how they use oral histories and that they need to be educated about the methods of historical research. Managers and other corporate executives often do not value or use their corporate archives and fear the consequences of allowing outsiders to see their records. They will not open records even for the historians they hire. They assume that oral historians, like journalists, can interview anyone, anytime, without extensive research. Oral historians have to explain their need to see records to prepare adequately for their interviews. Sometimes, however, these records will not be forthcoming. In the 1960s, for instance, interviewers for the John F. Kennedy Library were initially denied access to Kennedy's records.

Charles Morrissey has observed that corporate managers tend to select prospective interviewees depending on their rank in the corporate hierarchy, whereas oral historians want to interview those who actually shaped the issues being studied, "even if they are obscure figures in structured bureaucracies and do not command power or deference within their institutions." In fact, these seemingly anonymous members of the institution may have drafted the letters and speeches of higher executives and may have proposed the policies that the hierarchy adopted. They often have the least biased perspective on the institution. Lower-level staff members may actually have a clearer view of how policies evolved, be better able to evaluate people and programs, and have not only more detailed memories but a greater "willingness to impart what they remember."

Interviewers should try to align with one of the senior members of an organization, such as the chairman of the board, the chief executive officer, or the director of a public agency, who can open doors for the project and get access to records. The interviewer should brief top policymakers about the project as it evolves, giving them an idea of what methods are being employed and what information is being collected. Public historians are not public relations specialists and should not be required to tailor their work to reaffirm the picture of itself an institution may promote to the public. To be useful to clients, a historical study has to be honestly critical. The public historian's need to maintain professional standards works both ways: not only must historians be honestly critical, but they must also be willing to keep information confidential according to the policies of the organization that hired them.[52]

What will future historians want from our oral histories?

Researchers will want to hear the first-person observations of witnesses of events great and small, and to learn what sense those people made of the events in their own lives. Motivations and objectives are especially important. Other sources can usually provide the who, what, when, and where of history;

interviews can offer better insights into the how and why. The historian's job is to pull together a multitude of evidence from documents, objects, interviews, and other resources, weaving them together to create a narrative that makes sense of the often conflicting evidence.

Not all human activity is coherent and purposeful, the historian Elie Kedourie pointed out; it is more often a complex of choices producing unpredictable effects. Kedourie defined history as an account of people "in the peculiarity, idiosyncracy, and specificity of their personalities, outlooks, capacities, and positions, confronting or dealing with other [people] differently placed in respect to these things, and confronting or dealing with them in situations different from one another at least in respect of time and place, initiating, originating, taking measures, parrying, responding, reacting; the vocabulary we use to describe all this amply indicating that here are present and involved purpose and choice, mind and will." Or, as Ecclesiastes 9:11 instructs, "The race is not to the swift, nor the battle to the strong . . . but time and chance happen to them all." Oral history records both the purposeful and the accidental. Interviewers who give people a chance to assess why they did what they did will most likely capture the peculiarities of the history of our time.[53]

Historians writing a dissertation or a book, planning an exhibit or scripting a documentary, have their own questions they want to ask but may not have the opportunity to ask those questions personally. I first used oral history while writing a biography of a man who had died ten years earlier. Fortunately, he had given a lengthy oral history to Columbia University just months before he died. It was a thoroughly detailed, in-depth life history, amounting to 700 pages of transcripts. Since I could no longer question the man, Columbia's interviewer served as my surrogate. Today's oral historians are doing the preliminary work of tomorrow's biographers and researchers, hoping they will not have to agonize too often over the questions we failed to ask.[54]

Oral history is about asking questions. While researching the history of Methodist camp meetings in southern Mississippi, Charles Sullivan tried to visit every campground still operating. One day he mentioned to a student each of the camps that he had identified. "Yes, and Mt. Pleasant, too," the student responded, explaining that it was a black Methodist campground established after emancipation from slavery. Astonished, Sullivan wondered why no one had mentioned this camp before. "Probably because you never asked," came the reply. That is the reason for doing oral history: to ask the questions that have not been asked, and to collect the reminiscences that otherwise would be lost.[55]

2

STARTING AN ORAL HISTORY PROJECT

Where does an oral history project begin?

Every project should be started by determining its objectives. Not all goals need to be attempted at once, but they can be reached incrementally. For instance, having identified the likely pool of interviewees, oral historians will usually interview the oldest and most significant individuals first, while planning to move to younger or secondary figures later, depending on financial resources, available interviewers, and processing capabilities after the interviews are conducted.

After organizing a project, plan to start with a few well-conducted, in-depth interviews and then process them fully. The result will be something tangible to show when seeking additional funding. By concentrating on a few interviews, project organizers can establish a pattern of management and paperwork—from preparing and conducting the interviews to processing and transcribing them—that can expand along with the project. Similarly, projects may begin with only a few interviewers, paid or volunteer, who later can help train new recruits.

Always balance objectives with resources. Limited resources can frustrate ambitious objectives, and too many projects have ended with little to show for their efforts except boxes of tapes, unidentified, unprocessed, and unusable. Other well-intentioned projects have been stretched too thin; trying to interview too many people can produce superficial interviews that do not satisfy research needs.

What kind of goals should an oral history project set?

Decide what kind of a record you want to create, and for what purpose. Oral history should be collecting not what is already well known but information, observations, and opinions unavailable elsewhere. Oral history projects are often designed to supplement existing archival material, filling in gaps in paper sources with the contributions of people who did their business instead in person or on the phone. An oral history project may record a piece of community history that the local newspaper ignored or inadequately covered. Other projects have been designed to determine the contributions that individuals made to a movement—such as the civil rights movement—or to trace the impact of a movement on individuals and communities. Projects have been focused on various professions, ranging from journalism to architecture, medicine, and the law, recording the recollections of pioneers and other practitioners and tracing professional trends. Above all, oral history projects, by recording history in the words of those who lived it, can tell future researchers how people lived and how they perceived the events of their time.

A project may record the history of a church, a school, a business, or a philanthropic foundation, interviewing a cross-section of people associated with that institution. Project interviewers might follow members of a state legislature from session to session, capturing their versions of how legislation was enacted or defeated. An oral history project might be concentrated on a neighborhood or a particular ethnic group within a community. Oral history is appropriate not only for looking at the broad sweep of a community's history but for examining it at a specific time, say, during the Second World War or during the 1960s. An event (an election, a strike, the construction of a monumental building) or catastrophe (a hurricane, a flood, a major accident) can be its organizing theme. Or the subject can be the history of a group, such as women, African-Americans, or Hispanic-Americans, or a subgroup, such as immigrant women, African-American teachers, or Hispanic-American entrepreneurs. Some oral history archives focus their collections on the city, state, or region where they are located; others have built broad national and even international collections.

During the course of conducting interviews, it may be desirable to change or reevaluate the project's goals. Interviewers may find that some of the original objectives are impractical or that new avenues open up as additional interviewees are identified. Goals are often time-determined. Some oral history projects are ongoing, but others work on a year-to-year, grant-to-grant basis and must regularly do a certain amount of interviewing to ensure continued funding.

An oral history project will be judged by the significance of the goals its organizers set and the substance of the information they collected. Researchers will measure projects according to whom was interviewed, what questions were asked, and how ably the tapes and transcripts were processed. Users will also scrutinize oral history projects for new or different—or at least colorfully quotable—information on the subjects they are studying.

24

Should a project set a goal of how many people it intends to interview?

Trying to calculate in advance the exact number of individuals to interview puts unnecessary pressure on an oral history project. Rushing to meet numerical objectives causes both the depth of interviewing and a reasonable pace of processing to be sacrificed. Once interviewing begins, it will be discovered that some interviewees have much more to say than others, are more perceptive and cooperative, and have sharper memories. These are the interviewees to whom it is worth devoting more time. For reasons of age, health, or general disposition, other interviewees will have little to say of enduring value. Often not until an interview begins can the interviewer determine whether the interviewee is able to make much of a contribution. Sometimes a very old interviewee has a surprisingly sharp recall and even more stamina than the interviewer; sometimes not. Preliminary contact can help the interviewer to get a better sense of the abilities of the interviewee and to gauge how much time to budget for a session or a series of interviews. One oral historian went to considerable effort and expense to bring a crew to film an interview only to discover too late that the interviewee was distressingly senile.

Oral history projects invariably receive recommendations to interview the local raconteur, whom everyone says has a story about everything. Although more than willing to talk, this person may be unable to move beyond a store of set stories. Correspondingly, the most famous individual identified with an event may offer only a garbled, self-centered account. The most forthcoming interviewee may turn out instead to be a lesser-known, secondary figure who keenly observed what was going on and remembers it vividly. To do interviews of equal length with these varying individuals makes little sense. Remain flexible enough that interviewers can spend less time with those who have little to say and more time with those whose contributions are substantial.

In designing a project and in seeking funding, set the number of hours of interviews or sessions you intend to conduct rather than the number of individuals to be interviewed. A project that budgets for one hundred hours may spend one hour with one interviewee and ten hours with the next, giving each of them sufficient time to document the subject to the best of their abilities.

Is there an optimal number of hours for interviewing each person?

An interview session is usually best limited to an hour and a half to two hours—to avoid exhausting both the interviewee and interviewer—but there is no ideal length for an entire interview. Each interview depends on how much of value to the project the interviewee has to say, and whether the project is conducting life histories or concentrating on a smaller segment of a group of people's experiences. Whenever interviewers have to travel any great distance, they will have to estimate the number of hours of interviews in advance without knowing if that time will be sufficient. A second trip may be necessary, budget permitting.[1]

Be careful not to overschedule interviewing trips, forcing the interviewer to rush from one appointment to the next and cutting interviewees short regardless of what they have to say. Interviewees still actively engaged in their careers may set rigid limits on the amount of time for an interview (and may cancel at the last minute). Retired people tend to be more tolerant about giving longer, open-ended interviews that may or may not include lunch or other time-consuming diversions, such as a tour of the property or the town. Interviewers have to exercise personal judgment in deciding when the interviewee has become fatigued and is no longer thinking clearly. Interviewers frequently find that the interview situation is stressful for themselves and that their own ability to pay attention and interact diminishes the longer an interview lasts.

FUNDING AND STAFFING

How much does it cost to do an oral history?

How much can you afford to spend? Oral history can be expensive, but its costs are containable. The price tag may include research preparation and interview time, equipment, travel to and from interviews, lodging and meals if interviews are conducted out of town, transcription, indexing, cataloging, photocopying, postage for correspondence, supplies, and other overhead costs.

Some projects pay their interviewers, others rely on unpaid volunteers. Some purchase or rent their equipment, others take advantage of the equipment, services, and personnel of their parent organization, whether a church, library, corporation, university, or government agency. A project can include the work of transcribing, or tapes can be sent to professional transcribers, who are paid by the page, by the number of hours of tape, or by the number of hours worked. Some choose to abstract and index rather than transcribe. Using volunteer typists with access to word processors can reduce costs, but volunteers have to be trained and their work needs to be reviewed and edited. Rates for rental equipment, transcribing services, salaries, and overhead will also vary according to the geographic location of the project and the available labor pool.

If experienced oral historians are used, the budget will have to include pay for their services as interviewers and cover their research, travel, and processing expenses. Patricia Pilling, who does family interviews, has had clients question why her oral histories cost what they do when anyone can turn on a tape recorder and ask questions. She asks whether they can cook; if they say yes, she replies, "But can you make a gourmet meal?" Her analogy makes most clients see the value of professional expertise.[2]

How do oral history projects get funded?

Funding comes from an array of sources. More fortunate projects are based within institutions that provide them with office space, equipment, salaries, and travel expenses. Some institutions will meet part of those needs, such as office space and equipment, but expect the oral history project to raise the rest of its funds for salaries and expenses. Private granting agencies and many state humanities councils have long supported oral history projects. These grants often cover the conducting and processing of all or part of the planned oral histories, including interviewing, processing, and overhead. Some projects have done their interviewing and then turned to state humanities councils or other agencies for grants to transcribe the best of the interviews. State humanities councils have been especially interested in the public programs that can arise out of oral history projects and have therefore shown more interest in the results of oral history than in the interviewing itself. Transcription vastly increases the usefulness of oral history for publication, documentaries, stage productions, and museum exhibits. The National Endowment for the Humanities (NEH) has also funded oral history, although an enormous investment of time and effort is required to prepare NEH proposals, the competition is intense, and only about 20 percent of all proposals receive funding.

Seeking funds for an oral history project needs to be a creative effort. Volunteer groups have successfully sponsored receptions and other exhibits of their material as fund-raising events. If direct funds are unavailable, projects also seek such "in-kind" support as the loan of equipment and secretarial, printing, photocopying, and transcript-binding services.

Projects focused on a specific issue, such as women's rights or environmental policies, have often received support from individuals or organizations that support or promote the issue. The Washington Press Club Foundation's oral history project on women journalists, for instance, received funding from an array of media sources that included the Gannett Foundation, the Sulzberger Foundation, and Time Warner Inc. For a project centered on the career of a specific individual, such as a prominent politician retired from office, approach contributors to the politician's campaigns. A dinner in that person's honor could well serve as a fund-raiser for the oral history project. In addition, businesses, trade associations, and labor unions have funded oral history projects related to their fields. Families have underwritten interviews and whole oral history projects about an illustrious member.

Funding may determine who is interviewed. Corporate funding and support by wealthy individuals has accounted for much of the "elite" interviewing done by oral history projects in the past. Public and private funding agencies have supported community-based oral history projects, but these funds can fluctuate widely, depending on the financial or political climate. Although interviewee selection should be conducted separately from fund-raising, some project organizers have identified interviewees based on the likelihood of their financial contribution to the project or to the parent institution, slighting others whose interviews would have made a more significant contribution. Economic realities may be inescapable, but oral history projects should include as wide a range of interviews as possible and not be limited to those who can pay for it. Care must be taken not to allow funding sources to inhibit the choice of topics or interviewees.

How large a staff does an oral history project need?

There is no set number. Many projects are one-person operations, and others rely on a crew of volunteers or paid staff. Each project needs a manager or coordinator, who may also double as an interviewer or transcriber. Project managers prepare grant proposals, set up an advisory committee, recruit interviewers, identify likely interviewees, acquire equipment, handle correspondence, create the necessary filing system and other documentation (including legal release forms), arrange for transcriptions or abstracts to be made, organize workshops or training sessions for interviewers, and ensure that the interviews are deposited in a library or other institution where researchers can use them. The project manager may also handle publicity for the project or supervise the use of the interviews in publications, exhibits, and other forms of public presentation.

The pool of interviewers available to a project will influence the number of interviews that can be conducted. More interviewers can do more interviews but require more equipment and more processing time. Volunteers especially enjoy interviewing but are not as eager to do the less glamorous job of processing the interviews. Avoid doing more interviews than can reasonably be processed, to prevent large backlogs and delays in producing transcripts. Once processing begins to fall behind, it becomes increasingly arduous to catch up. If promises have been made to give copies of tapes or transcripts to interviewees, long backlogs create embarrassing delays.

In most projects, the interviewer is responsible for researching, conducting, and editing the interview. Sometimes a project can include research assistance, but the interviewer has to be thoroughly versed in the subject matter and cannot rely solely on prepared questions. An interviewer must be prepared to deviate from the outline at any moment and follow up on unexpected information from the interviewee. In some larger projects, interviews are contracted out for a set fee, which includes the interviewer's preparation of a finished transcript.

Whether the project or the contracted interviewer is responsible for the transcript, it is usually prepared by a trained transcriber. The transcriber may be a staff member of the project or of the host institution, a volunteer, or a professional hired from outside. Professional transcribers often advertise their services in oral history journals and newsletters.

Depending on funding, trained interviewers are paid a salary or a fee per interview. Fees may be set for entire interviews or by the hour, with reimbursement for any costs incurred in traveling to interviews. If using inexperienced volunteers, project organizers should ensure that interviews are properly conducted and processed by arranging for an oral history consultant to run workshop training sessions for interviewers and transcribers and to review their work periodically. The project manager may double as the oral history consultant. Consultants usually charge fees, but university oral history archivists will sometimes provide advice to smaller projects in their vicinity as a *pro bono publico* service.

Should a project appoint an advisory committee?

An advisory committee can help a project determine its goals, review proposals, suggest potential interviewees, assist in fund-raising, and offer general support to the interviewers. If the project is part of a larger institution, such as a library, archives, or university, whose administrators may not fully recognize all of the project's requirements, a wisely selected advisory committee can offer a strong network of support.

Select advisory committee members who are likely to be respected by the host institution or by the chief funding agency and who have the time and interest to attend occasional committee meetings. Keep the committee small enough to facilitate communication and meetings, but diverse enough to provide different areas of assistance. Potential members are scholars in the particular subject area (who can advise on the most pertinent topics and questions), experienced oral historians (who can advise on the interviewing process), prominent members of the community being studied (who can help make contact with potential interviewees), and perhaps fund-raising experts (who can help keep the project going).

Most funding agencies prefer some form of advisory committee, and grant proposals usually include funds to pay honoraria and sometimes travel expenses for advisory committee meetings. Some projects have blue-ribbon advisory panels that were created as showcases to appease funding agencies and whose members rarely convene meetings or are kept informed. This is a self-defeating practice. Any project can benefit from the experienced advice of advisory committee members, especially during the initial stages of design and development.

How should potential interviewees be identified?

The project advisory committee can often suggest the most likely interviewees. If a project is part of a larger organization, its leaders and members may have their own recommendations. Research into the subject will also identify those who were involved in the events at the time, and *Who's Who*, professional directories, phone books, pension lists, and other references can locate those still living.

Interviewees from particular groups or communities can be found through advertising in local newspapers, on radio or television stations, in the newsletters of companies, unions, churches, and civic organizations, and in alumni magazines. But mass appeals run the risk of stimulating massive responses, overwhelming the project with volunteer interviewees. Rather than disappoint people by not interviewing them, projects can limit their initial appeals to informal networks before going public through the media.

Then how should a project select interviewers?

Look first for those with previous oral history interviewing experience, those who have already done interviews or taken an oral history course or workshop. Ideally, interviewers should have some competence or experience in the project's subject matter. Occasionally, interviewers who fit both categories can be found, but usually the project organizers settle for one or the other qualification. Experienced interviewers coming into a new field need to do extensive research in the subject matter. Those already familiar with the subject material but who have not yet done any interviewing need training in interview techniques.

Inexperienced interviewers should attend training sessions conducted by an experienced oral historian, who can be located through the state, regional, or national oral history associations or through nearby universities and historical societies. It is essential that all interviewers be fully informed of the project's objectives, as well as of the ethical and legal considerations, before they begin interviewing.

Volunteers often come from the community or group being interviewed. Being part of the community gives them an advantage in researching the subject matter and in establishing rapport with interviewees. The disadvantages of using "intimates" lie in their reluctance to probe unpleasant topics and in interviewees' hesitation to disclose candid information to another member of their community. The "clinical" interviewer from outside the community may be seen as more neutral and discreet. Outside interviewers will take less for granted and encourage interviewees to talk over subjects that may be well known within the community but less recognized and understood beyond its boundaries. Be aware also that interviewers who share similar experiences will usually have their own stories to tell and may not be able to avoid interrupting and injecting themselves ("Oh, yeah? Let me tell you what happened to me") into the interviews. To forestall these temptations, it may be advisable to interview the interviewers. Let them tell their own stories on tape first. Being interviewed will also serve to further familiarize volunteer interviewers with the process.

Regardless of whether they are paid or volunteer, all interviewers should prepare written records of their preparation and methods, and the circumstances of the interviews. Interviewers should write a brief biographical statement about themselves to include with the tapes and transcripts. Future

31

researchers will find this information valuable in understanding the dynamics of the interview and will want to consider how the background of the interviewer might have affected the interview. Biographers will consider how the oral history itself became an incident in the interviewee's life, a time when he or she had the opportunity to reflect on past successes and defeats. They will want to know where and under what conditions the interview took place. Interviewers as well as interviewees deserve appropriate acknowledgment for their work in the tape and transcript and in all subsequent forms of citation or usage.[3]

How can the work of a variety of different interviewers be coordinated?

Maintaining consistency in the quality and standards of the oral history project is an issue when a number of interviewers, whether volunteers or paid, are used. Once again, a workshop for interviewers can be helpful, particularly at the beginning of a project—to help them not only to get some training but to appreciate the scope of the project and to have a chance to compare experiences and concerns. A core of common questions may emerge from these workshops or group meetings. Interviewers should be encouraged to read each other's transcripts, to measure their own work against the group's, and to offer some peer review. When many interviewers are employed over a protracted period of time, it is advisable to prepare a project handbook, with both general oral history procedures and information specific to the project. Model handbooks include *Working Womenroots: An Oral History Primer* (1980), designed for interviewing women trade union activists; *Oral History Techniques and Procedures* (1992), for army historians; and *Oral History in the National Park Service* (1984), which coordinates the myriad National Park Service oral histories.[4]

Better-funded, institutional projects have sponsored "memory-jogging" conferences to bring together a field's key people to discuss the topic and to fill in the gaps that scholars have found in the record. At these conferences, interviewers conduct preliminary interviews—with both individuals and groups—to determine how the attendees participated in the events being studied and to plan priorities for the full-scale interviews. Memory-jogging conferences have been held, for instance, to examine NATO's nuclear strategies during the cold war and the Cuban Missile Crisis.[5]

What credit should interviewers get for the work they have done?

Interviewers deserve full credit for their work. Display the name of the interviewer on the tape and the transcript. Whenever possible, cite the interviewer in any references to the interview in publications, exhibits, and other public presentations. Although the point of doing the interview is to collect the interviewee's story, it would not exist without the interviewer and might have emerged very differently if conducted by someone else. Increasingly, books heavily drawn from oral history interviews have cited the interviewer on the title page through phrases such as "with the assistance of . . . ," "as told to . . . ," and "based on an oral history with. . . ."[6]

EQUIPMENT

What basic equipment is needed for an oral history project?

Heavily dependent on technology, oral historians have adjusted constantly to introductions of new equipment. Fortunately, technological progress has resulted in lighter, easier-to-operate, and more affordable recorders. Dean Albertson, Allan Nevins's assistant at the Columbia Oral History Research Office, recalled purchasing Columbia's first wire recorders: "Instead of a reel of tape, they had a magnetic recording head through which passed a spool of fine wire. A more devilish machine was never invented. Quite apart from the fact that they weighed about 40 pounds was their propensity for jamming and spewing immense coils of wire all over the floor."[7]

Subsequently, oral historians moved to belt, reel-to-reel, and cassette tape recorders, and some to video cameras. Transcribing equipment has also advanced, from typewriters to word processors. Oral historians need to keep current with the latest and best equipment, being careful to adopt only those devices that adequately record and preserve high-quality sound. Pocket dictating machines, for instance, serve their own purposes but make poor recordings for oral history.

Purchase or rent the best that your project can afford. You need reliable equipment that will record clearly. Professional sound-quality reel-to-reel recorders are the best for archival preservation but are also the most expensive and least practical for interviewing. Most projects use good-quality, reasonably priced, portable cassette tape recorders. Some interviewers use earphones to monitor what is being recorded. Other useful accessories on the recorder are a signal to indicate when the tape is about to run out (so that the interviewer can change the tape with minimal interruption to the interview) and a register to indicate the strength of the sound recording (to alert the interviewer that batteries may be wearing down).

Electrical power is more reliable than batteries for tape recording, even though it may require some extra time or furniture rearranging to position the recorder near an outlet. Bear in mind, however, that the physical setting of the interview cannot always be determined in advance, and that you occasionally may need some mobility, say, to follow a craft worker through various stages of production in different locations. Always bring a supply of batteries to meet such contingencies.

Use only high-quality tapes. For cassette tapes, the recommended length is 60 minutes, although many prefer 90-minute tapes because they entail fewer interruptions to the narrative. Anything longer than 90-minute tape will be much too thin and likely to tangle and break.

Good microphones are also critical. Never use the tape recorder's built-in microphone; it will pick up all of the machine's operating noises. Many interviewers prefer to use lavaliere mikes, which attach to a lapel or other item of clothing and ensure clearer recording, especially if both the interviewer and interviewee have mikes. Lavalieres are a great advantage when interviewing soft-spoken people, the type who swallow their words, mumble, or unconsciously cover their mouths when they talk. If only one lavaliere mike is available, it should be used by the interviewee.

Table microphones should be placed close to the interviewee. Always test microphones in advance to be sure that the interviewee and interviewer can be heard clearly. Remember that most microphones have their own batteries that need testing and replacement periodically.

For transcribing, a separate transcribing machine is superior to a tape recorder. The foot pedal on the transcriber allows the operator to stop, reverse, and play back portions of the tape automatically while typing, since it may be necessary to listen to a phrase several times to ascertain the exact wording. Transcribing machines also permit the tape to be slowed down or speeded up to match the operator's typing speed and to help decipher muffled or slurred words. When outside transcribing services are used, transcription equipment is optional for a project, although a foot pedal-equipped transcriber can assist in audit-editing the transcripts.

Word processors have immensely advanced oral history transcription. Before the advent of the word processor, typists prepared a rough draft of the interview, on which the interviewee would make editorial changes, and then typed another clean copy. In fact, the principal transcript in some projects was the rough copy with handwritten corrections; this practice had the advantage of showing researchers where changes had been made, but the disadvantage of sometimes difficult-to-read handwriting that tended to reproduce poorly on microfilm and photocopies. Word processors speed typing time and allow editorial changes to be made more efficiently. Copies can be preserved on disk for instant retrieval and reprinting. Word-processing programs also check spelling and make the job of indexing faster and more comprehensive. Text-searching software is providing greater control and access for extensive oral history collections.

For any equipment, bargains can often be found by ordering via catalog. But the economy can be a false one if the equipment cannot be repaired nearby and must be shipped away at additional expense and for protracted periods of time. Work with reputable dealers and keep files on all warranties and guarantees.

What type of tape lasts the longest?

No audio- or videotape lasts forever. The National Archives and Records Administration recommends one-quarter-inch open-reel audiotape as the best for preservation, but since most oral historians use cassette rather than reel-to-reel recorders, archives will accept good-quality cassette tape for preservation. One compromise is to copy cassette tapes onto reel-to-reel. Regardless of the tape used, a master copy of the tape should be made for preservation purposes. Transcriptions and research use should be limited to the copies, never the master tape, since every replaying of a tape diminishes its sound quality. For videotape, archives prefer a one-inch or three-quarter-inch master tape.

Long-term preservation of tapes requires that they be kept under relatively constant temperature and humidity conditions, avoiding extreme heat and cold, excessive moisture, and dust and atmospheric pollutants. Tapes should be rerun every year or two at play speed to prevent blurring of their sound. Unfortunately, many projects do not have the facilities or the budget to maintain these conditions for their tapes or to go through the time-consuming process of regularly rewinding thousands of tapes.

Anyone who doubts that sound preservation is a problem should listen to audiotapes made a decade or two ago. These tapes often sound so muddy that both the questions and the answers have become indistinct. Documentary makers, after discovering that the sound quality of many oral history tapes has made them unusable, have been forced to use actors to re-create the interviewees' voices. These problems of long-term tape preservation highlight the need for oral history projects to transcribe their tapes and deposit master tapes in archives experienced in handling sound and video recordings, where they can be preserved for future use. The project can still retain copies of its tapes for its own ongoing uses.[8]

What sort of documentation should be kept on each interview?

The more interviews there are, the more control will be needed over the paperwork. The processing of each interview should move forward at a reasonable pace, and a "history" of each should be retained. The project manager should keep a log, or master project list, for each interview, including who was interviewed, by whom, for how many hours, on what dates, using how many reels of tape, whether the interview has been transcribed, whether it is open for research, what restrictions may have been placed on its use, and whether a microform copy is available.

A file for each interview should include whatever biographical information has been collected, letters arranging the interview, and an abstract of the interview that briefly summarizes (in not necessarily more than a single paragraph) the subjects covered and the names of the people most frequently discussed. The file should contain a copy of the deed of gift (the legal release form from the interviewee) and explanations of any restrictions on the interview. For ease of referral, it should note the libraries or other repositories where interested researchers can see copies of the interview.

Files should also be maintained on interviewers, with such basic information as home and work addresses, phone numbers, areas of expertise, interviews completed, and interviews scheduled. Keeping lists of potential interviewers and interviewees for later stages of the project is also helpful.

Where should interviews take place?

The location usually depends on the interviewee. Some people are so busy they will grant interviews only at their own office. This locale presents the problem of shutting out distractions and interruptions: a ringing phone, a secretary at the door, and all the reminders of the next item on the day's agenda will divert the interviewee's attention. Similarly, at an interviewee's home the phone, a spouse, children, the family dog, even noisy appliances, can interrupt the flow of the interview and create unacceptable levels of background noise on the tape. Too much background noise makes transcribing difficult and limits the eventual use of the tape for media or exhibits.

Try to conduct the interview in a quiet place away from everyday distractions. If not at the project office or the interviewer's office, then choose a room, or even a portion of a room, that the interviewee does not normally use. Get the interviewee away from behind the desk and sit in chairs at the other side of the office or in a conference room down the hall. Or conduct the interview at the dining room table. Politely request others in the home or office not to interrupt while you are recording. Shut the door if there is one.

Having the interviewee come to the interviewer allows for better control of the equipment and placement of the tape recorder or cameras and microphones. When going to the interviewee, allow enough time to set up the equipment. Not knowing where electrical outlets may be located, the interviewer should carry batteries or an extension cord. Always bring more tapes than you expect to use in case the interview goes longer than scheduled. Test the equipment just before the interview. The farther interviewers must travel to an interview, the less they can afford a malfunctioning piece of equipment. Murphy's Law applies to oral history: if it can break down, it will—precisely when needed.

What happens if the equipment fails?

Without any backup equipment, the interviewer will have to apologize and schedule another interview. Even worse is to conduct the interview and only later realize that the equipment failed. In addition to testing equipment before the interview, an interviewer must keep watch on it throughout the interview. I once had to call an interviewee to report that nothing could be heard on the tape but static. "Maybe that's all I gave you," the interviewee responded. That interviewee graciously agreed to do another interview, but repeat sessions are rarely as spontaneous and detailed as the original interview.

Failed equipment is the bane of the interviewer. The Oral History Association once invited veteran interviewers to testify to their "worst moments" in doing oral history. Tales of disaster included an absence of electrical outlets, tape recorders that picked up radio transmissions from passing police cars, tape that unraveled to fill an interviewer's car, and a long list of other calamities. It is reassuring to know that one is not alone, but such horror stories from experienced interviewers should encourage every project manager to test equipment regularly and be prepared to help interviewers meet any eventuality.

Is it ever appropriate to interview a group of people together?

The best oral history interview is generally done one on one. That way, the interviewer can focus exclusively on one person, whose stories will not be interrupted. Yet sometimes it is impossible to avoid having another person in the room, perhaps the interviewee's spouse or grown child, who may interrupt to contradict, correct, or supplement the testimony. Such interruptions can derail the interview, but they can also help by providing forgotten information and otherwise supporting an uncertain interviewee.[9]

Group interviews increase the potential for trouble. Facing a group, the interviewer becomes a moderator, trying to give everyone a chance to respond and ensuring that no one monopolizes the discussion. Transcribers have great difficulty identifying who is speaking in group situations, since all voices begin to sound alike. This problem is alleviated only if during the interview someone other than the interviewer (who has enough to do) keeps a sequential list of each speaker. Videotaping the group session can also facilitate identification.

Although more difficult, group interviews can gather fruitful information. Interviewees remember common incidents when sitting in a group that they might not have thought of by themselves. Self-exaggeration may also be tempered in a peer group situation. The John F. Kennedy Library has conducted several successful group interviews with journalists who covered the president and with the chairmen that Kennedy appointed to head the independent regulatory commissions. Nevertheless, group interviews should be considered only as supplements to individual interviews, not as replacements.

Can a team of interviewers conduct an interview together?

Using more than one interviewer distorts the one-on-one relationship that tends to work best for oral history. The anthropologist Michael Kenny warned that a group of interviewers, though it can sometimes work, holds a potential for disaster: "Illuminating as this technique can be, it can also turn into the worst type of press conference, wherein the informant is either thoroughly cowed or offended, and rightly so."[10]

But there can be advantages to using more than one interviewer. Younger students, nervous about the experience, often interview in pairs or are accompanied by a parent or teacher. Novice interviewers may similarly take along a partner for moral support. Some research projects have been done entirely by teams. For one project on racial violence in the South, a black interviewer conducted most of the interviews with white southerners but took the precaution of going as part of a team with a white interviewer. One team member may be better versed in a particular subject and can take the lead in questioning about that area. But in team situations, one interviewer usually serves as the principal interviewer, asking most of the questions and gaining the interviewee's primary attention. Accompanying interviewers should try not to interrupt, except perhaps to interject a follow-up question that the primary interviewer may have missed.

What are the differences between recording events that are still taking place and recording those that are long past?

Most oral history projects look back, but some have conducted "history while it's hot," in the words of Forrest Pogue, the World War II combat interviewer. Military historians since then have carried tape recorders to question troops from Vietnam to the Persian Gulf. During Eugene McCarthy's campaign for the Democratic presidential nomination in 1968, an oral history project recorded interviews with the candidate and many of his staff. Oral historians at corporations and university archivists have conducted ongoing interviews with their presidents and other high-level administrators, to review the past year's events and debrief the players in recent major events.

Scheduling is perhaps the biggest problem with interviewing as the events are occurring. The key players are often too busy or too likely to feel interrupted. They make and break appointments at a frustrating pace. Interviewers have to be patient and ready to take advantage of whatever opportunity comes along. Finally, when the subject matter is a current event, take it for granted that almost everything will be closed for some period. For the interview to be anything more revealing than a radio talk show, the interviewer must guarantee absolute confidentiality and allow the interviewee to seal the tapes and transcript for a safe period, until the events have passed into history.

PROCESSING

Must all our oral history interviews be transcribed?

The deteriorating sound quality of tape recordings over time is just one of many incentives for transcribing oral history interviews. Even with the best recording devices, listeners may find it hard at times to understand interviewees, especially older people whose voices have grown faint or those who speak with a pronounced accent or in regional dialect. Others may mutter and stumble over words. Background noises may obliterate the speaker's words. If the interviewer, who was present, finds it difficult to understand and transcribe all that was said, imagine the problem future researchers will have interpreting the tape. Transcribing enables both the interviewer and interviewee to review the interview and ensure that the transcript reflects what each intended to say.

Given a choice, researchers invariably prefer transcripts over tapes. Eyes can read easier than ears can hear. Transcripts can be scanned and photocopied. Information can be retrieved even more easily if the transcripts are indexed or if text-searching computer software is used. The tape will provide sound for television documentaries, radio programs, and exhibits, or for biographers, folklorists, and others curious about speaking voice, dialect, hesitations, and other verbal mannerisms. But archivists note that very few researchers ask to listen to the tapes if transcripts are available.

If a project cannot afford transcripts, what are the alternatives?

If transcribing is not possible, a project's work should at least include abstracting and indexing the tapes. A summary of the main individuals and subjects discussed, with notations of where they can be found chronologically on the tape, will enable researchers to find the portions they seek. The TAPE (Time Access to Pertinent Excerpts) system has been designed to prepare such abstracts. Oral history project managers must maintain control over their collections as they grow if they want to access portions easily in the future. Whether you transcribe or abstract, it is also essential to process as you go, to avoid creating overwhelming backlogs, which can paralyze a project.[11]

Should you transcribe your own tapes or contract them out?

Transcription is by far the most expensive and time-consuming part of an oral history project, requiring six to eight hours to transcribe each hour of interview as well as more time to audit-edit the transcripts—that is, to play back the tape while reviewing the transcript, making sure the two are consistent. Some project staffs transcribe their own tapes; in other projects, professional transcribing services are hired. In selecting transcribers, look for someone with previous oral history experience. Typing speed is far less critical for transcription than typing for comprehension. The estimated cost of transcribing should also include making corrections on the first draft of the interview. Request the transcript on computer disk as well as in a hard-copy version. It is advisable to continue with the same transcription service for all of your interviews to ensure consistent stylistic treatment of idiosyncratic vocabulary, acronyms, geographic place names, regional dialects, and any number of other factors that might hinder speedy and accurate transcription if the interviews pass through too many hands.

In some projects, interviews are transcribed after additional funds have been raised. Funding agencies, such as state humanities councils, have occasionally underwritten the transcription of already completed interviews, since the exact cost can be calculated and a finished collection guaranteed. The longer a project waits, the more difficult the transcription process becomes, owing to the deterioration of tapes and to the possibility that interviewees will die before having a chance to correct their transcripts.

What issues need to be worked out in advance with a transcribing service?

Transcribers want tapes that are clear and distinct, with little background noise. Provide a list of any proper and place names and technical terms that are mentioned on the tape, to reduce the chance of error and the time necessary for proofreading and editing. Label cassette tapes with the name of the interviewee, date of the interview, and sequence of the tapes (interview no. 1, tape no. 1, tape no. 2, and so on). As an added precaution, and for ready identification later, at the beginning of the first tape interviewers should introduce themselves, their interviewees, and the date of the interview. This formal preamble can be recorded before meeting with the interviewee to avoid jeopardizing rapport. Always retain the master tape and send only a copy to the transcriber.

Agreements should be made in advance with transcribers on the desired format of the transcripts, including spacing, type size, margins, and speaker identification. Make sure that the transcriber uses compatible computer equipment and software so that you can edit the disks and use them to produce copies as needed. Determine whether the transcriber will prepare the index, and what index terms are most important. Caution the transcriber about possibly confidential material on the tapes. (Some transcribers provide notarized assurances that transcripts will remain confidential.) Make the transcriber aware of whatever deadlines the project is operating under. Report any problems with the transcripts to the transcriber, especially at the beginning of the process before patterns have been established, to keep the final product consistent.[12]

Which is the oral history, the tape or the transcript?

Tape and transcript are two types of records of the same interview. Archivists generally consider the tape, being the original and verbatim record, the primary document. Looked at another way, the tape records what was said, and the transcript represents the intended meaning of what was said. Even the most slavishly verbatim transcript is just an interpretation of the tape. Different transcribers might handle the same material in different ways, including punctuation, capitalization, false starts, broken sentences, and verbal obstacles to presenting spoken words in print. Interviewers and interviewees should edit the transcripts, correcting errors, whether misspoken or mistranscribed. During the editing, interviewees may add material that was forgotten during their interviews, or they may remove comments that they have had second thoughts about.

Those in disciplines—particularly the behavioral sciences—more interested in the study of the actual speech warn against taking transcripts "too seriously as *the* reality." Viewing transcripts as only a partial rendering of the tapes, they note the importance of such additional features as pitch, stress, volume, and rate of speech, as well as facial gestures and body movements, which are not captured on audiotape. These disciplines often design particular modes of transcription to illustrate aspects of speech they consider important, such as measuring the pauses in an interviewee's responses. Some have devised symbols to express significant nonverbal responses. When the folklorist Henry Glassie interviewed the Irish at Ballymenone, he used a diamond-shaped symbol to signify "a smile in the voice, a chuckle in the throat, a laugh in the tale," suggesting humor visually but not verbally.[13]

In the United States, the transcript rather than the tape has generally served as the primary research tool. Created and directed by historical researchers, the pioneering Columbia Oral History Research Office during its early years produced transcripts and then, because of its limited budget, recorded over its tapes. As often happens, practical policies became elevated to the status of principle. Columbia noted that most researchers asked to use only transcripts and that only folklorists, linguists, and ethnomusicologists wanted to hear the sound recordings. Columbia thus felt justified in its deemphasis of the tape and spoke authoritatively on the matter. Many oral history projects followed its model.

Canadian oral historians, by contrast, adopted "aural history" and created impressive sound archives, often with no transcripts at all. Similarly converting a practice to a principle, some oral historians rejected transcripts as a distortion or corruption of the interview. To be accurate, they argued, every word, sound, or false start should be put down on paper. When the Oral History Association met in Canada in 1976, heated arguments erupted as to whether the tape or the transcript was the "real" oral history. Mercifully, most of this debate has since faded; oral historians now generally accept both tape and transcript as different but equally legitimate records of the same event. Computers have also made transcribing easier and more cost-effective, and transcribing services have blossomed for those who do not want to do it themselves.

Too great an emphasis on transcribing has caused many oral historians to ignore the quality of their sound recordings, so that many tapes are of such poor quality that they cannot be used for broadcasting or museum exhibition. Transcripts and high-quality sound recordings (and video recordings) involve considerable expense, and oral history projects have often been forced to take one path or the other. Still, tape and transcript should not be seen as an either-or choice but as mutual goals.

Does editing transcripts change and distort their meaning?

Editing is usually necessary to make sense of the spoken word when put down in writing. The transcriber may have made errors, garbled names, or been unable to distinguish exactly what an interviewee said. The interviewee may have given the wrong name or date or some other unintentionally misleading information. Speakers often do not complete sentences. The listener can get the gist of their meaning, but in written form these fragmented sentences can be a source of frustration.[14]

Oral historians are not the only people who edit transcripts. Members of Congress edit their remarks in the daily *Congressional Record*, and administration witnesses revise the testimony they have given before congressional committees. In his oral history, Carl Marcy recalled how during the 1940s he edited Secretary of State George C. Marshall's congressional testimony:

> Secretary Marshall called me to his office one day. He was very austere. He looked at me with a transcript in front of him that I had corrected. He said, "Marcy, you in charge of this?" I said, "Yes sir, I did that." He said, "Well, I don't know what it is, but I feel when I'm talking to the senators that I'm making sense and they understand me. But when I look at the uncorrected

transcript it doesn't make much sense." But, he said, "after you fix it up, it looks all right. You keep on doing it."[15]

There are advantages to having interviewees edit their own transcripts. Interviewees know what they said, or meant to say, better than anyone else. They can often spot misspelled names and mistranscribed sentences. Whether a word should appear at the end of one sentence or at the beginning of the next can affect the meaning of both sentences. Dropping a *not* can dramatically reverse the meaning. Words that sound alike and make sense in context may not be the words the interviewee used. Transcribers have heard *assumed* instead of *as soon*, *block aid* for *blockade*, and the *Duke of Wellington* instead of *Duke Ellington*. One transcript contained an astonishing comment about two Supreme Court justices: "Brandeis was concerned about marrying Frankfurter." The speaker had actually said that Louis Brandeis was worried about the health of Felix Frankfurter's wife Marion. Another transcript contained a mysterious reference to "I. C. Sping, head of the transition team." Replaying the tape revealed that the interviewee had actually said: "I ceased being head of the transition team."

Some interviewees will defer to the interviewer to make whatever corrections seem necessary. Others, especially professional people, feel chagrined at seeing their syntax set down in print. They will correct tenses, change *yeah* to *yes*, and otherwise make themselves appear as literate as possible. Interviewers need to remind their interviewees that an oral history is a spoken record, and that it is best to keep the verbal rhythms and flows rather than convert the history into a more formal text. Writers of fiction are always trying to re-create believable human dialogue; oral history is human dialogue. The vernacular is accessible and attractive to wide audiences. Too much tampering with the transcript compromises the qualities that make oral history so compelling. Some oral historians insist that any changes in the verbatim transcript be put in brackets. Others, seeking to avoid even the temptation of making alterations, prefer not to give the transcript to the interviewee for editing. Unless interviewees have already signed releases, however, their dissatisfaction or embarrassment may keep transcripts of their interviews from being opened for research. Although such issues can be negotiated, the ethics of oral history and the laws of copyright dictate that an interviewee's wishes be honored.

Some changes add to a transcript, as when interviewees realize that they did not finish a story on tape or left out related material, which can be inserted in the final transcript. More problematic are deletions of stories or commentary because interviewees have had second thoughts after completing the taped interview. Rather than eliminate this material altogether, interviewees should be advised to restrict its use for a safe period of time.

Transcripts may be edited, but the master tapes should be left exactly as spoken. Interviewers should inform interviewees that no changes or deletions can be made to the master tape. Interviewees may choose to set a longer restriction on use of the unedited tape than they do on the edited transcript, or to require listeners to quote solely from transcripts. Edited copies of the master tape may be released for research pending the lifting of any restrictions on portions of the master tape.

What is the interviewer's responsibility for reviewing and editing the transcript?

Oral historians should audit-edit the transcripts of their interviews. Having sat through the interview, the interviewer knows the material better than anyone except the interviewee. Sometimes interviewers transcribe their own tapes, but more often the interviewer serves as editor of the transcript. Listening to the tape, the interviewer reads the transcript to correct spelling errors, fill in words the transcriber could not discern, and generally make sense of what the interviewee said.

During the interview, the interviewer should note any unusual proper names and place names and afterwards ask the interviewee for the correct spellings. Some interviewers do this in the course of the interview, but others strongly prefer not to interrupt the interview and wait instead until the session is over. Their interview notes will facilitate the transcriber's job.

Listening to the tape while editing the transcript can also be an important—and excruciating—learning experience for interviewers, who thus get to listen to their own mistakes. Note the sound quality of the tape. Did you take into account the air conditioner or the grandfather's clock or the open window when you set up the tape recorder and microphone, and can you hear how these noises obscure the spoken word and make transcribing difficult? Did you interrupt before the interviewee was finished answering? Did you fail to follow up your initial question or leave an important question unaddressed? Did you pursue new leads in the interview or unwisely force it back to your prepared questions? Every editing session teaches interviewers more about their techniques and better prepares them for future interviews.

Should transcribers also edit?

The responsibility of transcribers is to reproduce as closely as possible what they hear on tapes. Transcribers should never rearrange words or delete phrases for stylistic purposes. Some projects permit a transcriber to remove "false starts," which are sentences that begin one way and then end abruptly as the interviewee changes gears. ("First we went . . . we started . . . well, actually, even before we went," might be tightened to, "Actually, even before we went.") But some false starts reveal mental processes, Freudian slips, and attempts to suppress information. Nor should transcribers try to correct ungrammatical constructions. A transcriber should leave the editing to the interviewer and the interviewee and only note those places in the transcript that were difficult to understand and any questions about spelling or syntax.

Working on a particular interview, a transcriber will soon become familiar with the speaker's verbal punctuation. Frequently, interviewees will use a word like *and* to start every new sentence, or *and so* to begin a new paragraph. If transcribed literally, the interview would read like one long run-on sentence. Instead, transcribers are justified in replacing constantly repeated cues with punctuation and paragraph breaks.

How should a transcript indicate sounds and gestures other than words?

Both the transcriber and the interviewer should add in brackets any additional descriptions—such as "[laughs]," "[snaps fingers]," "[uses hands to suggest height]"—that will help the reader understand what was happening or what the interviewee intended to express. Humor and sarcasm sometimes do not translate well and may be taken too seriously unless the laughter of the interviewer or interviewee is also recorded. The transcript should also elucidate otherwise unexplainable shifts in the dialogue by noting any break in the tape, mechanical failing, or prolonged lapse in the interview. In all of these cues, however, reasonable discretion and good sense should be employed. Their purpose is to assist the researcher, not to embarrass the interviewee.

Similarly, transcripts should be edited to provide—in brackets—the full name and any relevant title of individuals when first mentioned, such as "Bob [Senator Robert J.] Dole," or, "President [William J.] Clinton." When a city or town is mentioned, the state should also be added in brackets—such as Springfield [Missouri] or Springfield [Illinois]—unless a series of communities in a single state are under discussion. For stylistic questions about numbers, abbreviations, and so on, transcribers should consult the *Chicago Manual of Style* or whatever other style manual the project chooses to employ.[16]

Should transcripts reproduce accents and dialects?

If the interview is intended for folklore studies or other purposes for which regional speech patterns are important, then rendering regional dialect in a transcript might be desirable. But dialects are tricky business that should be handled carefully.

Educated interviewees who say *yeah* will insist on altering the transcript word to *yes*. They are sorely displeased when transcripts show them saying *gonna* or *talkin'* and would prefer to see their spoken words reproduced as they would write them. If oral historians allow these interviewees to correct their transcripts, they owe the same courtesy to those who are not used to seeing their words set down in print. As the Appalachian Oral History Project concluded, transcribing phonetically gives a pejorative cast to the speech and can "unintentionally demean the speaker." The Appalachian project discovered that its transcribers—student workers from the same area—were unaware of their own dialect's peculiarities (such as pronouncing *our* as *air*) and therefore spelled the words correctly. Only transcribers from outside the mountain culture tried to capture on paper what they imagined to be authentic-looking dialect. The Appalachian project trained its transcribers not to correct grammar, but also not to respell what was said to the approximate dialect. That way they kept the flavor of the speaker's style without indicating pronunciation.[17]

The historian Nell Irvin Painter came to the same conclusions about her oral history of Hosea Hudson, a southern black labor organizer. "Adapting Hudson's spoken language to the printed page meant abandoning its sound, for Hudson does not speak as I have rendered his words," Painter explained. A phonetically reproduced transcript would have been "condescending and difficult to read." She chose to use standard English spellings and to avoid apostrophes in words that showed variations from standard style, "because apostrophes and dialect in literature have long singled out characters that readers need not take seriously, ignorant folk who cannot speak correctly. With black people, the usage is centuries old." Yet as much as possible she preserved Hudson's vocabulary and such unique phrases as "howbeitsoever" to retain the spirit of the words without belittling the man.[18]

What should the transcript look like?

The word processor has revolutionized oral history transcripts and made obsolete many of the previously recommended styles of transcripts. At one time, either corrections were handwritten directly on the transcript or the entire transcript had to be retyped. Using typewriters, oral historians used triple-spaced lines and elaborately wide margins for making corrections. All of these techniques became unnecessary with the word processor's easy means of correction and reproduction.

Use common sense in setting margins. The practices of early oral historians led to so few words to the page that researchers complained about the inflated photocopying costs. On the other hand, too small a margin causes problems if a transcript is bound. Small type face and single-spacing will also make the transcript difficult to read when microfilmed.

Earlier, the anonymous *Q* and *A* were used to indicate questions and answers, but the word processor now makes it easy to insert the inter-viewer's and interviewee's last names each time they speak. If the interview extends over several sessions, the transcript should indicate at the begin-ning: "Interview no. 1 with Jane Jones, Wednesday, 18 October 1995," and at the end, "End of interview no. 1." Begin the next with, "Interview no. 2 . . ." The title page should list the interviewee's name, the name of the oral history project, the interviewer's name, the dates of the interviews, and their location.

Introduce the transcripts with a brief explanation of the purpose of the oral history project and an outline of the interviewee's life and career. Some projects will use a data sheet on each interviewee instead. A brief biographical statement for the interviewer will also be useful for future researchers, since different interviewers (historians, political scientists, folklorists, community members) will ask different questions. Put the deed of gift up front to establish the copyright and research use of the interview. Interview transcripts may also contain relevant documents as appendix material. Some projects include one or more photographs of the interviewee and of people and events de-scribed in the interview. An index will also greatly enhance an interview's research use.

Why is an index necessary?

It does not take long before even the interviewer has trouble remembering who said what in which interview. Collecting information is only the first step; retrieving it comes next. Word-processing programs now make indexing so much easier that there is less excuse for not creating them. At a minimum, indexes should include all names cited. Subject indexes are trickier but no less important. The program manager and interviewers should work out a general list of important terms for indexing purposes. Indexes help both interviewers and researchers. As interviewers prepare for future interviews, they will want to review pertinent portions of past interviews to prepare their questions. Researchers often do not want to read an entire transcript, but only those portions dealing with their particular subject. Text-searching software has also become a boon to users of oral histories, but since the transcript will often stand alone, particularly if it has been microfilmed, a separate index will still be useful.

Cross-referenced indexes add immeasurably to the research use of a collec-tion. Since 1948 Columbia University has maintained a name index of all of its interviews. Researchers have found this massive index to be a rich resource, since it identifies not only the major players in their subject but also the minor figures whose interviews they might not otherwise have consulted but who often offer the most perceptive observation and analyses.

Should the project director review all transcripts?

Someone other than the interviewer ought to review the transcript before releasing it for research. Depending on the size of a project, a project director or editor may read all interviews or may delegate some to members of the advisory board as reviewer/evaluators. This decision depends on whether the interviews are ready to be opened and therefore can be reviewed by an advisory board member, or whether confidentiality needs to be maintained and reviewing should be limited to the project director. The project director should review the material to determine whether the interviewer is following the project's guidelines, asking appropriate questions and follow-up questions, not interrupting, and collecting worthwhile material. Directors can use the review process to advise interviewers on recommended changes in style, or they may decide not to continue to use interviewers whose work is unsatisfactory. Project directors will also want to be sure that a consistent style is followed in the processing of different interviews in a project.

LEGAL CONCERNS

Journalists do not use legal release forms for their interviews; why should oral historians?

People who respond to journalists' questions assume that their words will appear in print unless they stipulate that something is "off the record" or otherwise not for attribution. Many journalists take notes rather than tape-record their interviews and generally use only brief excerpts from interviews in their stories. Few journalists retain their notes for posterity. Oral historians face different considerations.

Federal copyright law grants copyright automatically to anyone whose words and ideas are recorded in any tangible form, for a period lasting until 50 years after that person's death. That is, even without registering the copyright with the Copyright Office, interviewees retain the copyright on anything they have said in an interview. If the oral history project or any researcher publishes excerpts from their interviews beyond "fair use"—a relatively small number of words—without a deed of gift or contract that permits such use, then the interviewee could sue for copyright infringement.

For this reason, archives require a deed of gift or contract before opening an oral history for research. Similarly, publishers want to be sure that copyright concerns have been addressed before they publish interviews in a book. To avoid headaches later, interviewers should collect deeds of gift when the interview is conducted, or at least by the time the transcript has been prepared and edited.

The deed of gift or contract establishes who owns copyright in the interview and what may be done with it. Interviewees may retain the copyright and require that they or their heirs be consulted before anyone uses or publishes excerpts from the interview. This requirement makes the process complex and should be avoided if possible. Other interviewees will assign the copyright to the interviewer, the oral history project, or the repository but will stipulate that all or part of the interview must remain closed for a period of time, sometimes until the interviewee's death. Too stringent a time restriction should also be avoided, since archives do not want to store materials for protracted periods if they cannot be used.

A simple deed of gift can assign the copyright to the interviewer or the oral history project, to use as they see fit, and to deposit in an institution of their choosing. Some deeds jointly assign the copyright to the public domain, that is, both the interviewer and the interviewee waive the right to copyright the material. Assigning copyright to the public domain vastly simplifies administration but offers little control over uses of the material.

Projects should develop a standard deed of gift or contract that offers enough flexibility to meet the requirements of different interviewees. Interviewers should explain to interviewees ahead of time the potential uses and planned deposit of the interviews so that the interviewee knows fully what to expect. Usually, these explanations are outlined in the initial correspondence or conversation between oral historians and interviewees. Should the interviewee die before signing a deed of gift, the verbal agreement on the tape may serve as an oral contract. Otherwise, the oral history project will have to seek out the next of kin to sign the deed. (Sample deeds of gift are reprinted in appendix 2.)[19]

Must the interviewer also sign a deed of gift?

Since the interview is a joint product, the interviewer as well as the interviewee should sign a legal release. Projects that use volunteer or paid interviewers should require them to sign *before* they do any interviewing, to avoid any misunderstandings later on. By signing such releases, interviewers agree to assign whatever copyright they might have to the project to the interview repository or to the public domain (see appendix 2).[20]

Do interviewees have a right to close their interviews for a long time?

Before beginning an interview, when interviewees often feel nervous, interviewers will explain their right to close portions or all of an interview for as long as necessary. At the outset, more than one interviewee has announced, "Well, this is going to be hot and will have to be kept closed for a long time. I don't want to embarrass anyone." By the conclusion of the interview, however, the interviewee usually feels more relaxed, the information elicited rarely turns out to have been salacious, and it has become evident that the people discussed are usually long since retired or deceased and that the "hot" information has cooled down considerably. At this point, the interviewer should point out what a valuable research tool the interview will become, and what a shame it would be to keep it away from researchers for long. Quite often the interviewee may decide to open the interview within a short time, if not immediately. A little flattery and reassurance generally goes a long way to encourage early release.

What rights do interviewees have to publish their own interviews?

Interviewees may want the right of first use. That is, they may want to close the interview while they write their own book. The oral history may provide the outline and the core of what they are writing. Unless the project has its own deadlines for a publication, exhibit, or other public presentation of the material and thus needs to negotiate a mutually beneficial release date, there is no reason why the interview should not be kept closed for a reasonable period that will give the interviewee the chance to publish a book, or abandon the attempt. The book will most likely depart from the interview in many respects, or it may not use all of the interview material. In either case, researchers will benefit from the additional first-person material. Nevertheless, given your oral history project's investment of time and funds in the interviews, and recognizing that some interviewees will never be able to turn a transcript into a publishable book no matter how long they work on it, do not permit open-ended restrictions on interviews that give the interviewees exclusive use and fail to set a definite time when other researchers can gain access.

The *New York Times* noted that when the pilot Chuck Yeager first read the manuscript of his autobiography prepared by his collaborator, he exclaimed, "Hell, it's just like me talking." As it happened, the collaborator had drawn much of the book from 40 hours of taped interviews that Yeager had done with the Air Force Oral History Program. The Senate Historical Office interviewed George Tames, who had photographed Washington people and events for 40 years for the *New York Times*. Although never a member of the Senate staff, Tames had spent nearly every working day of his career on Capitol Hill, getting into the backrooms to snap his photographs. In his interviews, Tames gave vivid descriptions of the senators he captured on film and seemingly had a story for every photograph he took. When his interviews were completed, Tames dictated his own further reminiscences, which he published as *Eye on Washington: The Presidents Who've Known Me*.[21]

Future researchers may also find it useful to compare the original spoken interview with the polished publication. For example, the University of Kentucky Library contains the uncorrected typescript of the long series of interviews that Sidney Shalett conducted with the former senator and vice president Alben Barkley and used to produce Barkley's memoir, *That Reminds Me* (1954). The transcripts reveal a more hot-tempered, opinionated Barkley than appears in his genial autobiography, and the differences between the two versions offer useful insights for researchers.[22]

What if someone demands that the tapes and transcripts be returned?

Very rarely, an interviewee has second thoughts about an oral history and may refuse to sign a deed of gift or even ask to withdraw the interview from a collection. This unfortunate situation has also occurred when an interviewee dies without signing a deed of gift and the next of kin demands to have the interview back. It is necessary to impress upon these individuals the time and cost that it took to do the interview, and the breach that its removal would cause to the collection. Try negotiating a longer restriction on the interview rather than its removal. Sometimes the interviewee just needs a little reassurance that the interview is a valuable document and does not sound foolish. But if the interviewee is adamant, the tapes and transcripts must be returned. After a reasonable interval, a project can contact those who have removed their interviews, or their next of kin, provide some information on the continued progress of the collection, and encourage them to resubmit the interviews so that the story will not be lost.

Can something said in an oral history ever be considered libelous or defamatory?

Unfortunately, yes. Individuals whom interviewees may libel or defame can sue not only the interviewee but the interviewer and the repository that holds the interview. Such instances are exceedingly rare, but even the threat of a libel suit can be unpleasant. Use common sense. If an interviewee states something extremely negative about a living individual, something that is not widely known or previously published about that individual, and especially if the individual is not a public figure, then simply restrict that material for a period of time until the possibly defamed individual is no longer around to sue. The dead cannot be defamed.

Rather than close the whole interview because of one potentially libelous story, restrict that portion for a period of time until the closure can be safely lifted. It may be disappointing not to be able to open a juicy story immediately. But as a lawyer once advised an oral history project: "You could probably win a libel suit in court, but you wouldn't want to see the legal bills that would be the result."[23]

What should be done with the finished interviews?

If the oral history project is not part of a library, archives, historical society, or other institution that deals with researchers, then its tapes and transcripts should be deposited somewhere that is capable of preserving the interviews and of making them available for general use. Public libraries are usually eager to gather materials about a community, its longtime families, churches, and schools for their local history sections. Archives will be pleased to receive copies of interviews relating to any person for whom they hold manuscript collections. University libraries often collect interviews done by students and faculty members. Larger oral history offices are willing to take in donated collections on a wide array of topics.

Each interview's deed of gift should indicate that the interviewee knows, and approves, the interview repository. Supply the repository with basic information about the interviews, project goals, sponsorship, and funding and make sure that all interviewers have documented their preparation, methods, and interview circumstances.

Since oral history tapes and transcripts are easily copied, it is not necessary to limit the deposit to a single institution. Put copies of your oral histories wherever researchers are most likely to use them: in different libraries in a community, in archives that have the papers of the interviewee, or with institutions closely associated with the interviewee. In addition, plan to give at least one if not several copies of the transcript to the interviewee. Even in inexpensive loose-leaf or spiral binding, transcripts make treasured gifts for family members. Retain at least one copy, or the computer disk, for the oral history project's own future reference.

How do you let people know where to find your project's oral histories?

Having gone through all the steps of conducting, processing, and preserving oral history interviews, it can be a source of immense frustration when researchers fail to use them. Your oral history project is really not over until you have made an effort to publicize the existence of the collection. Send announcements to professional organization newsletters for oral history and local history groups or for other disciplines whose researchers are likely to be interested in the subject. Consider writing a brief article, drawing from the interviews, for publication in a newsletter or local newspaper. Oral histories can be included in library catalogs. Archival projects also report their collections on the Research Libraries Information Network (RLIN) or the Online Catalog Library Center (OCLC) cataloging systems. A number of microform publishers also reproduce and distribute oral histories, with the permission of the oral history projects. The possibilities for making interviews available on computer networks are also being explored.

In addition to scholarly researchers, you should also make the interviews available to the community from which they came. The library or archives where the interviews are deposited may be willing to mount an exhibit based on them. Local newspapers and broadcasters may draw from the collected materials for articles, programs, and documentaries. Pamphlets and other publications can be planned to give the material a wider distribution. Documentaries, slide-tape productions, and radio and theatrical performances have all tapped into the abundant resources of oral history.

3

CONDUCTING INTERVIEWS

What qualities make a good interviewer?

For Studs Terkel, the trick to interviewing successfully is "engaging in conversation, having a cup of coffee." His interviewing style is unobtrusive, straightforward, and sympathetic, but challenging when necessary. One interviewee described him as easygoing: "He doesn't ask particularly *probing* questions, and yet he's able to get people to open up and tell these marvelous little stories about themselves. He's a good listener." All interviewers need to put their interviewees at ease, to listen carefully to what they have to say, to respect their opinions, and to encourage candid responses. Listening skills do not come automatically, and interviewers have to work hard to achieve these results.[1]

Interviews are partly performance. Not only do interviewers want to handle themselves well, but interviewees often feel nervous about their ability to recall and describe events long past; they also want to do well. No one wants to sound forgetful or inarticulate. Interviewers should become a partner in the process, helping interviewees become as comfortable, forthcoming, and accurate as possible. Interviewers need to guide without leading, providing names, dates, and other information to keep the dialogue moving. A critical task is to move interviewees beyond reluctance to an honest and perhaps self-critical evaluation of the past.[2]

Fundamental rules and principles apply to all types of oral history interviewing: do your homework; be prepared; construct meaningful but open-ended questions; do not interrupt responses; follow up on what you have heard; know your equipment thoroughly; promptly process your tapes; and always keep in mind and practice the ethics of interviewing.

PREPARING FOR THE INTERVIEW

How should an interviewer get ready for an interview?

Familiarize yourself with whatever information is available about the general subject matter and about the people to be interviewed, their families, communities, jobs, successes, and failures. Interviewers first get acquainted with the outline of interviewees' lives and then allow them to fill in the details. Read any published sources, such as family histories, histories of the town or institution, and histories of the events that the individual experienced, to understand and formulate questions.

Back issues of newspapers and magazines, published and unpublished genealogies, and other sources likely to be found in the local history section of a library are natural beginnings for research. Some interviewees have deposited their papers in a library, although most still have their papers, scrapbooks, and other memorabilia in their closets, attics, and basements. Ask them to make these records available prior to the interview. Others bring relevant memoranda, letters, and photographs to the interview. When all else fails, ask interviewees to give brief descriptions of themselves and to suggest what other sources you might consult.

An especially instructive way to prepare for an interview is to read or listen to other oral histories. Investigate other interviews from your project or the tapes and transcripts deposited in a library. Techniques vary, even from interview to interview, depending on the interviewer's expertise and the interviewee's cooperation and loquaciousness. Analyzing different types of questions, and ways of asking them, will help you construct your own questioning style. During the 1970s, Former Members of Congress, Inc., interviewed more than 100 former senators and representatives and gave the tapes and transcripts to the Library of Congress. A number of interviewers participated, and their transcripts reveal a variety of styles and approaches: historians asked questions that fit a mostly biographical framework; political scientists asked organizational questions about seniority, staff, committee assignments, leadership, and other aspects of congressional group behavior.[3]

When preparing a budget, count on doing as many as ten hours of research for every hour of interview conducted. Usually, only the initial interview sessions require this much advance research. Subsequent interviews will build on the original research and require less preparation time. The cost of preparation decreases when several interviews can be conducted from a single investment in prior research.

Is so much research really necessary?

Yes. It is the only way to determine what questions to ask. The more an interviewer knows about the individual and the subject matter, the easier it is to build rapport and conduct the interview. Interviewees become impatient with interviewers whose questions show they do not know the subject matter.

Research also helps an interviewer supply information that an interviewee has forgotten. As they backtrack through their lives, few people remember names and dates accurately. An interview can come to a standstill while the interviewee gropes for a forgotten name ("that tall man, you know, what's his name, the economist, who smoked a pipe"). If the interviewer can provide the name ("Do you mean John Kenneth Galbraith?"), the interviewee, with great relief, will continue as if uninterrupted. If you do not know it, promise to look up the name later to fill in the transcript. Many interviewees, especially older people, lack confidence in their memories and tensely view an interview as a test. Interviewers should try to put them at ease. Dates are also significant, since people often jumble the chronology or merge events that took place at different times. By interjecting "Didn't that happen in 1960 rather than 1970?" the interviewer can help the interviewee get back on track.

Interviewers need to be sufficiently prepared to know what to expect and what not to expect from an interview. If interviewees make claims that conflict with other accounts, encourage them to explain further. Interviewees may bring up some entirely new subject that was not part of the original research. Explore this new topic by saying, "I didn't know about that. Can you tell me more about it?" Although interviewers work hard to prepare questions in advance, they must be willing to deviate from them sometimes to follow the interviewee's detours, which may provide valuable information.

How many questions should be prepared for each interview?

It is safer to have too many questions than too few. Some interviewees talk at great length in response to a single question. During a soliloquy, they may anticipate several questions on the interviewer's list and discuss these issues without being prompted. Others answer briefly and need several follow-up questions to draw them out. Whenever Senate Majority Leader Mike Mansfield appeared on "Meet the Press," the program's interviewers prepared twice as many questions as for other guests because the senator habitually abbreviated his responses to "Yep" and "Nope." If an interviewer has prepared more questions than time permits, another interview session would be in order.

Avoid asking the type of question that elicits a brief answer, such as, "You grew up in Grand Rapids?" "Yes." "And you went to public school there?"

"Yes, I did." Instead of simply verifying your research notes, ask, "What was Grand Rapids like when you were growing up there?" and, "Tell me about the schools you attended." Transcripts showing a string of single-sentence answers indicate poor interviewing techniques. Oral historians seek broader, longer, and more interpretive answers.

Do not ask more than one question at a time; most interviewees would address only one of them. Either the interviewer has to repeat the other half of the question later or it is simply forgotten in the flow of the narrative.

How many times should one person be interviewed?

Single-session oral histories are like "audio snapshots." Depending on the objectives and budget of your project, try to conduct more than one interview with each person. It often takes more than one interview just to break the ice. Repeated visits establish an intimacy that encourages candidness. Both interviewer and interviewee need some time together to develop the rapport necessary to ask difficult questions and to give honest answers. One interviewee began his fourth interview session by saying, "Up till now I've been giving it to you sugar-coated," and went on to discuss his most disagreeable professional relations. It took the first three interviews to gain his confidence before he lowered his guard.

Interviewees do not necessarily hold things back deliberately; it takes time for anyone to remember all the relevant details. Most minds do not work in a precise and orderly manner, and most of us cannot call forth recollections in perfect chronological order, grouped together logically. Memory usually works by association. An interviewee may talk at length about President Harry Truman's administration and seem to have completely exhausted the subject, until a later session when a question about John F. Kennedy elicits the response, "Kennedy handled that differently than Truman." The interviewee then recounts an aspect of the Truman years that had not come to mind earlier.

Some interviewees just do not have much to say. They may suffer from "mike fright" and become tense. They may not have been very perceptive. Their memories may be clouded. One interviewee in a nursing home drifted off to sleep twice during his interview, awakening each time the interviewer began to pack up the equipment and continuing the interview as if uninterrupted. There was no second session. Other interviewees will surprise you with their volubility, the depth of their recall, and their articulateness. In these cases, it is best to return for several sessions until the interviewer feels they have exhausted the subject matter.

But beware of the lonely interviewee who seeks to prolong interview sessions unnecessarily. Some interviewees have few visitors or are not taken very seriously by their families, and they revel in an audience. Take care to be sensitive to the needs of older interviewees, but remember that you are not a psychiatrist offering free and unlimited therapy sessions.

How long should an average interview last?

Unless you are traveling and have a tight schedule that requires lengthier, even full-day sessions, plan each interview session for no longer than two hours. Longer sessions often have a "narcotic" effect on the interviewee, who can become fatigued and distracted. The interviewer will also have trouble listening to what is being said. If prolonged sessions are necessary, arrange for several breaks to give both parties a rest.[4]

SETTING UP THE INTERVIEW

Who should be interviewed first?

Logically, you should start with the oldest and the most significant players in the events or community that you are pursuing. For any number of reasons, some people develop more influence, respect, and standing with an organization, profession, or community. A significant player may have been the one who held a critical post, had a warm and caring personality, or served as the institution's unofficial historian and record-keeper. If interviewed early in the process, they can help identify and locate other potential interviewees and help persuade them to be interviewed. Called the "gatekeepers" by oral historians, their assistance is often indispensable. The gatekeeper may have been a longtime employee who still communicates with former colleagues, or a surviving spouse, other relative, or close friend of a key figure in the events. Others often wait until the gatekeeper has sanctioned the interviews. While trying to interview Benjamin V. Cohen and Thomas G. Corcoran, the "Gold Dust Twins" who shaped much New Deal legislation, I received no response to my letters and phone calls to Corcoran. But the day after I interviewed Cohen, Corcoran's secretary scheduled an appointment, indicating that I had passed inspection.

Always keep actuarial realities in mind. Planning an oral history project can be so time-consuming that when a project is ready to begin interviewing, the best prospective interviewees may either have died or become too ill to give a useful interview. Potential interviewees should be grouped according to age, significance to the theme of the project, and availability in terms of time and location. Save for a later stage of the project those who are younger, more peripheral, and further away. Travel constraints, however, frequently require that interviewees living in a particular location be bunched together. Remember also the practical journalism advice of starting with those "who are most likely to cooperate." Less cooperative subjects require repeated invitations and patient persuasion. In the end, they may agree to be interviewed only to keep others whom they opposed, distrusted, or held in contempt from monopolizing the historical record.[5]

How do you locate potential interviewees?

The oral historian has to play detective. Word-of-mouth referrals will unearth many potential interviewees, but quite often oral historians have to hunt for their subjects. If interviewing for a biography, the interviewer who has read the subject's papers will know which people corresponded with the subject and may have found return addresses on their correspondence. Phone books may identify people who have moved. (Many phone directories around the nation have been compiled on CD-ROM for ready retrieval.) Certain individuals within a family or an organization make a point of keeping in contact with other family members, neighbors, and colleagues and can provide current addresses and telephone numbers. Various professions also maintain directories of their members, such as the *Martindale-Hubbell* guide for lawyers. Other associations and corporations publish newsletters that reach current and retired employees and can carry stories and advertisements about an oral history project. Newspaper advertisements may also locate potential interviewees, but indiscriminate calls for volunteers may inundate the interviewer with an unmanageable number of willing interviewees and not necessarily identify those who can make the most valuable contributions.[6]

What is the best way to initiate contact with interviewees?

By letter or phone call, state the purpose of the interview and the nature of the project. Explain what will happen to the tapes and transcripts, and describe the legal release that the interviewee will be asked to sign. Follow up any phone conversations with a letter to establish a record for your own files. It is especially important for older interviewees to have your name, address, phone number, the purposes of the interview, and the scheduled date, in writing.

Sometimes the interviewer plans a preliminary meeting, perhaps over lunch, to get acquainted with the interviewee and to get a better idea of the major subjects that will be discussed during the actual interviews. Being able to have preliminary meetings clearly depends on the time available, for both the interviewer and interviewee, and the project's budget. In some projects, preinterview sessions are discouraged, to avoid losing the spontaneity and candidness of unrehearsed questioning. The television interviewer Brian Lamb complains of having "ruined" some of his interviews by asking questions before the cameras were turned on, since a question asked the second time rarely elicits as fully satisfying a response as it did the first time.

Schedule the interview at the interviewee's convenience, and make sure you arrive on time. With more prominent interviewees, scheduling can pose problems, especially if the interviewer must travel any distance to the interview. Reiterate to the interviewee the purpose of the project, and be sure to mention your difficulty and expense in arranging it. When planning to go to the interviewee's home or office, ask directions on how to get there. Nothing starts an interview more disagreeably than an interviewer arriving late and tense after a frantic search for the right address. Interviewers are guests and should act accordingly. Interviews can easily go awry if the interviewer arrives late, smokes, chews gum, dresses inappropriately, or otherwise offends the interviewee's sensibilities.

CONDUCTING THE INTERVIEW

Where should you position the tape recorder?

Place the tape recorder where the interviewer can easily see it and periodically check its functioning, but where it is out of the interviewee's direct line of vision, to keep it from becoming a distraction. Equipment sometimes makes people nervous, but after a few minutes most will ignore the tape recorder if it is not right in front of them. The microphone should be situated near the interviewee, preferably pinned on as a lavaliere microphone. Electrical outlets, or their absence, may also determine the position of the recorder. Either use rechargeable battery packs or bring batteries in case there are no convenient outlets or the original batteries wear down. Tape recorders should never be completely concealed, however, since hidden recording is antithetical to the trust and confidence on which oral history depends. Surreptitious recording is unethical, and in most states illegal.

Become familiar with your equipment, both the recorder and the microphones. Failure to test equipment may cause the entire interview to be lost or so poorly recorded that it is difficult to transcribe. Every interviewer should try transcribing a tape at least once to grasp the critical necessity of good sound quality.

Most interviewers try to set up their equipment in a quiet place where the interview will not be interrupted by children, inquiring spouses, secretaries, ringing phones, open windows, street traffic, air conditioners, loud clocks, and the like. Interviewees will want to be good hosts, but clinking coffee cups and plates, ice twirling in drinks, and other extraneous noises will all be picked up on the tape. The interviewee may be unperturbed by this everyday commotion, but it will distract the interviewer and make the tape more difficult to use for transcribing, editing, and research purposes.

By contrast, folklorists, linguists, and anthropologists will often try to capture the "sound environment" of the interview, including ambient sounds, from church bells to ocean waves. Some noises are undesirable for any purposes. An interviewer once recorded at a table under a bird cage, not noticing the sound until he played back the tape and found that "noises of the parakeet scratching in his cage all but drowned out the interviewee."[7]

What if the tape runs out while the interviewee is speaking?

Keep an eye on the recorder. Some tape recorders have signals that warn when the tape is about to run out. As the tape comes close to the end, take advantage of the interviewee's next pause and ask to stop while you change the tape. Always keep a new tape nearby, and remember that there is no third side to a tape! When turning the tape over, let it run a few seconds, long enough to get past the "leader."

Make a mental note of the subject being discussed when the tape ran out. Interviewees sometimes have trouble picking up the thread, even after a short pause, and will need some prompting from the interviewer: "You were saying that . . ."

Should questions be arranged chronologically or topically?

The scheme of interviewing depends on the goals of the project. For some projects, the entire life story of the interviewee will be relevant; for other projects, the focus will be on the events in which the interviewee participated. For instance, Andrew Young might be interviewed for his entire life, for his tenure as United Nations ambassador, or for his role in the civil rights movement. Biographical interviews usually proceed chronologically. If the focus of a project is on an event, then the questions will be more topical.

Jumping right into the main question is not the best approach. Avoid making the first question too abrupt and confrontational; instead, build up to the climactic questions by first establishing the historical setting and making the interviewee more comfortable with the process. People tend to recall things chronologically. Set the stage with general questions, and then follow with more specific, pointed questions. Strictly topical questions may elicit responses that lack depth and context. Topical questions, however, can follow quite appropriately within a chronological framework.

Are open-ended questions preferable to specific questions?

Ideally, interviewers should mix the two types of question. The first questions should be open-ended, such as, "Please tell me about your childhood." Specific questions can follow: "What schools did you attend?" Starting with too specific a question gives the interviewer too much control of the interview. Interviewers should let interviewees explain what they think is most significant before beginning to narrow the questions. "The best oral history is a quasi-monologue on the part of the interviewee," the oral historian Sherna Gluck has observed, "which is encouraged by approving nods, appreciative smiles, and enraptured listening and stimulated by understanding comments and intelligent questions."[8]

Use open-ended questions to allow interviewees to volunteer their own accounts, to speculate on matters, and to have enough time to include all of the material they think relevant to the subject. Use more specific questions to elicit factual information, often in response to something the interviewee has mentioned while answering an open-ended question. Political reporters and courtroom attorneys use this type of mixed questioning in an approach that has been called "funnel interviewing." Their search begins with general questions and then constantly narrows until the subject has difficulty not answering the final, more specific questions. Oral history is a much less adversarial means of interviewing, but the funnel approach remains useful when the subject is controversial.[9]

In framing an open-ended question, the oral historian Charles Morrissey postulates that the two-sentence format often works best. The first sentence should state the problem; the second poses the question: "The records show you were a leader in establishing the zoning laws that shaped this town. Why were zoning laws your objectives?" There are a number of possible follow-up questions: "How did these laws specifically affect your neighborhood?" "What complaints were raised about these laws?" "How effective would you judge these laws to have been?" "Looking back from today, what would you have done differently?" Questions also might relate to specific zoning incidents drawn from newspaper clippings. For such a topic, a map can serve as a good visual prompter during the interview and as appendix material for the transcript.[10]

Keep in mind that interviewers are not restricted to asking questions. Statements of fact, concise restatements of what the interviewee has said, brief observations and comments can stimulate responses from the interviewee as well as inject more spontaneity into the discussion. Mixing occasional comments among the questions provides some relief and can prevent the interview from sounding too much like a cross-examination. But interviewers should always use such interjections in moderation to avoid skewing the content of the interview with their own opinions.

The use of open-ended questions has also been cited as a means of "empowering" interviewees—that is, by encouraging interviewees to relate and to interpret their own stories, such questions shift the balance of power from the interviewer to the interviewee. Those who talk of empowerment view the interviewee as an "informant" and the interviewer as a "reporter." The interviewer may be asking the questions, but the interviewee is actively shaping the course of the interview rather than responding passively. These notions have raised the consciousness especially of those sociologists, anthropologists, and linguists who do not identify—or create fictional identities for—their oral sources, and of interviewers who work outside their own cultures and struggle not to impose their cultural assumptions on the people they observe and interview.[11]

Can the framing of a question distort the answer?

Pollsters say that if you can tell from what position a question is being asked, then the question is loaded. "Do you support a balanced budget amendment to end waste and fraud in the government?" is loaded. "Do you support a balanced budget amendment?" is neutral. Journalists often ask leading and manipulative questions; the preface "Wouldn't you say . . ." is designed to produce a response that fits a particular hypothesis. Many politicians have regretted letting a reporter put words into their mouths with such questions. Researchers working on a specific book or article similarly ask questions to fill holes in their evidence, usually having in mind the answer that they *hope* to hear. The danger of this approach is that interviewees want to please and will pick up the clues—from the type of question asked to the tone of voice used—as to what type of an answer they think the interviewer wants to hear. The result is the opposite of the way an oral history should proceed.[12]

Start with open-ended questions, allow the interviewee to talk broadly, ranging as far and wide as possible. Listen and make notes as the interviewee speaks, but do not interrupt. When it is clear that the person has exhausted the subject and stopped, go back and ask specific follow-up questions, clarify points of confusion or contradiction, and pursue details.

What if the answers are perfunctory?

Short answers may be a sign that an interviewer is asking too many specific questions and not enough open-ended "how" and "why" questions. Interviewees are not always sure of how much detail interviewers want. They may give answers that are to the point but short, unrevealing, and unreflective. Never be satisfied with brief answers, and follow up with more detailed questions to draw the interviewee out.

Short answers may also indicate that the interviewer has been too quick to jump in with the next question. It requires some discipline to remain silent after asking a question, and to remain so until absolutely certain that the interviewee has finished answering. Try not to speak immediately after the interviewee stops, since it may just be a pause for a breath of air or for gathering additional thoughts. Silence indicates that an interviewer expects more. Ten seconds can seem excruciatingly long if neither party is speaking but can encourage the interviewee to give a more detailed response.[13]

Sometimes answers are perfunctory simply because the interviewer has not engaged the interviewee's interest. Try varying the types of questions and the subjects they cover. Studs Terkel has described his interview of the 90-year-old philosopher Bertrand Russell. Allotted only half an hour, Terkel knew he would be escorted out promptly when his time was up. His first theoretical question elicited only a short reply. He switched to more provocative questions and noted that as Russell became engaged, his answers grew longer. With time running out, Terkel sought "the home run question." "Lord Russell," he asked, "what is the world you envision?" Russell's response summarized his hopes and frustrations, ending with a touch of weariness. Although he might have ended there, Terkel tried for "a parting shot." "You liked Shelley when you were young, in your formative years," he said. "Do you still feel the same way?" That charming, personal question showed that the interviewer knew his subject and had come well prepared (although it might have been more effective if he had asked it earlier in the interview). The interview succeeded because the fully engaged interviewer was constantly evaluating his interviewee's responses and changing gears to provoke more stimulating responses. Terkel reminds us that every interviewer ought to be looking for the "home run question."[14]

How should you deal with an uncooperative interviewee?

A former secretary of state once greeted an interviewer by pointing out that he had given his papers to an archives so that historians would not bother him. Anyone who expected him to remember and comment on events that happened years ago "must live in the realm of the ridiculous." The interviewer was well aware of his subject's reputed temperament and had come with a plan. He knew that the secretary retained a strong attachment to his home state, and although the interview dealt with foreign policy, the interviewer asked about the foreign policy concerns of people in this town or that. The questions appealed to the secretary's interests, and he began to speak at length, well beyond the mandated time for the interview.

For many personal reasons, ranging from their state of health to their unhappiness over the way their lives and careers developed, some people will be uncooperative interviewees. Perhaps they disliked or resented the individual whom the interviewer is researching. They may not like "dredging up the past." By preparing as thoroughly as possible for an interview in advance, interviewers should be able to anticipate some of the causes of such behavior and to develop strategies for dealing with them. If one line of questioning elicits bitterness, shift to another approach. Seek areas that the interviewee enjoys talking about before raising the disagreeable questions. Be prepared to justify the need to "stir up those old ashes" after so many years and to explain why scholars are seeking answers to these questions.

Some interviewees will answer evasively. They may be testing the interviewer's knowledge. If the interviewer allows them to respond incompletely or evasively, however, they will continue to do so. Following up with more specific questions on the same subject, thereby indicating that the answers were insufficient, may elicit more complete or informative responses. If this tack does not work, then clearly and respectfully point out that the interviewee seems to be less than forthcoming. Perhaps the interviewee will make some explanation or finally give a fuller response. If not, the interview should be ended.

How personal should an interviewer get?

The degree to which an interview explores personal matters is something that each interviewer and interviewee will have to work out between themselves. Like the media, historians increasingly want to know about the private side of public figures. The feminist notion that "the personal is political" has also contributed to the merging of the public and personal spheres in historical analysis. Whether individual interviewees will answer personal questions is another matter.

Different people have different concepts of what is personal. When Ronald Steel was interviewing Walter Lippmann for his biography, Lippmann volunteered to cooperate so long as Steel did not ask anything personal. Steel soon learned that Lippmann defined the word quite broadly. Once when Steel asked him what his father had done for a living, Lippmann stared at him silently and then replied, "I wouldn't want you to make a novel out of this." (Lippmann was not proud that his family's fortune rested on rents from tenement houses.)[15] In fact, Lippmann's lawyer, Louis Auchincloss, did turn a major turning point of Lippmann's private life into a novel, *The House of the Prophet* (1980), in which the protagonist complains: "Biography is a whole new ball game. It is possible now, even in the lifetimes of our very greatest men, to persuade their friends and acquaintances to record on tape their most intimate impressions of these individuals. All you have to do is wave in their faces the sacred banner of history."[16]

How should you bring up subjects that may be embarrassing?

Having gone to great lengths to put interviewees at ease and to establish rapport, it is often hard to confront them with embarrassing questions. The sociologist John Gwaltney, author of *Drylongso* (1993), an oral history of Newark's inner-city blacks, once chided members of the Oral History Association for often being too polite and discreet "to ask the embarrassing question." He argued that with some gentle and persistent prodding, interviewees will talk about difficult subjects. Playing tapes to demonstrate his point, Gwaltney showed that his questions were humorous and playful, but unrelenting. Being blind, Gwaltney also had the advantage of his interviewees wanting him to understand them; they would go on at length and punctuate their responses with, "Don't you see?"

One way to bring up difficult or embarrassing issues is to quote someone else. During the Gerald Ford and Jimmy Carter administrations, the National Archives maintained an office near the White House where they interviewed officials as they left the administration, many of them involuntarily and under some cloud. The interviewees were often agitated and unnerved over their experience and not happy to talk about it. Conducting preliminary interviews for the Ford and Carter presidential libraries, the Archives interviewer had to ask some embarrassing questions but tried to connect them with published sources: "The *Washington Post* reported that you left office because of such and such. Was this a fair assessment?" Since the matter was part of the public record, and the interviewees were being asked to give their own side of the story, they invariably offered their own defense. Having made the focus the newspaper versus the interviewee (rather than the interviewer versus the interviewee), the interviewer needed to be sure to follow up with questions about the subject's self-defense, its inconsistencies, and its contradictions with other accounts.

When confronted with embarrassing subjects, an interviewee's first response may be brief, defensive, inconclusive. The interviewer should return to the topic later in the interview. The more the interviewee attempts to explain, offers more details, and strains to make the interviewer understand, the more candid—and less canned—the responses become. This approach takes time; once again, multiple interview sessions are important.

Some interviewees stipulate before an interview that there are certain subjects they will not discuss. Although it is possible to allude to such topics during the interview, the interviewees may break their own rules and venture into the forbidden areas themselves. Ultimately oral historians must accede to an interviewee's request. It is legitimate, however, to note the interviewee's demand in the files for that interview, thereby explaining to future users why certain subjects were not addressed.

Difficult, embarrassing, or confrontational topics should be deferred until later in the interview, after the interviewer has established some rapport. While working on a history of an abortive plan to use nuclear weapons to dredge a harbor in Alaska, an oral historian arranged to interview the crusty nuclear physicist Edward Teller. Time was limited, and Teller arrived late. Rather than ask his "warm-up" questions, the interviewer decided to jump right in with an opening question about the most controversial part of Teller's involvement with the project. "This interview is over," snapped Teller as he got up and left.

To appear interested and sympathetic, an interviewer does not have to act obsequiously. If a point of disagreement is reached with an interviewee, one solution is to try to restate the interviewee's point of view. The interviewee will usually respond by further defining the position, and the dialogue is thus extended rather than terminated. Finally, keep in mind Oscar Wilde's observation that "questions are never indiscreet. Answers sometimes are."[17]

What if the interviewee asks that the tape recorder be turned off?

An oral history is not a journalistic interview, so there is little to be gained by hearing a story "off the record." Politely but firmly, interviewers should decline to interrupt the interview. Explain that the tape can remain closed until the interviewee is ready to release it, and that the transcripts can be edited. At times, however, interviewees may want to stop the tape to explain their hesitancy about answering a question or to ask the interviewer's advice about the propriety of discussing a person or issue. Interviewers can halt both the interview and the tape to hear their problems, counsel them, and offer some reassurance before resuming the taping.

How can interviewers get beyond stories that have been "rehearsed" through frequently retelling?

Oral historians are frequently encouraged to interview the favorite storyteller and unofficial local historian. These individuals often have wonderful stories that may have folklore value, and they will tell their stories regardless of how relevant they are to the interviewer's questions. To a lesser degree, everyone tells stories about past experiences, to relive glory days, celebrate shared experiences, or make comparisons with the present. Each telling of the story embeds it all the firmer in the mind. Columbia has an interview with Ferdinand Pecora about the highly publicized investigation he conducted during the 1930s of Wall Street banking and stock market malpractice. Although he gave the interview 40 years after the events took place, his memory was remarkable for its detail and precision. But Pecora's family pointed out that he had been telling these stories for years, and even after the interview was still telling them on his deathbed to the hospital nurses.[18]

Although important for memory retention, rehearsal can create stumbling blocks for interviewers. Every telling of a story embellishes it, thereby moving it further away from reality. Events are telescoped, chronology tightened, order rearranged and edited, drama or humor heightened. Rehearsed stories tend to omit negative events and concentrate on triumphs. Interviewees have not necessarily forgotten old wounds and mistakes. When questioned, they can recall past defeats, even if they do not always feel comfortable talking about them. By the time the oral historian asks the question, the answer may simply be the oft-told story.

The best defense against a well-rehearsed story is a well-prepared interviewer who can spot inaccuracies and gently challenge inconsistencies. But interviewees may have told their stories so often that they cannot remember it any other way. Some interviewees prime themselves for the interview, and others have stories that they will tell anyone under any circumstances. If the interviewer tries to cut them off, they may become confused or, more likely, will simply wait for another occasion to insert the stories in the dialogue. Since these stories have special meaning to the interviewee, it is usually worth giving them time to tell their set speeches. (You will probably find it impossible to stop them.) After the supply is finally exhausted, try to ask questions that will lead down less familiar paths.[19]

Rehearsing a story, through its retelling over the years, also serves as a form of self-interpretation. People not only remember their past but try to make sense of it, rationalizing it so they can live with it. An interview with a divorced couple will probably elicit two very different versions of the marriage and why it ended. Defeated politicians have similarly reconstructed their pasts. Interviewers need to ask these interviewees to stop and think about what they have said.

Not all stories have been rehearsed mentally or anecdotally. Questions may cause interviewees to recall events long buried in their memories. They often express amazement at their recall of seemingly forgotten memories, then recount them in explicit detail and at surprising length.

How can an interviewer assist an interviewee's ability to recall?

An interviewee once commented that he felt as if his memory was on trial. Recognizing that most people do not readily remember names and dates, interviewers attempt to become familiar with the major players in the interviewee's life and with its basic chronology, not only to keep the interviews moving but to put the interviewee's mind at ease. Oral historians have similarly explored the use of photographs and familiar artifacts to trigger recall. Family photo albums, newspaper clippings, and letters have all served as tools for unearthing otherwise forgotten information. Some interviewers have even experimented with the sense of smell, to see what memories different smells elicit.[20]

Looking through family photographs not only prompts commentary from the interviewee but can provide illustrations for the interviewer's publications. The historian Pete Daniel traveled down the Mississippi River to interview people in the towns along the way, recording their recollections of the great flood of 1927 fifty years after the event. The photograph albums that many interviewees brought out helped sharpen their memories and provided stunning illustrations for his book, *Deep'n as It Come* (1977). By contrast, Andrea Hammer began her research with a set of the New Deal's Farm Security Agency photographs taken in southern Maryland between 1935 and 1943. During the 1980s Hammer located many of the subjects who still lived in that region and who could talk about the people and places in the photos. Her object was to reconstruct the social context of the photographs, an exercise that demonstrated again that photographs can be misleading, and misinterpreted, without help from those who were there.[21]

Do differences in race, gender, or age between the interviewer and the interviewee make any difference in the interview?

Interviewees take the measure of interviewers, make assumptions about what they will want to ask, and to some degree try to please them by telling what they want to hear. A study of the Federal Writers Project interviews with former slaves, conducted in the 1930s, discovered that an elderly black woman was interviewed twice, once by a white woman and again by a black man. She gave starkly different accounts of her memories of slavery, painting a relatively benign account for the white woman and a much harsher account for the black man. She may well have spoken even more differently to another black woman.[22]

Differences in age, race, gender, and ethnicity may influence both the questions asked and the responses elicited. There are no set prescriptions to overcome such differences. Some may want to match interviewers closely with interviewees, but men and women of different races and ethnicity should be able to interview each other. In seeking to make interviewees feel comfortable, interviewers might reveal a little of themselves—where they live, where they went to school, where they work, what their families do—to establish points of commonality that might cut across some of the barriers between them.

Even without any common reference, the interviewer can compensate by having thoroughly researched the subject and being familiar with names, dates, and events long past. A well-prepared interviewer becomes, for the duration of the interview, the contemporary of the interviewee. "Oh, do you know about him?" the interviewee will say. Or, "I haven't thought about that in years." During the interview, older people seem younger and more animated as they relive the past with a sympathetic listener.

The Oral History Associations's principles and standards encourage interviewers to

> work to achieve a balance between the objectives of the project and the perspectives of the interviewees. They should be sensitive to the diversity of social and

cultural experiences, and to the implications of race, gender, class, ethnicity, age, religion, and sexual orientation. They should encourage interviewees to respond in their own style and language, and to address issues that reflect their concerns. Interviewers should fully explore all appropriate areas of inquiry with the interviewee and not be satisfied with superficial responses.[23]

Are there any differences between interviewing the famous and interviewing average individuals?

The difference lies largely in the interviewee's previous experience of being interviewed by the media. The average person has not been interviewed and may initially feel intimidated by the tape recorder and microphone. For the more prominent interviewee, the interviewer's problem will be to draw a distinction between an oral history and a newspaper interview. Interviewees must recognize that what they say will not appear on the front page of tomorrow's newspaper or on the evening news, a revelation that may actually disappoint some of them but that for the most part enables them to speak candidly. They can leave a complete record but keep it confidential so that it will not damage their careers.

Professional people can also prove difficult to interview. Lawyers, for instance, have been trained not to volunteer information. Even worse are law professors, who seem to be judging questions to see how much the interviewer already knows. If prepared and able to ask probing follow-up questions, interviewers can earn their respect and perhaps a little more of their cooperation. Business executives may need some coaxing to think of the interview as something other than a promotional device. Most professional people and all politicians have been interviewed before as part of their jobs. They are used to responding to questions, and they have developed certain patterns of response. As a result, their answers may be superficial and packaged, and it can be hard to break through their veneer. Some oral histories with politicians sound more like radio scripts than candid interviews.

When interviewing within an organization or a group of people who participated in a common event, it is just as important to interview the "little fish" as the "big fish." Those on the middle or lower tiers of any hierarchy usually have more time to do interviews, a broader perspective on events, and less ego invested in the operation. Those at the top may be too preoccupied and perhaps too self-centered to provide much new information. If they are still in power, those at the top are often more cautious in responding and may give little more than a press release. Interviewing at the periphery provides information that makes it easier to interview those at the center. Conversely, interviewing the top people early in the project reassures anxious subordinates that management sanctions the project. Interviewers have to take advantage of whatever scheduling opportunities they encounter and develop their own tactics in determining which individuals in any group to interview, how many, and in what order.[24]

Is there more advantage to being an "insider" or an "outsider" as an interviewer?

Sometimes you have an advantage if you are part of the same organization as the interviewees. Even if years younger than the interviewees, you will know the names of their contemporaries and will probably have heard many of the stories and much of the gossip, so you can be trusted as a colleague. If you come from outside the group being interviewed, you have to research all the harder to be sure to know the basic organizational facts and nuances. In building rapport, you do not want to sound like an outsider.

At the same time, there are disadvantages to "intimate" as opposed to "clinical" interviewing. An interviewer from within the same group often takes too much for granted and may neither ask for explanations nor follow up with questions about matters that seem to be common knowledge to the interviewer but are obscure to outsiders. Moreover, interviewees sometimes perceive the inside interviewer as a partisan or player in the events and may feel less uncomfortable discussing certain people or issues with someone from outside their organization or community.

Whether an insider or an outsider, you do not want to look like a "know-it-all." The purpose of interviewing is to collect and record for the first time what other people know, thought, and perceived. An interviewee who gathers that the interviewer is thoroughly versed in the subject may not see much point in going into detail. "You know what that is, right?" they may say, then skip the explanation. You may indeed know what that is, but someone reading the transcript years hence may not have a clue. The best strategy is to play student to the interviewee as teacher. You have done the homework but want to know more, so you ask questions like: "Why was that?" "I don't understand; can you explain that to me?" "I've always wondered why that was." Such questions cause interviewees to want to make you understand the situation the way they understood it, and to see it the way they saw it.

Never be afraid to admit that you did not understand what an interviewee meant. Some interviewers prepare elaborate questions and then never follow up on them. If the first responses are glib, short, or shallow, press the interviewee further on the same subject until you are sure the subject has been exhausted.

Should interviewers use a questionnaire?

When dealing with a group that has a common identity or was involved in a common event or organization, be sure to direct the same core questions to everyone. Especially if different interviewers are working for the same project, you should agree on a common list of themes and certain questions for all to ask. But individual interviewees have had their own unique experiences that no questionnaire can anticipate. You must be willing to deviate from the prepared questions whenever something unexpected and interesting develops. Oral history, after all, addresses neglected areas of knowledge. The best items uncovered are often subjects that you were not prepared to ask questions about and perhaps had read nothing about in your research. A good interviewer hears an unexpected statement and follows up with additional questions.

Behaviorists, who prefer questionnaires that can be coded and quantified, often bemoan the "subjective" nature of oral history. But oral historians deal with individual memory and perception, which are hard to squeeze into a structured format.

Can follow-up questions be prepared in advance?

Follow-up questions require both prior research and spontaneity. A thoroughly prepared interviewer will sense when the interviewee is being incomplete and will press for a fuller discussion. Research also helps you spot new information or information that conflicts with other accounts. "I didn't know that, can you tell me more about it?" can be the best follow-up question, since it encourages the interviewee to devote more attention to the issue and provide more details. Interviewees are often surprised when an interviewer seems to care about a particular subject and would not have mentioned it more than in passing if interest had not been expressed.

The most important skill in asking questions is being able to listen carefully to what interviewees are saying. Those who study listening have concluded that people generally hear only a small portion of what is said to them, a phenomenon that every parent and teacher can confirm. Even in an interview situation—so much more focused than a normal conversation—the interviewer is keeping an eye on the tape recorder, concentrating on choosing the next question to be asked, and growing fatigued and distracted as time elapses. Listening to a tape of one of his interviews, Theodore Rosengarten, the author of *All God's Dangers: The Life of Nate Shaw* (1974), realized that he had "set out to question, not to listen." Thinking ahead from question to question, he had allowed the tape recorder to listen for him. "Let the machine record," he admonished, "and you listen!"[25]

Training themselves to remain alert saves interviewers from the embarrassing position of asking a question that the interviewee has already answered—a clear signal that the interviewer has not been paying attention—and helps them flag the unexpected revelations that deserve to be followed up. In listening to the tapes after their interviews, even the most experienced interviewers hear things that eluded them during the interview. These areas can be pursued in subsequent interviews, but not as spontaneously as when they first arose.[26]

How should interviewers react to statements with which they strongly disagree?

The hardest part of listening is having to pay attention to ideas and information with which you differ. You may be inclined to interrupt and argue, but you need to hear the interviewee out fully before confronting areas of disagreement. Challenge answers that seem misleading, and pursue responses that seem mistaken. Interviewees may misspeak or poorly express themselves; sometimes they are misinformed or just wrong. But they may also possess a more accurate version of events than the interviewer has seen in other sources and, given the opportunity, may be able to present their version convincingly.[27]

Oral history collects the interviewee's recollections and opinions, not the interviewer's. Interviewers are not responsible for converting interviewees to any true faith, nor do they need to demonstrate that they are purer than the people they are interviewing. A true test of both the interviewer and the oral history project is whether they conducted interviews with representatives of all sides of an issue, including those whom they considered less than admirable.

But what if the interviewer suspects that an interviewee is lying or shading the truth?

Never be too quick to assume that an interviewee is wrong or lying. Your objective is to record the story from the interviewee's point of view, even if that includes some exaggerated claims or boasting. You need not embrace totally whatever the interviewee is saying. Try to draw interviewees out further on any dubious assertions. Return to troublesome issues at different points during the interview, as a means of prodding interviewees into defending or refuting their previous statements. Do not hesitate to cite contrary evidence in newspaper accounts and other sources. Conflicting information can be attached as an appendix to the transcripts, for future researchers to consider. (First, however, be sure to alert the interviewee to the added material.)[28]

There is always the possibility that an interviewee is lying to him or herself. The interviewee may have consciously or subconsciously distorted memories of an unpleasant past. In Germany and Italy, oral historians have encountered a mass amnesia about fascism and the Holocaust.[29] Some people dramatically change their positions but convince themselves of their consistency and correctness. The oral history interview, usually taking place years after the events occurred, can have a cathartic effect that allows some interviewees to confront painful, long-buried memories. In such cases, the interview serves as therapy as well as to set the record straight.

But even a psychiatrist would have trouble getting some interviewees to confront the past honestly. The lie sometimes takes on a mythic significance of its own, and the interview may become valuable not for the story's accuracy but as a means of analyzing the roots of its distortion and measuring an idealized self against less favorable perceptions.

Should an interviewer pay any attention to the interviewee's "body language"?

Even interviews that are not being videotaped have a visual component. Sitting in close proximity, interviewers and interviewees communicate nonverbally through facial expressions and body movement. Always focus your gaze fully on the interviewee. Looking around the room, staring into space, examining your nails, suggests that you are not paying attention, just as frowning indicates disagreement or disbelief. Interviewees will either interpret such behavior as rudeness or, fearing that they are boring you, begin abbreviating their answers. Except for glancing periodically at the tape recorder or looking over photographs and other items relating to the interview, maintain eye contact diligently throughout the interview. A smile or a nod signals that you got the point and encourages the interviewee to keep talking. Quiet signals are preferable to verbal interruptions ("oh, yes," "uh-hmmm," "you don't say"), which sound foolish on the tape and clutter the transcript.

Interviewees also send nonverbal cues. A person leaning toward the interviewer and pointing a finger projects an aggressive, take-charge attitude; sitting back with crossed legs and arms and leaning away suggests a closed, self-protected attitude. Body language may indicate nervousness about the interview, and topics that make interviewees particularly uncomfortable may cause them to shift in their seats, drum their fingers on a table, and engage in other such noticeable behavior. Some interviewees glance at the interviewer to see how an answer has registered. Amelia Fry reported that when she interviewed the former California senator William F. Knowland for a life history, he never looked at her but stared fixedly at the ceiling, "as if he was answering to a higher authority." It later became evident that Knowland was undergoing a crisis in his personal life and found it distressing to reflect on his past. This crisis caused him to commit suicide before she could conduct another interview.[30]

In another extreme—but still instructive—case, an oral historian who conducted a series of interviews with prisoners at the state penitentiary detected that the inmates had "a great deal of practice at perfecting their intentionally deceptive statements." He identified such nonverbal cues as tapping a cigarette and loss of eye contact during specific replies as signals that a statement might be deceptive.[31]

Sounds also play a part in nonverbal communication. Voice pitch, hesitation, emphasis, sarcasm, and muttering of asides provide indications of attitude. When people become emotional, they tend to talk faster and raise their voices. Interviewers need to catch these nonverbal cues, since they are almost impossible to transcribe. A sarcastic inflection, for instance, can completely change the meaning of a sentence. The interviewer might point out a sarcastic response and ask the interviewee to explain the sarcasm.

Is there a role in oral history for what social scientists call "continuing observation?"

Oral historians have never shared the interest of social scientists in observation as part of the interviewing process. Historians tend to isolate interviewees from their environment and to put them in a quiet place where they will not be interrupted during the interview, whereas in other disciplines subjects are examined in their natural setting. Anthropologists, for instance, live in communities to record their day-to-day observations along with their subjects' testimony.

Richard Fenno has encouraged political scientists to collect data by "interactive observation," by which he means "following politicians around and talking with them as they go about their work." Fenno accompanied politicians through their home districts, through elections, and through their legislative service:

> Much of what you see, therefore, is dictated by what they do and say. If something is important to them, it becomes important to you. Their view of the world is as important as your view of the world. You impose some research questions on them; they impose some research questions on you. That interaction has its costs—most notably in a considerable loss of control over the research process. It also has benefits. It brings you especially close to your data.[32]

Fenno's prescription describes what many social sciences consider effective fieldwork. Although oral historians often travel to the area where their interviewees live and are interested in their environment, participatory observation has not been a major component of the oral history interview. Oral historians frequently interview those who have retired and live in different communities from where they spent their careers. Observing current daily routines would not offer many clues about the past that oral historians seek to capture on tape. Sometimes, however, interviewees want to show interviewers buildings and other sites that played an important part in their past. Oral historians should take advantage of such offers and visit the sites, bringing along their tape recorders, cameras, and possibly video cameras to illustrate and supplement the interviews.[33]

CONCLUDING THE INTERVIEW

What's the best way to conclude an interview?

Look for a natural "wrap-up" question, something that causes interviewees to reflect on their lives, to compare recent events with their earlier years, to draw conclusions about major events, or to look ahead to the future. Ask the interviewee whether there are any other issues that could be discussed. Occasionally, an interviewee has anticipated a question that the interviewer did not raise. The interview itself may have triggered memories of long-forgotten people and events that the interviewer had not researched. Encourage interviewees to put whatever they consider important into the record.

At the conclusion of the interview, remind the interviewee of how the tapes will be processed and where the tapes and transcripts will be deposited. Explain what their role will be in editing the transcript and in signing the deed of gift. Sometimes the interviewee is asked to sign a tape release immediately after completing the taping session and another release later approving the transcript; other times no release is signed until the interviewee has reviewed the transcript. The timing depends on how quickly a transcript can be produced and on whether the interviewee is likely to request that the interview be restricted.

It is customary to present copies of the tape or transcript to the interviewee and to sometimes make additional copies for family members. If the object of the interview is an article or book, try to give a copy to the interviewee. Plan to invite interviewees to exhibit openings or other public presentations based on the interviews.

You cannot simply walk out the door with someone's life story, their candid reflections, and sometimes their extremely personal observations. Interviews can be difficult, emotional experiences, and sometimes you need to spend time talking with the interviewee after the interview, without the tape recorder running. Let interviewees know how important their interviews will be to the oral history project, and reassure them that they were helpful. Give them some idea of how long it will take to process the interview, when they can expect to receive copies of the tape or transcript, when they will sign the deed of gift, how you expect the materials to be used, and where the interview will be deposited and opened for research.

Should interviewees ever be paid for their interviews?

Most oral history projects work on such limited budgets—sometimes depending on volunteer staff—that they rarely can afford to pay interviewees. They operate on the valid principle that having one's life story recorded for the future is reward in itself. A very few projects, however, especially those in which the interviews are with musicians and others commonly paid to perform, have recognized some financial obligation to their participants. Blues and jazz projects have further justified their decision to pay on the potential profitability of the interviews. "Since blues is a marketable form of oral history," wrote Walter Liniger of the Blues Archives at the University of Mississippi, "we felt morally obliged to secure the rights of the informants and to pay them a fee for their contributions."[34]

Obviously, any financial arrangement depends on the resources of the sponsoring project or institution. Some projects have written stipends for interviewees into their grant proposals, similar to the honoraria paid to their advisory committee members. But whether or not payments are made, all oral historians have a responsibility to inform interviewees of the anticipated uses of their interviews, whether in publication, radio or video documentaries, or other means of public presentation that might generate royalties or other monetary compensation.

4

USING ORAL HISTORY IN RESEARCH AND WRITING

Oral history methodology seems geared to large projects; how much of it can the individual researcher apply to interviews for a book or an article?

Individual resources may be more limited than those of a group project, but an individual researcher is no less concerned about making interviews fully usable. Since researchers are the primary users of the information they collect, they ought to set their own standards to at least equal, if not surpass, those of an oral history project or archives. Both projects and individual researchers want to collect oral documentation that is complete, accurate, and reliable, but researchers scrutinize even more intensely than do project interviewers what they hear in the interviews they conduct and apply a higher degree of professional skepticism to them. They seek verification in other sources for information gathered through interviews, and they evaluate contradictory material to draw their own conclusions.

Despite their focused efforts and self-defined goals, individuals doing their own interviewing bear definite professional responsibilities. In 1989 the American Historical Association issued the following recommendations about interviewing for historical research:

1. Interviews should be recorded on tape but only after the person to be interviewed has been informed of the mutual rights and responsibilities involved in oral history, such as editing, confidentiality, disposition, and dissemination of all forms of the record. Interviewers should obtain legal releases and document any agreements with interviewees.

2. The interviewer should strive to prompt informative dialogue through challenging and perceptive inquiry, should be grounded in the background and experiences of the person being interviewed, and, if possible, should review the sources relating to the interviewee before conducting the interview.

3. To the extent practicable, interviewers should extend the inquiry beyond their immediate needs to make each interview as complete as possible for the benefit of others.

4. The interviewer should guard against possible social injury to or exploitation of interviewees and should conduct interviews with respect for human dignity.

5. Interviewers should be responsible for proper citation of oral history sources in creative works, including permanent location.

6. Interviewers should arrange to deposit their interviews in an archival repository that is capable of both preserving the interviews and making them available for general research. Additionally, the interviewer should work with the repository in determining the necessary legal arrangements.

7. As teachers, historians are obligated to inform students of their responsibilities in regard to interviewing and to encourage adherence to the guidelines set forth here.[1]

Why bother to record interviews on tape? Why are notes not sufficient?

After years of scribbling notes during class lectures, many researchers feel perfectly able to take coherent notes during an interview. They consider a tape recorder an unnecessary expense, a bother to lug about and operate, and a possible barrier to a candid interview—whether with public figures, who may be overly cautious about having their words recorded, or with nonpublic figures, who may be intimidated over talking into a microphone. Some researchers consider note taking superior to tape recording. Barbara Tuchman, for instance, complained that tape recorders simply encourage people to "ramble effortlessly and endlessly." She described note taking as a "crystallizing process" in which the writer automatically distinguishes the significant from the insignificant. Others have cited the risk of the tape recorder breaking down at crucial moments as their rationale for not tape recording.[2]

Such responses combine cogent truths and unnecessary rationalizations. Tape recorders are no longer such an expense or a novelty. They can be purchased or rented for a reasonable cost, are easy to operate, and have become so commonplace that few interviewees will be surprised or uncomfortable to see one. More important, tape recorders radically expand and improve the interview. The longer interviews last, the more interviewers tire and miss nuances. Later, when they play back the tape, interviewers inevitably hear more than they did during the interview itself. Note takers may make honest mistakes in what they hear or find their handwriting hard to decipher. Note takers also run the risk of hearing only what they want to hear rather than what the interviewee actually says—a recurring phenomenon to which anyone interviewed by the press can readily attest.

Note taking makes some researchers feel more comfortable because it helps focus their attention—as they listen to what is being said—on the exact points they anticipate later using. But there is no reason not to tape-record and take notes at the same time. The notes can serve as the tape's index, which is especially useful if a full transcript cannot be made.

Tape recording is the researcher's best means of self-protection. Interviewees may object to how they were quoted or may not be willing to stand behind statements they made in their interviews. A tape recording of the interview provides the documentation to defend against such reactions. Some interviewees, especially the more prominent, may be so skittish about being misquoted that they will insist that the interview be tape-recorded. For his biography of Henry Kissinger, Walter Isaacson interviewed former President Richard M. Nixon. Isaacson took notes, while Nixon recorded the interview. When the tape recorder broke down, Nixon commented, "I've never been very good with these things."[3]

What if a potential interviewee refuses to be recorded?

Interviewers operate under ground rules that interviewees set. For an oral history project, such an objection would likely cause that person to be stricken from the list of potential interviewees, since there usually remains little reason to conduct an oral history if it cannot be recorded. But the individual researcher may consider the person a critically important source, regardless of the ground rules. Notes may be inferior to tape, but they are better than nothing. As soon as the interview session is over, the interviewer needs to write down as full an account as notes and memory permit.

An interviewee may decline to be recorded out of fear or vanity, emotions that can sometimes be overcome by reassurances and flattery. The late historian Gordon Prange, whose ego matched the monumental books he wrote on the Second World War, refused to be tape-recorded during an interview on the grounds that Gen. Douglas MacArthur had never allowed his interviews to be recorded. The interviewer took notes for a few minutes and then injected, "What a shame that this isn't being recorded, Professor Prange, because my notes will never do justice to your cogent thoughts and beautifully crafted sentences." Accepting that as a point well taken, Prange permitted the tape recorder to run for the rest of the interview.[4]

But why make a tape when you cannot afford to transcribe it?

You can make notes from your own tapes without having to transcribe them entirely. Having the tape allows you to quote accurately and to pick up nuances you may have missed during the interview. The tape serves as a record to be quoted, cited, deposited in a library, and referred back to for proof should any queries arise about the accuracy of the material.

Transcripts are costly and time-consuming to create, but they increase the usefulness of an interview to everyone, including the original interviewer. Researchers planning to conduct extensive interviews for a dissertation, book, or other project should seek a logical repository, whether it be a university library, a state archives or historical society, or a community library, to which to donate the completed tapes. The repository will most likely have legal release forms that the interviewer can use. If the interviews meet the repository's standards, it may be able either to have its own staff transcribe the interviews or to join the interviewer in seeking a grant for transcription.

Why should independent researchers make their interviews available to anyone else?

Scholars have a professional obligation to permit access to their sources. A footnote citing "personal interview in the author's possession" leaves much open to question, especially if the interviewee has died. Readers may question how accurately the researcher quoted or paraphrased the interview. Even when a researcher quotes an interview meticulously, in all probability he or she needs to cite only a small portion of it. Future researchers may make different use of the same material.

While writing her doctoral dissertation on the Office of War Information, Holly Cowan Shulman discovered that another historian had conducted an interview with a key official of the agency. Her graduate adviser, however, dissuaded her from asking to see a copy of the interview, on the grounds that it was someone else's work. Although she complied at the time, she came to feel that it had been wrong not to examine the interview for her research, since interviews "were a piece of historical evidence just as much as letters or diaries." Seeking to raise the consciousness of the historical profession on the issue, Shulman has argued:

> When we conduct interviews, we are creating evidence. When the next historian comes along interested in another aspect or interpretation of the same topic, he or she should have access to the interviews we did. This is the very nature of the rules of history. Otherwise, I could hide all of my evidence to protect myself from competition and argument. Or I could make up anything I wanted and assert its truth citing interviews I supposedly conducted but would let no one else see. In other words, if we historians don't treat interviews seriously, we raise a series of problems which could hurt the profession as a whole.[5]

Must individual researchers get signed legal releases for their interviews?

A legal release is essential if the interviewer intends to deposit the tape or transcript in a library or archives. By signing a legal release, the interviewee indicates that he or she understood what the interview would be used for and establishes its ownership. Just having tape-recorded another person's words does not give the interviewer copyright on those words, and making quotations in the resulting publication beyond "fair use" length might stimulate a legal challenge. The problem may not come from the interviewee but from the interviewee's heirs, who may seek compensation from the interview's publication.

Unfortunately, graduate advisers have too often assured individual researchers that they were just doing interviews, not an oral history project, and therefore did not need to get releases. This oversight unnecessarily limits the interview's future use. When depositing the interviews in an archives, the interviewer must go back to get signatures on legal releases. Sometimes interviewees have died and their next of kin must be located. It is always easier to have the legal releases signed when the interview is conducted.

With limited time and resources, why should independent researchers ask questions beyond their immediate research interests?

Researchers understandably think of interviews as filling in gaps in their work or expanding their own knowledge of the particulars and want to ask questions precisely about those areas and nothing else. But this attitude is counterproductive in a number of ways. First, the interviewee's memory may not immediately be able to dredge up the specific information that the interviewer is seeking. Interviewers need to spend some time establishing rapport, building up to the central issue, and understanding its context in the interviewee's life. Interviewers need to be sensitive to the feelings of interviewees and to not dismiss other areas of their lives they may consider relevant to the interviewer's questions.

In the 1970s I interviewed the New Dealer Benjamin V. Cohen about his role in creating the Securities and Exchange Commission in the 1930s. Watergate was the news when the interview took place, and Cohen wanted to talk about Richard Nixon. But for my dissertation, I needed to hear about Franklin Roosevelt. Not willing to follow his tangents, I constantly steered the interview back to my immediate interests. Not until later did I realize that I had missed the opportunity to capture Cohen's thoughts about Watergate and to find out whether the development of the "imperial presidency" had in any way changed his opinion about the expansion of the executive branch during the 1930s.

Within a few years of completion of most oral history projects, many of the interviewees will have died. There is no guarantee that these people will have been interviewed by any other programs. A researcher's notes, tapes, and transcripts of interviews therefore become valuable sources for other researchers, who no longer have access to the deceased.

Does the independent researcher have any advantages over the oral historian in a group project?

Anyone working on a specific book or article becomes far more steeped in the subject matter and has a much more personal stake in the process. Their interviews lead to publications and promote their professional advancement, perhaps even earn them royalties. Researchers can verge on obsession with their projects, wanting to know *everything*. They press interviewees to go into greater detail than does an interviewer for a more general project. A number of interviewers participated in the Former Members of Congress oral history project, and not surprisingly, one of the lengthiest and most detailed interviews was conducted by an interviewer who was also writing a doctoral dissertation on the senatorial interviewee. The interviewer pressed the senator on any number of issues, even persuading him to sing his campaign song.[6]

Individual researchers may express disappointment with the project-directed interviews they read in oral history archives because the project interviewers did not dig deep enough into the subject. The main themes may have been covered, but not enough of the smaller details are included. Because individual researchers generally are seeking answers to specific questions, they may undervalue the parts of an archival interview that do not directly address their needs. The curse of oral history is failure to pursue details.

Can an independent researcher's interviews be considered an oral history?

There are differences between interviews conducted for one researcher's express purposes and those conducted as oral histories for general use. Oral histories are broadly conceived and conducted, then processed, preserved, and made available to other scholars in an archives. Research interviews fill the narrow needs of the individual interviewer, are rarely tape-recorded or transcribed, and generally wind up in the interviewer's file cabinets or in boxes in basements and attics.[7]

These distinctions become blurred when a researcher's interviews are recorded on tape or transcribed and deposited somewhere so that other researchers can use them. Oral historians have long objected to the use of the term "oral history" to describe every interview, regardless of whether it was recorded on tape or simply in handwritten notes. "Historians have been interviewing people for hundreds of years; there's nothing new about that, and I don't think they've been doing oral history," observed Philip Brooks of the Harry S. Truman Library in 1966. "I think there's a *real* distinction here between a researcher who interviews people for *his own* purpose to derive information for *his own* book, and that of what I sometimes call a 'pure' oral historian, who is accumulating a stock of evidence for the use of other researchers, any and all researchers, as we do in an archival agency. I think this is related somewhat to the question of objectivity." More recently, oral historians have conceded that all interviewing—archival or individual— is subjective, and that the earlier distinctions posed a false dichotomy.[8]

Similarly, when the Oral History Association first issued its *Evaluation Guidelines* in 1980, they were directed almost exclusively toward group or archival projects. When the revised guidelines were promulgated in 1992, they addressed the "independent/unaffiliated researcher" as well. Fully half of the guidelines involve the transfer of the independent researcher's interviews to an archives. Some interviews may not be worthy of permanent preservation, particularly if the researcher has not followed other criteria for oral history interviewing, preparation, and processing or has not been sensitive to oral history ethical considerations. Still, in the long run, institutions— whether public libraries soliciting and collecting family history interviews for their local history sections or major research archives working with authors and documentary film producers to collect oral history project interviews— stand to gain from a closer partnership with individual researchers.

It would be a mistake to define oral history so narrowly that it applied only to large archival collections. But to do oral history, interviewers must live up to its standards and assume its legal, ethical, and methodological responsibilities, including that of making their interviews available to other researchers for verification and further use.

ORAL EVIDENCE

How valid is oral history as historical evidence?

Treat oral evidence as cautiously as any other form of evidence. Documents written at the time have an immediacy about them and are not influenced by subsequent events, and yet those documents can be incomplete, in error, or written to mislead. A statement is not necessarily truer if written down at the time than if recalled later in testimony. Whether written or oral, evidence must be convincing and verifiable. A federal court jury on which I served was presented with a written statement that the prosecutor described as the defendant's "signed confession." The defense insisted that the prosecution had misinterpreted the statement, whose many grammatical errors obscured its meaning. In the jury room, jurors repeatedly read the statement, trying to decipher exactly what it meant, before concluding that it failed the test of convincing evidence.

Oral history can be unconvincing. Some interviewees' remarks are self-serving; they remember selectively, recall only events that cast themselves in a good light, and seem to always get the better of opponents. Interviewers may be too polite or too timid to ask probing questions about events that did not turn out well. Sometimes interviewees honestly cannot remember. They jumble names and dates and confuse people and places. Whole series of interviews can be faulted for paying attention to only one side of an issue, or for interviewing only people who spoke positively about the individual who was the subject of the project.

Enough bad oral histories have been done to satisfy the worst suspicions of traditionalists, and yet enough good interviews have been conducted to validate the process. Properly done, an oral history helps to interpret and define written records and makes sense out of the most obscure decisions and events. An interview with a thoughtful participant and perceptive eyewitness can generate new ideas and avenues of inquiry that a researcher might have never thought of pursuing. Interviews can explore the use of language by subgroups—such as jazz slang, black English, shop-floor jargon, and even the acronyms of government bureaucrats—and discover word meanings that might otherwise have eluded researchers outside the subgroup.

Oral evidence does not always derive from oral history. The French historian Emmanuel LeRoy Ladurie published what amounted to an oral history of a fourteenth-century village in the Pyrenees, Montaillou. His sources were depositions taken during the Inquisition by Bishop Jacques Fournier, who interrogated some 500 suspected heretics between 1318 and 1325. Scribes copied the questions and answers and gave the accused the opportunity to correct the transcripts. The final copies were deposited in the Vatican archives, where six centuries later they enabled Ladurie to quote the words of the common folk of Montaillou, people who stood in stark contrast to the nobles who dominate the chronicles of the Middle Ages. *Montaillou* (1979) became a best-seller in France and elsewhere, possibly because of its explicit accounts of sexual relations within the village. Prurient interests aside, the first-person accounts make the book compelling reading even for nonmedievalists.[9]

Similarly, the pension application process for militiamen in the American Revolutionary War amounted to what the historian John C. Dann has called "one of the largest oral history projects ever undertaken." In 1832, when Congress agreed to pay a yearly pension to any militiaman who had served for more than six months in the Revolution, thousands of elderly veterans applied. Since written records were scarce, the government required them to dictate their reminiscences to court reporters, giving as many names, dates, and other details as possible. Government clerks then scrutinized these testimonies to determine their accuracy. Selecting from a great mass of applications a century and a half later, Dann published the first-person eyewitness accounts of foot soldiers, runaway slaves, and women who followed their husbands into combat. Their accounts authentically describe not only combat but everyday life in the camps, wounds, diseases, and the whole social setting of the Revolutionary War.[10]

Oral history makes a critical addition to oral evidence: a trained interviewer can guide an interviewee's recital of events that he or she may not have thought about for years but can recall vividly when asked. Questions prompt interviewees to discuss issues they might otherwise have skipped over. Interviewers can question inconsistencies between the oral account and written documentation. A good oral history can present and preserve convincing evidence and put it in quotable, first-person prose that enlivens historical narratives. But oral history should not stand alone as a single source. Researchers seek out available material to substantiate both written and oral evidence. If written and oral information contradict each other, then the researcher must dig even deeper to determine which is more accurate.

While preparing to interview the former chief clerk of the Senate Labor, Education, and Public Welfare Committee, Stuart McClure, much of the research centered on the National Defense Education Act. In 1957, when the Soviet Union launched *Sputnik*, the first earth-orbiting satellite, McClure wrote a memo to the committee's chairman, Lister Hill, suggesting that the public attention generated by Sputnik might help pass the education bill that had stalled in Congress—if they called it a "defense education act." One account of the bill's passage devoted a chapter to the fight between the Senate, which wanted to make the money available as grants in the form of scholarships, and the House, which insisted on making it available as loans. During the interview, when asked why the Senate lost this battle, McClure laughed and replied:

> Oh, that was another clever, clever ploy. That was done on the House side. They narrowed the issue. There were millions of dollars for all kinds of other things, but Carl Elliott [the Alabama representative who chaired the House subcommittee on education] and his guys narrowed the issue to whether we should have the federal government hand out scholarships or loans. . . . The House denounced scholarships, it was a waste of money and socialism and all of that. And the minute the damn scholarship issue was done for, dead, the bill swooped through. I don't think anybody had read any other title in it. Oh, that was clever stuff. Carl Elliott was a brilliant strategist, as good as Lister Hill in his way, in different houses.[11]

Here oral history exposed a legislative ploy that not only fooled most members of the House of Representatives but the scholar who had published a history based on the official documentation. The debate over loans versus grants had been a subterfuge designed to allow the House, which had previously defeated federal education bills, to save face and claim victory. McClure's story has the ring of credibility—first, because it is logical, and second, because Senate staff rarely give credit to House members, except to express sheer admiration for a brilliant legislative tactic.

Can information from an oral history ever be cited by itself, with no other supporting evidence?

It depends on the information. A personal description, the expression of an opinion, or the telling of a colorful anecdote would permit citation of the interview as the single source. But the more controversial the subject, the less an interview can stand alone. Critics could question the authority of the interviewee. Was that person in a position to know, or does the interview constitute simply secondhand speculation? When in doubt, employ the journalist's practice of seeking at least two witnesses before asserting a statement of fact—if indeed a second witness is still alive.[12]

Independent researchers can also borrow from journalists the practice of having one interviewee comment on what another has said. A novice reporter, sent to cover a dispute involving a local developer, interviewed the developer and wrote his story. "Did you talk to the architect?" asked his editor. The reporter dutifully interviewed the architect and added his comments to the story, but his editor was still not satisfied. "Take what the architect said back to the developer and get him to respond," the editor instructed, "then take what the developer said back to the architect, and after they've answered each other's charges, then you write your story."

In cultural resource management projects that have included oral history interviews despite the misgivings of archaeologists and others on the team who are not oral historians, efforts have been made to determine the quality of evidence that the interviews gathered. The oral historian Dan Utley has described how, in one project collecting information about a defunct farming community, each interviewee was encouraged to talk at length about the annual hog killing, a universal experience in the community. "The hog killing stories were then compared and used as a rough guide to evaluate the memories, descriptive abilities, and involvement of the interviewees," he explained. "It was not easy to sit through numerous descriptions of the slaughter process, especially after breakfast, but they did provide an important comparative dimension to the overall project."[13]

Isn't most oral history anecdotal?

People naturally recount events and personalities anecdotally, in small self-contained stories that illuminate or instruct. Anecdotes often focus on humorous situations and characteristics and in conversation are designed to stimulate a smile or a laugh. In many ways, the anecdote is a writer's freshest material. The term derives from the Greek word *anekdota*, meaning "things unpublished," and it is often the telling stories taken from interviews that make a book original and different from previously published sources. *Anecdotal* is not synonymous with *apocryphal*, meaning spurious or unverifiable information. Names, dates, and other facts can usually be more reliably obtained elsewhere, but each interviewee has a unique store of anecdotes.

Although scholars sometimes denigrate anecdotes as the antithesis of analysis, these accounts can actually be informative, offering their analysis in a vivid and colorful manner and enlivening a narrative. Good writers have an eye and ear for a lively and believable anecdote that can make their points both memorably and compactly. Critics also dismiss oral history and other forms of narrative history because anecdotal information, by its nature, is randomly gathered and not statistically significant enough to make generalizations from. Social scientists look to census data, marriage licenses, death certificates, and voting statistics rather than to interviews, unless they are using a standard questionnaire and questioning a large, representative sample. Oral historians tailor their questions for individual interviewees, and time and financial limitations tend to restrict their pool of interviewees.

Although anecdotal information has a personal flavor, the collected stories from a group reinforce each other and show common threads in the lives of the group's members. Mixing anecdotal information with the hard data of statistical abstracts, the skilled researcher and writer can re-create a colorful as well as convincing portrait of the past.

Can an interviewer argue with interviewees if they seem wrong in what they are saying?

Individual researchers have more liberty than archival oral historians to inject the interviews with their own opinions and to challenge the interviewees. Remember, however, that all interviews are voluntary and last only as long as the interviewee desires. Keep in mind that too forceful an intervention by the interviewer may also distort the interviewee's responses.

Deliberate carefully when trying to decide whether interviewees' stories are accurate, misleading, or erroneous. An individual researcher usually approaches an interview with a thesis to prove and may assume that anything contradicting that thesis is wrong. Give the speaker a fair hearing, and then challenge any inconsistencies in the testimony with other sources. When pressed, the interviewee may be able to provide some additional rationale or even hard evidence to support previously unsubstantiated assertions. An impaired ability to listen can be a dangerous affliction for interviewers.[14]

"Research involves the shedding, not the confirmation, of our preconceptions," the historian Blair Worden has asserted. "If historians go to the archives expecting certain answers to their questions, careful study of the evidence will almost invariably change their minds." Living sources can magnify this condition by looking interviewers in the eye and telling them they are wrong and by revealing unexpected information. Interviewees may see things entirely differently from the researcher, and although interviewees might be biased or just plain wrong, so might the researcher's thesis. The best information to emerge from an oral history is often completely unexpected: a different way of looking at something, turning preconceived notions upside down. An interviewer may want to argue points with an interviewee, but it is self-defeating to seek out people to interview and then ignore what they have to say. Or as Lyndon Johnson used to say, "I ain't never learned nothin' talkin.' "[15]

Although interviewers strive to take a neutral role during the interview, neutrality may not be acceptable in its publication. When James Green published his interview with the historian C. Vann Woodward in the *Radical History Review*, it stimulated a series of angry letters to the editor expressing outrage that Green had not rebutted Woodward's critical remarks about the Marxist historian Herbert Aptheker. The opinions had been Woodward's, but Green took the blame for his silence and apologized for not challenging Woodward's assertions. "My purpose in interviewing Woodward for RHR was not, however, to expose our political differences," Green explained, "but to examine his contribution to the Left's understanding of Southern history and to the study of race, class and region in U.S. history."[16]

Is it possible to get a worthwhile interview from someone with whom you profoundly disagree?

The emphasis on interviewing "from the bottom up" has presumed that interviewers at least admire their interviewees even when they do not agree with them. But some researchers record the lives of people whose politics and ideologies they find "unsavory, dangerous, or deliberately deceptive." The sociologist Kathleen Blee, who interviewed former Ku Klux Klan members from Indiana, had no sympathy for the Klan's anti-Semitic, anti-Catholic, and racist politics and violent attitudes. She found it unnecessary to appear empathetic when interviewing Klan members and made little effort to shy away from controversial topics. She anticipated "no rapport, no shared assumptions, no commonality of thought or experience" and expected her interviewees to be too wary of her to reveal their true attitudes. But her expectations proved groundless. Not only did the former Klan members seem at ease during their interviews, but they assumed that she, "a native of Indiana and a white person," had to agree, even if secretly, with their views. "Even challenging their beliefs had no effect on their willingness to talk," Blee noted, concluding that despite their profound differences, rapport was disturbingly easy to achieve in an oral history interview.[17]

Won't interviewees try to convince their interviewers to adopt their viewpoints?

A certain amount of intellectual seduction—interviewees trying to make interviewers agree with them—may take place. Sitting down to talk with prominent figures can be a heady experience, and it is all too easy to slip into a false sense of intimacy that can diminish scholarly distance and detachment. The makers and shakers who spent their careers assiduously trying to manipulate the media may treat historical researchers in much the same manner. They want the researcher to see events from their perspective, to validate their positions. Some of them are campaigning for historical vindication just as energetically as they did for public office.

Researchers can also be captivated by less prominent individuals who have lived noble lives, suffered oppression, or been crusading spirits. Empathy helps greatly in conducting interviews. Allan Nevins once said that an interviewer needs *gemutlichkeit*, an "obvious sympathy with the person whom he interviews, friendliness and tact, as well as courage." But researchers must also demonstrate scholarly skepticism. Interviewees were players and partisans in the events and often have positions and reputations to defend. Researchers are observers, not players, and must not let personal admiration keep them from weighing the evidence dispassionately and creating a convincing account of people, movements, and past events.[18]

How does a researcher go about finding oral history interviews that have been collected and are open for research?

Although researchers may feel an impulse to grab a tape recorder and begin interviewing for themselves, the best place to start is with oral histories that have already been collected, transcribed, and opened. Many authors have used these collections, and many books have cited them, but only a small portion of these vast resources have been tapped.

Several directories to oral history collections exist, and various states, regions, and individual archives have published catalogs (many listed in the bibliography to this volume). Oral history archives have been collected at Baylor University, the University of California at Berkeley, California State University at Fullerton, Columbia, Cornell, Duke, Radcliffe, UCLA, and the universities of Connecticut, Kentucky, and Vermont, and at many other colleges and universities. Presidential libraries conduct their own oral histories, as do many corporate and labor archives. A sizable portion of these oral histories have been microfilmed and are available in a library's microform division or through interlibrary loan. The Library of Congress, for instance, holds copies of most of the microfilmed oral history collections.[19]

Interview tapes and transcripts are also interspersed through the manuscript collections of both interviewees and interviewers and in numerous agency files within larger archives. A great many of these collections are included in the National Union Catalog of Manuscript Collections, unwieldy as that multivolume guide can be. Ideally, oral history collections of all sizes and subjects will eventually be included in national on-line databases. Until then, finding oral histories will require as much ingenuity as locating relevant manuscript collections.

Is it legitimate for a researcher to use interviews conducted for someone else's earlier book?

As researchers's periods of study move further into the past and survivors are no longer available to interview, they have to rely more on a "second-generation" use of oral history, reexamining interviews that were conducted for other publications. The original interviewer may have cited only portions of the material or may have overlooked significant clues buried in the testimony. Seemingly innocent remarks may take on new meaning in the light of later developments. New trends in historical research may highlight issues that earlier researchers considered marginal or insignificant. Second-generation research potential increases the importance of depositing and preserving interviews in libraries and archives—for verification, reinterpretation, and reuse long after the interviewee, and the interviewer, are gone.

When Mark Stoler wrote his concise biography of Gen. George C. Marshall, he worked in the shadow of Forrest Pogue's monumental four-volume biography of Marshall. Although General Marshall had steadfastly refused lucrative offers to write his own memoirs in the 1950s, Pogue persuaded him to give interviews. Eventually, Marshall warmed to being interviewed and left behind a rich, reflective commentary on his impressive career, particularly his earlier years. Since General Marshall died years before Stoler began his research, the historian made use of Pogue's interviews at the Marshall Research Foundation in Lexington, Virginia. Repeatedly, Stoler quoted from Pogue's interviews for Marshall's evaluations of his colleagues and self-assessments of his actions. Although drawing from the same sources that had been available to Pogue, Stoler's book was a fresh interpretation of the material he thus shared with the earlier researcher.[20]

How reliable are an interviewee's reconstructions of conversations with others?

People often recall events in the form of conversation ("so she said to me . . . "). They remember the words of presidents and other famous people they have met; they remember arguments, warnings, humorous and ironic remarks, and beautifully turned phrases. People reconstruct dialogue not only in oral histories but in their letters and diaries; the results can be colorful but treacherous.

Interviewers hear only one party's version of a conversation, generally years after it took place. In evaluating such evidence, think about whether the comments are characteristic of the person to whom they are attributed and whether they make sense in the context of the time and place of the conversation. Be suspicious of interviewees who always managed to get the last word or administer the perfect squelch. They may be recalling what they wish they had said or may be claiming credit for lines spoken to them rather than by them. The humorist Garrison Keillor once confessed in a radio monologue that his childhood reminiscence about an overripe tomato thrown with perfect aim was absolutely true—except that his sister had thrown it at him, not the other way around.

The historian Arthur Schlesinger, Jr., noted that remembered dialogue helps to "impart immediacy to narrative" but warned that such information should only be used when the remarks are "plausibly supported by context or other evidence." He added: "I have extended this tolerance to oral history and employed the literary convention with the same critical caution I hope illustrious predecessors have applied to written documents. It remains a convention."[21]

How legitimate is it to cite anonymous interviews?

Journalists and other writers often rely on anonymous sources. Like Bob Woodward's "Deep Throat," journalists have interviewees whose identities they promise to keep secret and would go to jail over rather than divulge. Reporters know they would not get sensitive information if they interviewed only for attribution. Social scientists employ pseudonyms to protect the privacy of the communities they study. Anthropologists, linguists, and sociologists often interview people as representatives of types rather than as identifiable individuals. Their fieldwork techniques permit the creation of fictional identities for people and places. They believe that anonymity encourages interviewees to speak more candidly and that it protects interviewees, their families, and their jobs from retribution.

Oral historians influenced by the social sciences have felt a similarly strong need to protect interviewees' well-being by not revealing their names. They feel that sometimes the general message carries more significance than the particular speaker. For instance, the historian Sherna Gluck regretted that the political climate of the Middle East prevented her from revealing the real names of the Palestinian women she interviewed. "They have made it clear, however, that this personal recognition is less important to them than making their story public."[22]

Yet anonymity clashes with some of oral history's most fundamental objectives. Having sought to give "voice to the voiceless," it is inconsistent to render them nameless. Oral historians conduct life review biographical interviews because they consider interviewees important as individuals and want to record their unique experiences and perceptions. Future historians using these interviews will also expect some verification of sources. They will want to know where the information came from and what biases may have affected the testimony. Just as critics of journalistic practices have complained that unbridled anonymity allows public officials to evade responsibility for their views, oral historians believe that their interviewees should be held accountable for what they say for the record. Nothing based on anonymous sources can be proven, and the evidence remains at the level of rumor and innuendo. "When sources choose anonymity," the oral historian William W. Moss warned, "whether out of privacy, humility, or fear, the record produced not only suffers the loss of user confidence that accompanies any anonymous testimony, but the primary assertion of oral history that the individual indeed matters is also lost."[23]

The issue of anonymity created the greatest single area of disagreement when the Oral History Association revised its principles, standards, and evaluation guidelines in 1991. After protracted debate, the OHA adopted guidelines that ask whether "the interviewee understands his/her right to refuse to discuss certain subjects, to seal portions of the interview or in extremely sensitive circumstances even to choose to remain anonymous."[24]

By accepting anonymity under dire circumstances, oral historians indicated that it should never be a routine practice. When authors claim that their books are based on hundreds of interviews and cite none specifically, or assert that none of their interviewees chose to be identified, there is a strong suspicion that anonymity was part of the researcher's design and that interviewees never were encouraged or given the opportunity to speak for the record. The use of blanket anonymity also raises the question of the expiration of that anonymity. Was the promise of anonymity eternal, or can the interviewees' identities be restored to them at some safe point in the future?

One solution for writers seeking to balance their interviewees' anonymity with scholarly verification is to deposit the tapes and transcripts in a library or archives with provisions for identifying the interviewees after a safe interval. The political scientist Richard Fenno has given his interviews with members of Congress to the National Archives. Since these interviewees had left public life, they could be identified without fear of political embarrassment, thereby enhancing the future research value of the collection. A history of the U.S. space program drew heavily from interviews with past and present employees of NASA (National Aeronautics and Space Administration), asking about their personal backgrounds, the type of work they did in the space program, and their perspectives on how the agency changed over time. Given that many of the interviewees were still NASA employees, they were assured that their names would not appear next to any quotations used in the published history—which identified each interview only by number—but that the transcripts, linking names to the numbers, would be preserved in the NASA History Office.[25]

PUBLISHING ORAL HISTORY

How much editing of interviews is acceptable for publication?

Transcripts of tapes are edited, and most published oral histories have been further edited, condensing and highlighting remarks and in some cases rearranging testimony for chronological and narrative purposes. But how much is too much? Oral historians have expressed suspicion over the popular books of Studs Terkel, who usually removes his own questions and sometimes reorders his interviewees' answers. When Charles Morrissey questioned some Vermonters quoted in Terkel's *American Dreams, Lost and Found* (1980), they objected to the way their remarks had appeared in print. One complained that Terkel "applied his thoughts to my words and came up with the version in his book." Another felt that his words had been rearranged "in such a way that I can't make sense of it."[26]

Some of the best-known "oral history" books have been produced by professional writers who lacked training in historical research and handled oral documentation rather loosely. Serious questions were raised about the authenticity of Alex Haley's *Roots* (1976); many felt it was a work of historical fiction more than history. Merle Miller's *Plain Speaking: An Oral Biography of Harry S. Truman* (1974), in a similar fashion, seems to mix Truman's recollections with Miller's own creative writing. Miller did not publish his interviews until after Truman's death, and some of the statements he attributed to Truman strain credulity. Miller's rambling remarks to an Oral History Association meeting in 1975 augmented the audience's worst suspicions. "I don't consider myself an oral historian," Miller later admitted. He then added, "Oral historians don't either. I spoke at their national convention several years ago and they loathed me, detested me, because since I don't know the rules of oral history—and operate as a reporter, which I consider myself—I violate them."[27]

Editing and rearranging interviews for clarification and cutting away tangential material are appropriate so long as the original meaning is retained. The goal is to sharpen the focus without putting words in the interviewee's mouth or altering the essence of what was said. For instance, if an interviewee spoke at length about someone's positive characteristics and fleetingly of one negative quality, it would be misleading and unfair to quote only the latter.

In reproducing large sections of oral history interviews for publication, researchers should consider including the questions as well as the answers. Some subjects may not have been discussed simply because the interviewer asked nothing about them. Other subjects came up precisely because that was what the interviewer wanted to know about. By leaving as many of their questions in the text as feasible, oral historians not only show what questions elicited the responses but demonstrate that the interviewee did not necessarily volunteer the information and may even have had to be coaxed to reveal private and potentially embarrassing information. Without the questions, the basic dialogue of an oral history is lost, creating the impression that people raised the issues when in fact they were responding to queries. Similarly, when several interviewees focus on a particular trait or make a similar observation, it could be simply because they are all responding to the same question.

Oral history has become fashionable among popular writers and other purveyors of popular culture who are not always careful about its presentation. Cullom Davis, who directed the oral history program at Sangamon State University in Illinois, warned of its "debasement" by those who fail to "observe the canons of our profession." He charged that publication of oral history without interpretation produces little more than a scissors-and-paste scrapbook and a disorganized mass of recollections. "As serious practitioners, whether lay or professional," Davis argued, "we must identify the hucksters and charlatans who exploit oral history's intrinsic appeal for their own shallow, ahistorical and even unethical ends."[28]

Should oral history interviewees speak for themselves, or do they require scholarly interpretation?

The compelling nature of the spoken word, the enjoyment of reading the vernacular, the honesty and humor of so many interviewees, has kindled a strong interest in allowing oral sources to "speak for themselves." This approach, which often involves little interpretation on the part of the compiler, sometimes results in books that resemble collages. The literary critic Elizabeth Hardwick has dismissed "tape recording without an interpretive intelligence" as "a primitive technology for history" designed to relieve the author of the burden of writing. Hardwick insists that a book requires an author's "signature of responsibility."[29]

Reviewing the biography of Robert F. Kennedy by Arthur Schlesinger, Jr., Henry Fairlie dismissed oral history as testimonials of dubious value. It is up to the historian "to do the hard work of sifting," wrote Fairlie. "When we are given the personal words of various actors, that is all we are given, and we have either to take or reject their word that something happened as they say. . . . That is what we have historians for: to take their word that this was so." Historians act as judges, interpreters, and critics, compiling and analyzing sources of the past. Historians are rarely themselves eyewitnesses to the events they write about. They reconstruct events and the temper of the time from a mixture of sources, balancing the reliability of one piece of data against another, arranging them in a coherent pattern to make sense out of what happened.[30]

The very act of editing and arranging interviews shows that the author has not simply allowed interviewees to speak for themselves. Editorial intervention begins with determining whom to interview, what questions to ask, which interviews to include in the volume, in which order, and how much of the original interviews to publish. Even if the editor refrains from adding an overt interpretation, he or she is still deciding which interviewees are most worthy of being recorded and published. Having gone that far then, the editor owes something more to readers. At the minimum, authors of oral history collections should provide some background for their interviews to place the interviewees in context, offering suggestions about why they said what they did and took certain positions and sometimes spelling out where interviewer and interviewee did not agree.

A certain romantic belief has developed that putting a microphone in front of people will miraculously provide the road to truth. In his influential reviews of oral history literature, Michael Frisch has argued that what historians do—interpreting evidence, weighing, testing, connecting people and events—is still critically important. "And yet, at the same time the exciting thing about oral history is that the process becomes a less exclusive one," he added. The scholar and the subject collaborate: "They come together and provide a good advantage for understanding the meaning of the experience." This is the notion that Frisch calls a "shared authority": "the grounds of authority are very different, and have very different meaning, but there is a kind of sharing in the process of the interpretive authority, which is one of the exciting things about doing oral history."[31]

If writers quote from interviews they conducted, do they need to first submit them to their interviewees for review?

Some researchers allow their interviewees to check their quotes before they use them. "I think it's only fair," Arthur Schlesinger, Jr., reasoned, "that when you talk to people, you should give them the same kind of control over an interview as they have over an oral history transcript." Other researchers might chafe at this idea, given that an interviewee might change or delete something entirely. Yet anyone who has ever been interviewed by a reporter and then misquoted in the newspaper article can appreciate how differently the teller and the listener can hear the same story. Context is essential for accuracy, and even a perfectly quoted sentence can have its meaning altered if taken out of context.[32]

At the same time, interpreting what the interviewees said remains the historian's domain. A researcher and an interviewee may form entirely different opinions about the events under discussion. Even though interviewees were eyewitnesses, their perspectives could be distorted, and their memories incorrect. By collecting evidence from a multitude of sources, the historian may come to a different conclusion. The author's duty is to quote the interviewee correctly and not distort the remarks to fit a thesis. Otherwise, the author is entirely responsible for the finished product.

What do reviewers look for when reviewing oral history books?

Reviewers have been notoriously inconsistent in dealing with oral history. Too often a review begins with an admission that the reviewer knows little about oral history or does not trust oral sources, characteristics that never seem to disqualify them from reviewing the book. They distance themselves from the methodology and consequently add little to our understanding. At the root of their complaints, however, is a fairly common call for the author to assume a more interpretive role. Commenting on the increasing appearance of books based on interviews, the novelist and frequent reviewer Diane Johnson asserted, "There does seem in this technique an almost cowardly reluctance to think."[33] In the same vein, Timothy Foote began a review of an oral history of the Second World War by noting: "Anything calling itself oral history probably ought to be approached with deep suspicion. Time is short. There is much to read. We're already awash in ill-chosen words. And though tape recorders are splendid gimmicks, people who present interviews as history are farther from the mark than a cook who insists that a loose collection of eggs, sugar, milk, vanilla, flour, and a few squares of bitter chocolate are in fact a chocolate cake."[34]

Reviewers more experienced with oral history have reacted to the literature through the lens of their own disciplines or tailored their reactions to fit the publications in which their reviews appear. After conducting a survey of oral history reviews, the book review editor Linda Shopes observed that reviewers in the *Oral History Review* generally wanted to know more about the interviewing process and procedures than about the subject matter and particular findings of a project, although the accuracy of the information gathered was often a major touchstone of *OHR* reviews. Reviewers commented on whatever unique insights and perspectives emerged from the interviews but took authors to task for not testing the accuracy of oral evidence through corroborating sources. Reviews in the more theoretically oriented *International Journal of Oral History* were more likely to be interpretive, focusing on subjectivity and on how oral tradition and narratives "can reveal the complex consciousness of a culture." Reviews in the British journal *Oral History* tended to raise questions of a political nature, reflecting the journal's socialist leanings.

Reviewers for general, non-oral history journals express more concern about oral history's substantive contributions to historical knowledge. These reviews emphasize the importance of first-person narrative in conveying a sense of people as historical actors and actresses. General historical reviewers tend to respond best to authors who use a variety of interviewees together with other documentary sources, and who place the data in a broad analytical context. The chief conclusion that emerges from this sampling of reviewers is that the author of an oral history volume is inevitably judged as a historian and cannot escape that role by suggesting that the sources "speak for themselves."[35]

How should oral histories be cited as references?

How to cite interviews is a question that touches on the one of how seriously researchers take oral sources. Of all the academic disciplines engaged in interviewing as a research tool, professional historians have devoted the least amount of methodological attention to its problems and potentials. This laxity contrasts sharply with the intense seriousness historians bring to written sources. Authors dutifully list every manuscript collection, book, and article consulted and then limit the bibliography of oral sources to a few lines acknowledging those who "shared their knowledge" in "conversations" with the author. Footnotes identify the interviews with cryptic initials and often without dates or other information that would tell the interested reader how the interview was collected. Some interviews are not cited at all. Substantial numbers of histories drawn from oral sources give no indication of whether the tapes and transcripts are deposited somewhere, either for other researchers' use or for verification. It remains puzzling why professional historians have accepted on faith an author's reliability in note taking, transcribing, and even interpreting oral information.[36]

Guides to historical writing specify that the standard reference should begin with the name of the interviewee. The title of the interview (if there is one) should be in quotation marks. The citation should include "interviewed by [name of interviewer]" and mention whether the interview is a tape or transcript, and whether it has been published as part of a book or journal article or in any other medium, with standard references to such publication. The citation should indicate whether the interview is in the author's possession or has been deposited in a library or archives. Keep in mind that the purpose of a footnote is to show where the information comes from and to help the reader find the original source. Page numbers for transcripts, or other publications, should be provided.[37]

106

The following are examples of citations of interviews from oral history archives, from independent research, and from published sources:

Beth Campbell Short, interviewed by Margot H. Knight, 23 April–17 August 1987, transcripts, Women in Journalism Project, Washington Press Club Foundation, Washington, D.C.

Sen. Hugh D. Scott, interviewed by the author, 27 January 1986, tape and transcript deposited at the Senate Historical Office, Washington, D.C.

David Montgomery, interviewed by Paul Buhle, in *Visions of History*, ed. Henry Abelove, et al. (New York: Pantheon, 1983), 169–83.

5

VIDEOTAPING ORAL HISTORY

Should oral histories be videotaped?

Memories are recounted with more than words. Transcripts can indicate laughter, sobs, finger pointing, or fist shaking. But some expressions and gestures are too complex or subtle to reduce to words. When Richard Sweterlitsch tape-recorded an interview with the Italian-American Sophia Bielli about the granite industry in Barre, Vermont, he realized that her language was not just verbal. "Sophia spoke with her hands punctuating her oral statements, and with her face and eyes she communicated her intensity and reactions to what she was saying," he observed. "It was obvious that I had to document the visual along with the aural."[1]

Transcripts, audiotapes, and videotapes all impart the same basic information, but videotape provides an extra dimension to oral history interviews. Transcripts reduce language to written symbols. Tape recordings convey tone, rhythm, volume, and speech patterns. But the facial expressions and body language captured by videotape reveal even more of an interviewee's personality. A smile, a wink, a frown, or a look of perplexity would be missed in an audio interview and convey more than what can be reproduced in a transcript.

The setting in which the interview takes place can also add color and context. For many families, videotaped oral histories with elderly relatives are treasured keepsakes. For museums and archives, video interviews expand the potential uses of oral histories as valuable resources for exhibits and documentaries. The Smithsonian Institution has used video interviews with zoologists not only to talk about but to show changes in zoo facilities and animal care. Harlem's Schomburg Center for Research in Black Culture has videotaped African-American dance traditions.[2]

Videotape is highly practical when recording group interviews. Anyone who has tried to transcribe an interview with multiple interviewees knows the frustration and helplessness of not knowing who is speaking, since voices in a group sound impossibly alike. Speakers will interrupt each other, cut in, and speak simultaneously, all chaotic conditions for the transcriber. One solution is to assign someone to sit in the session and note the order of speakers, but a videotape provides a much more precise means of distinguishing speakers.

Videotape is the favored medium for recording oral history visually. Although film is a perfectly acceptable alternative, it is infrequently used because of its expense, production complications, and inconvenience. Videotaping also has drawbacks in that it usually requires the use of cameras, lighting, sound equipment, and crew. Some video historians prefer to work in studios, where they can better control sound and light conditions. Others argue that the latest portable camcorders, particularly those using digital technology, perform well in low light conditions, need only a single operator, and allow the interview to take place in more natural settings.

In either case, the increased equipment and personnel requirements make videotaping more expensive than audio interviewing and can also make it harder for the interviewer to put the interviewee at ease and establish rapport. People may not warm up as quickly to the cameras, may become more self-conscious, and may have more trouble speaking candidly. A video interview can result in hours of visually dull "talking heads." Oral historians also want to be assured that videotape has the same recording and preservation capabilities as audiotape; that the technology has advanced to the point where it is worth the investment; that the video can be considered reliable; that the recording will last; and that the demands of the technology will not alter the interview situation too much. Before adopting video, therefore, consider carefully what you want to achieve and measure the benefits of videotaping against its liabilities.[3]

Behind these pragmatic reasons, the reluctance of many oral historians to try videotaping also suggests a widespread "technophobia," or nervousness about any new technology. Similar fears caused some interviewers to use reel-to-reel tape recorders long after the majority had switched to more portable and affordable cassette recorders. There are always good reasons for caution—reel-to-reel tape remains preferable to cassettes for archival preservation—but "we've never done it that way before" is a poor excuse for not exploring and trying new equipment. Although some veteran oral historians hang back, National History Day judges can attest that high school–age students have been quick to master new technologies and that the videotapes they produce are often impressively polished and professional.

Should every interview be videotaped?

Videotaped interviews are expensive. A few projects can afford to videotape every interview, but most use video only selectively. Generally, it is advisable to conduct audio oral histories first, to collect basic information, and then return to videotape a portion of the interview, allowing the camera to illustrate the oral history. The video interview may cover new ground or repeat some questions to recapture highlights of the previous sessions. The video segment of interviews with artists and craftspeople might be devoted to recording them at work or to having them describe and explain their creations. Having recorded most of the interview on audiotape gives the interviewer and the interviewee a better idea of what to expect during the videotaping session, making them both a little more comfortable in front of the camera.[4]

To retain some of the interview's spontaneity, a few weeks should elapse, if the schedule permits, between the audio and video segments of the interview. People never say things exactly the same way twice, however, and the video-taped rendition may simply not be as lucid or entertaining as the earlier audiotape version. Documentary makers often have to coax an interviewee to repeat a phrase, louder, with different emphasis, or in more complete sentences. That some staging is necessary in video may offend those practitioners who believe an oral history should always be authentic and unrehearsed. In fact, there has never been any truth to the adage that "photos never lie." Just as Civil War photographers rearranged bodies on the battlefield to heighten the visual effect, modern documentary makers often choose to meld history with artistry.[5]

If the ultimate objective of a project is to produce a documentary or mount an exhibit, it makes sense to video every session of every interview. But if the objective is an archival collection for all types of research, selective videotaping is more cost-effective. Vivian Perlis, director of the Oral History and American Music Project at Yale University, has described the video component as "the finishing touch" of their oral histories. Initially, the project historians conducted videos of all their interviews at the homes of such interviewees as Aaron Copland, but they came to realize that some musicians are "more filmic" than others and that the expense of regular on-site interviewing was growing unmanageable. They did subsequent videotaping at a studio at Yale and even then videotaped only major figures rather than all interviewees.[6]

Won't the camera make interviewees nervous and uncomfortable?

Undeniably, the use of a camera and crew, lights, and the possible shift of the interview to a studio may intimidate some interviewees. Video specialists recommend that interviewers explain the equipment to interviewees, demonstrating how it works, making sure that they are seated comfortably, and encouraging them to look at the interviewer rather than at the camera, which should be placed off to one side.[7]

Yet television has become so commonplace in modern society that interviewees are far less likely to be put off by cameras than might be expected.

Video interviews with elderly residents in nursing homes, for instance, show that even people never before videotaped quickly feel at ease and talk naturally on camera. Keep in mind, however, that interviewees can become fatigued and not look their best for the camera. Some video historians have raised the ethical question of what obligation a project has to interviewees who, because they slumped or were nervous or made awkward gestures, are disappointed or embarrassed over their video appearance.[8]

Sometimes the interviewer can be even more nervous than the interviewee on camera. Listening carefully to what is being said and thinking ahead to the next question, interviewers also have to wonder about how they appear themselves (although interviewers may not necessarily be seen on camera). It takes some practice to switch from audio to visual taping. In 1983 the Oral History Association sponsored a debate between a video supporter, who conducted all of his interviews on videotape, and a video skeptic, who had previously expressed deep-felt reservations that the camera destroys the intimacy needed to establish rapport in an interview. When the debate took place, however, the skeptic announced that, to be fair, he had decided to try doing a video interview himself. To his astonishment, he admitted, it was the best interview he had ever conducted. Not only was he freed from watching the tape recorder and changing the tape, but the crew was unobtrusive and the interviewee had no problem talking on camera. Delighted with the results, the skeptical interviewer had become an enthusiastic convert to video-taped interviews, forcing the video supporter to interject a few words of caution about video's potential problems into his presentation on its benefits.

What about those interviewees who do not look well enough or talk clearly enough for videotaping?

Timing is a critical element in conducting any oral history. Interviews ideally take place at a point when the interviewee is appropriately reflective and still has full mental capabilities. Sometimes the oral historian arranges the interview too late, after the interviewee has grown forgetful and confused. Taking videos of very elderly interviewees may be problematic if they look infirm and speak indistinctly (a dilemma for audiotaping as well). It raises the question of whether a visual record of people at the end of their lives does justice to the stories they can tell of their youthful, active years. Nevertheless, an oral history is not cinema, and interviewees should not have to look and sound like trained actors.

The Afro-American Labor Leadership Oral/Video History Series con-ducted a video interview with Hosea Hudson, who at 86 suffered from respiratory problems, spoke with a slurred drawl, and appeared physically frail. Yet the producers found that Hudson's condition only underscored his firm rhetoric, positive outlook, and mental spryness. "Thanks to his video-taped interview," the interviewer James Wilson asserted, "one can now more easily appreciate what a fiery young orator Hudson was during the CIO's [Congress of Industrial Organizations] southern organizing drives of the 1930s."[9]

The speech of some interviewees may be so indistinct, or their accents or regional dialects so thick, that subtitles are necessary to render their words understandable. Gallaudet University has also employed subtitles for its video interviews with deaf students. A split screen records both the interviewer and the interviewee, captures the sign language they are using, and simultaneously provides written translations.[10]

Should interviewees be prepared in advance of a video interview?

Interviewees should be informed of the purposes of the interview, of any special requirements for videotaping, of their legal rights, and of the need for their signature on a release form. For videotaping on location, the interviewee needs to know about, and give permission for, setting up cameras and lights in his or her home. Interviewees should also be reminded of the expense and difficulty of sending a crew to videotape an interview, to encourage them not to cancel or postpone the interview without sufficient notice.

Some interviewers also recommend to interviewees appropriate dress, or at least advise them on the types of colors and patterns to avoid (white or black, and clothes with bold stripes or patterns). Interviewers should be available to talk with interviewees in advance of the interview, to answer their questions and satisfy their concerns. Such information and reassurance often helps interviewees feel comfortable with the video medium, encouraging them to speak as candidly as possible.

Does the use of video versus audiotape affect the types of questions that an oral historian asks?

The medium definitely affects the message. Oral historians who have worked with video report that they have had to reformulate questions to elicit the type of information that makes for better visual presentation. They replaced abstract and generalized questions with more specific inquiries, asking fewer "why" questions and more "how" questions. They asked interviewees to demonstrate how equipment worked or to go through their usual routines, eliciting the type of detail that an audio interview could never approach.[11]

Shifts in questioning become more pronounced when curators, exhibitors, documentary film makers, and material culture specialists conduct their video interviews with specific ends in mind. The museum curator might be seeking a videotape of a worker talking about and demonstrating a mechanical or artistic process, to accompany the actual machinery on display in the museum. The questions therefore would be aimed precisely toward that end. The National Park Service set up lights and cameras in the home of Jimmy Carter in Plains, Georgia, and had Carter conduct a tour of the house and grounds. Although the interview raised questions about Carter's life and career, and particularly about his postpresidential years, the chief focus was on the architecture of the house and an inventory of the Carters' furniture, memorabilia, and other belongings. Eventually, when the house passes to the National Park Service as a historic site, the videotapes will enable curators to re-create the environment in which the Carters lived. Excerpts from the tapes will also be shown at the visitors' center.[12]

Although the type of question may change, the way in which questions are posed should not. However complete their transfer from the aural to the visual medium, oral historians must maintain their professional standards and avoid the temptation to emulate the more aggressive television news interviewers. Interviewees may pose, but oral history interviewers should never play to the cameras.

SETTING, EQUIPMENT, AND CREW

Should a video oral history be conducted in a studio or in a more natural setting?

Since studios are artificial—perhaps even intimidating—settings for interviews, interviewers often want to bring the camera to interviewees' homes or equally familiar surroundings. The natural setting provides a more interesting backdrop and usually an abundance of stimulants for interviewees' memories. The Smithsonian Institution has conducted video oral histories in the laboratories and workshops of its scientists and curators. The Minnesota Historical Society similarly has videotaped on location, from farmyards to boat docks, after first completing audio interviews. After the audio segments are made, several interviewees are selected to retell portions of their stories on camera and to point out places or demonstrate activities related to their testimony.[13]

Although it is more visually interesting, a natural setting adds to the problems of doing a video interview, including the cost of moving a crew and equipment, maintaining sound quality, and the unpredictability of light, sound, and background noise when videotaping outdoors. Video interviewers need to know the limitations of the equipment and have to be prepared to solve technical problems in the field. They need to prepare checklists so that equipment is not forgotten. Videotaping at an interviewee's home or place of work may require an advance trip to the site to decide how to set up the equipment. The camera crew will need to be careful to place the interviewee away from the glare of a window and to avoid noisy rooms, to be conscious of outdoor noise and wind, and to watch out for inquisitive neighbors and dogs. When taping outside, the wind may create noise or play havoc with the interviewee's hair, distracting viewer attention. The sun may cast unflattering shadows, and clouds may cause the light to fluctuate during the taping.[14]

For quality control, a studio or other indoor setting is preferable for video interviewing. Studio interviews, however, more often result in "talking heads" and do not offer the variation in picture that improves and enlivens a documentary. A reasonable compromise is to conduct part of the interview in a studio and then take a camera to follow interviewees through more natural settings—walking around their homes or neighborhoods, at a factory, going down a road by themselves or with the interviewer. These images can later be edited into the studio tapes, with the studio audio used as a voice-over. Still photographs also can be interspersed.

After the interview has been completed, the production crew can do a "sweeping pan" of the room where the interview took place, to capture the interview environment for the historical record. Photographs from a family album can also be videotaped at the end of the tape. Known as "cutaways," this additional footage can be interspersed later throughout the interview to vary the visual effects.

If a project has a limited budget, how can it afford to use a studio?

Video oral historians have a number of affordable options to get technical assistance and access to equipment. Numerous community colleges and universities maintain broadcasting facilities, often as part of communications departments. These studios, together with student assistants, can be rented for reasonable costs. Their managements are often open to cost-sharing proposals to reduce charges further.

Another avenue for low-cost or free use of studios and equipment is the local community-access cable channel. These channels were made possible by the Cable Communications Policy Act of 1984, which entitled communities to require the creation of a community-access channel as part of their franchise agreements with cable television companies. An estimated 1,500 public channels have been established nationwide, providing local citizens with an outlet to express their views. Services, fees, and expertise vary widely, but these facilities have been used successfully by oral historians in different regions to produce video interviews and documentaries.

Community-access channels generally provide free use of their equipment, and since they are always seeking new material, they often offer to show the resulting programs and documentaries. For a nominal fee, the channels usually offer training for individuals or groups in the use of video cameras, lighting, audio mixing, scripting, directing, and producing. The studios may provide free tape stock for the programs they air but probably will charge for any duplicate tapes. Oral historians who must travel to do their interviews can look for a local resident to sponsor their use of the local community-access studio. To identify community-access channels, contact the local cable programmers or the Alliance for Community Media.[15]

How large a budget is necessary to do video oral histories?

Consumer video cameras are relatively affordable and produce a reasonably good interview for limited purposes, but a full-fledged, good-quality video oral history is not an inexpensive process. Costs range widely, but the basic costs always include fees for the interviewer's preliminary research, interview time, travel expenses, and editing of the interviews. Producers and directors also require payment for services before and after the interview. A crew may have to be hired, and equipment leased for the day, at the going rate where the interview takes place. The crew may also incur transportation, lodging, and meal expenses. Tape and other supplies must be purchased.

When the interview is completed, transcribers or indexers are needed. Duplicate tapes must be made for archival preservation and use, and sometimes copies of the tape or transcript must be given to the interviewee. General office expenses and supplies cannot be overlooked. These costs all mount up. When applying for grants to do video histories, it is essential not to underbudget, or operating expenses will evaporate well before the project is completed. In fact, most granting agencies and foundations have acquired a good sense of the financial requirements of video oral history and dismiss applications that are underbudgeted—a sure sign of the applicant's inexperience.

Why have a camera operator? What is wrong with the interviewer simply setting the camera on a tripod to run by itself?

By all accounts, the interviewer makes a grievous mistake by trying to play camera operator. An interviewer needs to concentrate fully on the give-and-take of the interview. Running a tape recorder offers distractions enough, but the cameras, lights, and sound requirements of a video interview require trained technical assistance. It is possible, however, for the interviewer to act as producer-director, consulting with the camera operator over camera angles and the type of picture sought.

The camera operator should be fully aware of the project's objectives, of the mood it is seeking, and of any interviewee mannerisms to be recorded. The video interview is therefore a collaborative effort, not only between the interviewer and the interviewee but between the interviewer and the technicians responsible for the quality control of the video recording.

How many people are necessary to run a video oral history project?

Numbers vary according to project budgets, but the functions that have to be handled are the same, regardless of the size of the staff. In better-funded projects, these functions are divided among several staff members; the staffs of smaller projects wear many hats. All oral history projects, audio or visual, need a director who will set the agenda, raise and administer funds, handle contracts, maintain the paperwork, and supervise the rest of the personnel.

A video oral history requires a producer (who may be the project director or the interviewer doing double duty) to choose interviewees, the times and sites of the interviews, and the crew to conduct the interviews. The director (who may also be the producer) supervises the technical crew and the setting of the lights and cameras and maintains the general aural and visual standards of the day's taping. The camera operator (who may also be the director) composes the shots, tapes the interview, and keeps the interviewer informed of when the tape is running out. Larger projects may employ a sound operator to handle the microphones and monitor the audio recording levels, and a "grip," or assistant, to set up and take down the equipment before and after the interview. It is also beneficial to have a production assistant present at the site of the interview to take care of the paperwork, get release forms signed, handle the master tape, and deal with problems as they arise.[16]

What kind of videotaping equipment should be acquired for an oral history project?

The better the quality of the equipment and tape, the better the video interview. Despite the impressive results from consumer video recorders, long-term preservation and use in exhibits or documentaries require that professional-quality cameras and studio videotapes be used.

A camera is only as good as its lens. Use lenses that are wide enough for videotaping in close quarters. A zoom ratio—from telephoto to wide-angle—of at least 8:1 is recommended. Avoid using the microphone mounted on the camera, since its sound quality will be undependable. Instead, use a "boom mike" that extends to the speaker. To be safe, also record the interview on a tape recorder as a backup system. The audiotape can be used for transcribing and archival purposes. As in audio interviewing, a lavaliere mike, pinned unobtrusively onto a scarf, necktie, or lapel, promotes good sound quality. Work with reputable dealers, and while taking advantage of whatever discounts are available for equipment and tape, make sure that you understand the warranties and guarantees.[17]

Since purchasing professional, studio-quality equipment will most likely be too expensive, consider either renting equipment or hiring a crew with its own cameras and equipment for specific interviews. Rental costs will vary according to the interview location and can be considerably higher in some cities—variations that need to be taken into account when setting budgets and applying for grants.

What's the optimal way to set up the cameras for an interview?

A video oral history needs a competent camera operator who knows how to frame and light a picture properly. Poor camera work can make even the most interesting interview dull. If you have gone to the trouble of using the visual medium, you need to be conscious of the picture you are getting. Although oral historians interview to gain information, video offers the observer an array of new insights. The aim is to present the picture so that it does not overwhelm or distract viewers from the substance of the interview but enhances the meaning of what is being said.

Videotapes and documentaries are almost always viewed on television-sized screens, and television is a close-up medium; head and shoulder shots predominate. In framing the picture, it is important to give the speaker adequate "head room" and "look space." Balanced head room prevents the head from appearing too close to the top of the frame or sinking below it. Eye room similarly suggests the amount of space from the face to the side of the frame. For variety, the camera can move in for a close-up that shows the face only from the eyes to the mouth. Viewers mentally complete the picture. The video specialist David Mould also notes that "the human body has certain natural divisions—at the neck, at the waist, at the knees," and he warns against framing an interviewee so that the bottom of the picture breaks at one of these divisions.[18]

The way a subject is framed can constitute a subtle form of editorializing. The popular television news show "60 Minutes" frequently shoots its interviewees in extreme close-up, cutting the top of their heads from the picture and focusing on their eyes. By contrast, when the camera turns to the program's own interviewers, it pulls back to give them full head and shoulders and "lots of visual breathing space."[19] Shooting below or above the interviewee also distorts the picture. A more neutral picture of the speaker is the one taken at eye level, so that the viewer sees the speaker at the same level. Interviewees should sit at a slight angle to the camera and talk to the interviewer rather than to the camera. The background should be relatively uncluttered to avoid diverting viewers' attention. Interviewers should dress appropriately for the particular interview and should avoid wearing unusually patterned clothing that would clash with the backdrop or otherwise prove distracting.

Camera angles differ when videotaping a group. Video oral historians have experimented with many different arrangements of interviewers and interviewees. A particularly successful arrangement is to place the interviewer, back to the camera, in the open end of a V-shaped table at which the interviewees are sitting. The interviewer can maintain eye contact with whomever is speaking, just as the camera can focus easily on the speakers, either individually or in groups.[20]

Is it appropriate to use a zoom lens during a video interview?

Zoom lenses change the picture composition to create more diverse and interesting visual effects, to provide close-ups, or perhaps to capture an artifact or a speaker's expressive hands. But video specialists cringe at "unmotivated" zooming and recommend that the zoom-in or -out take place during the question rather than during the answer. Documentary makers inevitably edit the tape for their particular needs, cutting out false starts, phrases, and whole sentences and paragraphs; they prefer a standard camera angle and position and head size because the speaker's head remains a uniform size when they cut back into the tape. Editors also favor some variety in shots, however, and suggest that at least two standard framings be used. Video historians must consider all the possible uses of their product and proceed accordingly.

Should both the interviewer and interviewee be seen on camera?

The chief focus always should be on the interviewee. The interviewer's questions shape the dialogue, but the reason for doing interviews is to hear what interviewees have to say and, on video, to watch them saying it. When the budget covers the use of only one camera, as is most often the case, tape the interviewee during the interview. If necessary, the interviewer can be taped asking questions and reacting (that is, listening quietly) after the interview is over. Television news broadcasts have long employed this technique, which is a pivotal point in the movie *Broadcast News*. As in the motion picture, staged "reaction" shots raise ethical issues and should be handled very carefully.

Some oral historians object strongly to taping only the interviewee. Noting the collaborative nature of an interview, they ask, why videotape only one party to it? "The integrity of the document may be compromised if only half of the interview 'team' is photographed and recorded," Thomas L. Charlton of the Baylor University Institute for Oral History has written. He recommends using two cameras: one to focus exclusively on the interviewee, the second to focus alternately on the interviewer and on group shots containing both the interviewer and interviewee. Some video oral historians have also used a split-screen technique. Multiple cameras are easier to use in a studio than on location.[21]

PRESERVING AND USING THE VIDEOTAPE

What type of documentation is needed for a video oral history?

Just as with an audio interview, video oral histories require some basic data for research use. At a minimum, documentation should include: the date of the interview; the names of the interviewee and interviewer; a summary statement on the interviewee and the subjects covered; whether there are transcripts of the interview; whether the tape is audio or video; the running time or length of the interview; and any restrictions on the use of the material.

Are deeds of gift also required for video oral histories?

Federal law specifies that any tangible recording of a person's words is protected by copyright. Interviewees retain ownership of their words until they sign a deed of gift, contract, or release form, which usually transfers intellectual property rights in the interview from the interviewee to the sponsoring institution or documentary maker. Video release forms can be the same as those for audio oral history, with one difference: the use of an interviewee's face as well as voice in a documentary can be unsettling if unexpected, so some video releases include a statement that the interviewee has been notified of the uses to which the material will be put.[22]

What archival considerations should be taken into account when making video oral histories?

As with sound recordings, archives face the problem of new technology making current video equipment obsolete. Some video interviews have been recorded in formats for which archives have no playback equipment. The tapes have to be converted or they are not usable.

Because picture quality decreases each time a videotape is played, a master video recording must be preserved. "Dubbing masters" are used to make copies for showing and editing. Archivists recommend the use of "larger, thicker, wider tape" for quality sound and image recording, reproduction, and preservation. They recognize, however, that such high-quality recording requires large and cumbersome equipment and considerably higher costs. Moreover, manufacturers are increasingly abandoning the one-inch and three-quarter-inch videotape that archivists prefer in favor of Betacam and digital formats such as Super VHS and Sony's Hi-8.[23]

How long will videotape last?

Not as long as the initial—optimistic—estimates said it would. Pointing out that color photos in family albums appear washed-out over time as their dyes change color, videotape manufacturers declared that color videotape recordings would not deteriorate any more than black-and-white recordings, and that both would be stable "for long periods of storage." It was estimated that deterioration would become noticeable only after several hundred plays of the tape.[24]

But the life span of home videotape, stored at optimal conditions, has since been downgraded to about 15 years. Archivists and museum curators who have accessioned older government videos into their collections have opened the cassette to find only a ribbon of clear acetate and a pile of brown powder. According to one report, "the oxide was dropping off videotape like so much dandruff." Heat and moisture will make the tape deteriorate all the quicker, making it even more important to store the tape at temperatures between 59 and 77 degrees Fahrenheit, and at a midrange of humidity.

Video archives must plan to regularly copy their videotapes before the images deteriorate. Each copy is considered a generation, and it is estimated that consumer VHS tape can make it to three generations. To ensure longer preservation, a digital reproduction master can be made from the original tapes. Every copy made from the digital master is the second generation— that is, as good as the first copy of the original. But digital reproduction is expensive; archivists are not wholly convinced of its longevity; and archival budgets must still include wholesale reproduction of the videos.

In a reversal of the current trend of converting home movies into videos, consider converting videos into film, which has a lifetime of 50 to 100 years. The decay of videotape, the fading of color photographs, and the disintegration of highly acidic paper has created the ironic situation, one photographic specialist noted, "that we're the most fully-documented people in the history of the species, yet ours is the epoch most likely to vanish from the record."[25]

Is it not true that television networks already save extensive video interviews?

Network collection and preservation of video has been less extensive, and more recently initiated, than is generally assumed. Nations with publicly owned television networks took the lead in depositing their film and video at their national archives. The Canadian Broadcasting Company's collection at the Canadian National Film, Television, and Sound Archives in Ottawa provides an outstanding example. By contrast, the privately owned American networks went for decades blithely unconcerned about preserving their film and video heritage and either discarded film or routinely erased and recorded over videotape. Universities made the first efforts to save broadcasting materials; in 1968 the Vanderbilt Television News Archives, for instance, began collecting an extensive backlog of television news programming. More recently, the National Museum of Broadcasting in New York has also begun preserving and exhibiting old television programs and news broadcasts. Purdue University houses the C-SPAN archives, and the University of Maryland is home to the National Public Radio and Television Archive.

Much video remains uncollected, however, especially interview segments (or "out-takes") that were not used in documentaries or broadcast on the news. In Hawaii, a video producer's "sheer frustration" in seeking resource material led to the creation of the Film and Video Archive Project. Chris Conybeare realized that as soon as a televised documentary is finished and goes on the air, its producers go on to other projects, rarely stopping to think that, though they used only three minutes from an interview, the "other twenty-five minutes they didn't use might be very interesting, historically, to people who are scholars, or even just the general public who has a curiosity about history or culture." Those working on the Film and Video Archive Project also realized that because the shelf life of videotape is so short, these out-takes, without proper maintenance, may be entirely lost within a few years.

Supported financially by Hawaii's public broadcast channel and its state legislature, the Film and Video Archive Project began by compiling an inventory of the condition of videotaped interviews in the state. The archives also has encouraged groups applying for funding to produce video documentaries to make provisions to archive all of their interviews. Since documentary makers usually operate on budgets tight on both time and funds, stopping to preserve the material they do not use in their finished documentaries can be an expensive nuisance. They are more likely to comply with this provision if they have built preservation into their budgets and scheduling from the start. Doing archival work as an afterthought, when the documentary has been completed and shown and new projects are beckoning, is not nearly as successful.[26]

Other oral history archives with extensive audio interview holdings have also begun collecting video interviews and out-takes from producers and projects in their region. The University of Kentucky Library, for instance, has the interviews done for such documentaries as *Harlan County, U.S.A* (1976) and *Long Road Back: Vietnam Remembered* (1985). The deposited tapes and transcripts are available for others to research.[27]

What is the difference between a video oral history and a documentary?

A video oral history in itself is not a documentary. Few people would want to watch the many hours of videotape necessary to conduct a full life review oral history. Instead, the video interview is source material for documentaries and exhibits. One oral history project included 30 hours of video interviews, of which 25 minutes appeared in the 78-minute documentary. But even this product was cut down to "a television hour," or 56 minutes, requiring further reductions in the interviews shown. In another project, 50 hours of interviews were condensed into a one-hour program. In any documentary film or video project, an interviewee who speaks for an hour on videotape usually appears for only a few minutes, or even a few seconds, in the final product.[28]

Video interviews are more than just another source, however; they have profoundly influenced the nature of documentaries. Older documentaries relied heavily on newsreels and television film. "The producer usually centered on some sort of theme like *The Roaring Twenties* or *The Depression Thirties*," noted the pioneer oral historian Dean Albertson. "A snappy narrative against a background of contemporaneous pop music would be provided, and voilà, a history film." Since the 1970s documentary producers have drawn increasingly on oral histories, and the availability of interviewees from particular times and places have shaped the subject and focus of their projects. The old-style documentary showed newsreel clips of women working in a World War II airplane factory, with an omniscient voice-over narration explaining how women went to work during the war. But *The Life and Times of Rosie the Riveter* quoted the women themselves, reflecting on their own experiences, talking decades after the war, but often seen in earlier photographs.[29]

Oral histories have helped documentaries become more intimate, more compelling, and more complex. Such recent projects as *Vietnam: A Television History* (1984) and *Eyes on the Prize* (1986 and 1990) appeared on national television and have been far more widely used as educational tools in schools.

Video interviewing requires making choices as to whom to interview. Turning video interviews into a documentary requires further choices as the documentary maker selects material from the interviews. The editing of the interviews also reveals how much documentary makers value the video interviewees as interpreters of their own experiences who can provide anecdotes about people and pivotal moments and help re-create the drama of a moment. By minimizing the role of the narrator and allowing interviewees to speak for themselves, some documentaries have carried the message that only those who "were there" are allowed to speak for history. In reviewing the popular documentary series *Vietnam: A Television History*, Michael Frisch complained, "It is as if students of the Pentagon Papers or journalists or historians, over the years, have not learned more about these events than immediate participants can possibly have experienced, much less remembered and willingly discussed, and as if we had not, in the process, arrived at any alternative ways of understanding these events."[30]

Academics also have been troubled that documentaries do not fit the generally accepted notions of scholarship. Films and videos have no footnotes or bibliographies. Rarely do they explain their methodologies for determining what was included and what was left out of the final film. They offer little means of verification or corroboration to written sources. "Perhaps this is one of the reasons why a scholarly book or article seldom if ever cites a video documentary as its source," noted Richard Sweterlitsch, an academic who has produced video oral histories. "We simply don't trust productions which lack the critical apparati of scholarship."[31]

Do artistic considerations take precedence over accuracy in video?

Being a visual medium, video makes the picture a primary consideration, a priority that can frustrate those more concerned with the information an interview generates. It is a common complaint among television journalists. The veteran broadcaster Daniel Schorr has commented that whenever a television reporter offers a story, the producer will ask, "What do we see?" Dramatic pictures can blow a story entirely out of proportion on television. The evening news opens with pictures of a dramatic rescue from a burning building, while the next morning's newspaper relegates the same story to a paragraph or two buried deep in its pages. On Capitol Hill, television commentators have complained that they could get better coverage for senators and representatives if they could get them to ride around in fire engines.[32]

At an Oral History Association meeting in 1987, Ken Burns, whose documentaries include *The Shakers: Hands to Work, Hearts to God* (1985), *Huey Long* (1987), and *The Civil War* (1989), discussed the ethical problems of using illustrations to tell the story though they are not always accurate. Burns once decided to use a photo of Huey Long surrounded by uniformed policemen to illustrate a voice-over explaining that Long traveled with armed bodyguards because he feared for his life. Long's guards dressed in street clothes rather than uniforms, but a photo of plainclothesmen would not have made much of a visual point. Burns selected an untypical picture because it told the story better. To justify his decision, he related the practice of a football coach who would ask an injured player what time it was. If the player could not answer correctly, he would be sent to the hospital for observation—unless the coach really needed the player, in which case he would tell him what time it was and send him back into the game. If an illustration is really needed, Burns advised, use it. Just be careful, he cautioned, not to make cutting such corners an automatic practice.

The video interview presents an unvarnished look at the interviewee; a documentary doctors both the audio and the visual to produce a more polished product. The practice of some documentary makers of not always distinguishing between generic and specifically identified photographs raises questions about the integrity of the process. By using illustrations that make the point that the speaker is discussing, but show someone other than the speaker, a video misleads viewers into thinking that they are looking at historic photos and film of the speaker. Documentary makers may choose to leave in a statement that, though they know it to be slightly erroneous, is told colorfully by an important source. They may coach an interviewee to repeat a line, over and again, until it is said the way they want it. Even more troublesome is the technological advance in video editing that allows documentary makers to trim and even rearrange a speaker's words without the audience being aware that it is not hearing the remarks strictly as spoken. (Advances in digital imaging permit editors to alter elements of the picture as well.) Careless or devious editing can make speakers seem to be saying exactly the opposite of what they intended.[33]

How much control does an oral historian have over how interviews are used in a documentary?

Oral historians' control depends on their role in making the documentary, particularly on whether they were producers or consultants. "Consultants are at a disadvantage; they only consult," observed E. John B. Allen, who did interviews and consulted on a documentary on skiing. "The director and cameraman work full time on the film. As the cutting, editing, i.e., the finalizing of the film takes place, it enters on a life of its own." The oral historian as consultant may find that advice previously taken is discarded in the editing process, that misleading, historically inaccurate film footage has been used because of its visual impact, and that the final product does not correspond to the consultant's personal and professional standards.[34]

Historians who have worked as consultants for documentaries are often appalled at the filmmaker's blatant manipulation of people's words and disregard for facts in order to create a more visually exciting product. Unlike historians, however, documentary makers are eager to attract and appeal to large audiences. They seek to be enlightening and educational, but also entertaining and provocative. Recognizing these dual and conflicting needs, the American Historical Association has promoted standards that encourage historians to "be sensitive to the artistic and dramatic rights of film and video collaborators and seek solutions that respect both historical and artistic-dramatic concerns."[35]

Besides documentaries, how else have video interviews been used?

Museums quickly embraced video oral histories as a means of presenting information in a visually appealing manner. As collectors of objects, museums are always seeking ways of placing them in context and showing how people used them. Oral history reconstructs the context, but audiotape alone rarely goes into great detail about objects and the ways they were used. Video interviews, however, can be directed far more toward objects.[36]

Video also makes speakers more real, providing them with faces and gestures and emotions. The U.S. Holocaust Museum in Washington, D.C., illustrates its message with both audio and visual interviews. In the stark "Voices of the Holocaust" hall, visitors listen to audiotape of a series of survivors telling their stories. The disembodied voices have a haunting quality. Later, in a small amphitheater, visitors watch videotaped interviews with concentration-camp prisoners recounting their experiences. A woman recalls sharing her soup with a friend; a man weeps as he remembers talking with his father in the camp barracks; another former prisoner describes a guard with a bulldoglike demeanor who saved her life. Their faces—some stoic, some wrenched with emotion, solemn but occasionally smiling—complement the words and capture the audience. Viewers gather in larger numbers and tend to stay longer for the video than for the audio presentations. A less emotional topic might need more artistic staging—these films are nothing more than talking heads—but tears welling in a speaker's eyes make their point vividly.

At the Boott Cotton Mills Museum in Lowell, Massachusetts, the National Park Service has set up a self-guided tour of the factory with an emphasis on realism. At the shop-floor level, the machinery and other artifacts and authentic background noise help visitors "hear, smell, and feel" what workers experienced. Upstairs, in a more traditional museum setting—an exhibit on the broad history of weaving—video monitors present the testimony of retired spinners and weavers about their relations with other workers, salaries, and working conditions. One reviewer noted that "seeing and hearing the interviews of individuals such as Valentine Chartrand, a spinner who witnessed the fatal accident of a co-worker, and Victor Sherbon, who talked about the death of the mill, elicit emotional responses that no label or artifact could match."[37]

What is the potential for individual research in video oral history?

Although researchers prefer transcripts, which can be skimmed and photocopied, when they turn to the tapes they often learn more than they would from an audio interview. By viewing a film or video, noted one video specialist, the researcher not only hears voice inflections but sees raised eyebrows, hand motions, and unspoken body language, "everything, in short, from clothing to reaction gestures and mannerisms." And gestures combined with words sometimes convey very different meanings.[38]

Some researchers have used the video camera themselves to gather material and information for their work. David Seaman videotapes artists in the process of creating. While interviewing the West Virginian artist Ruth Rodgers, Seaman showed her meditative process: sitting and visualizing what she wanted to put on the canvas. Then, as she painted, he crawled on the floor and reproduced what she had seen in her meditative state. Seaman found that people who communicated in the visual arts—painting, photography, sculpting—also communicated well with words and could provide articulate running narratives for his videos.[39]

Do archives face any particular problems in using video oral histories?

Those archives that have compiled substantial video oral history collections report increasing use of the interviews by television producers for documentary purposes. That television producers tend to demand material in a rush can be an aggravation for an archivist, but more troublesome are the questions about how the material will be used. With sometimes hundreds of interviews on videotape, an archives cannot consult with each interviewee about the uses of their interviews beyond whatever the interviewee specified in the deed of gift. Still, it can be disconcerting for interviewees to see themselves unexpectedly in a broadcast. Archives must explain the copyright provisions for their videos and should obtain some written confirmation from the producers concerning their intended use of the material. The Smithsonian Archives, for example, initially makes available only a copy of the video interview in half-inch VHS format with time code displayed on-screen, which discourages its use for broadcasting. Broadcasters and documentary makers view the video and determine what portions they want, then formally apply for the three-quarter-inch broadcast-quality film.

In at least one instance, an archival videotaped interview was requested for use in a court proceeding—although not subpoenaed—and the interviewee agreed to its use in court.

Considering all the expense and problems involved, is videotaping worth the effort?

The video oral historian Brien Williams has commented that even the most poorly produced and wretchedly preserved videotape of Abraham Lincoln would still have enormous value. Arthur Schlesinger, Jr., concurs:

I think if we had videotaped interviews with Emerson, Socrates, Charlemagne, it would be marvelous. On the other hand, videotaping compounds all the problems of expense, storage, dilapidation, and so on. Obviously it would have to be used selectively. But, for commanding figures, particularly those who haven't been amply documented on television, it would be particularly useful. Eric Sevareid's interviewing Walter Lippmann, for example, would be invaluable to historians a hundred years from now wondering what Lippmann was like. But only an unusual case would justify the expense. There are not that many Walter Lippmanns.[40]

Some video historians envision a time when all oral history will be videotaped. Costs, however, are likely to remain a barrier to universal videotaping. Because the oral historian cannot always control the location of an interview, audiotaping on-site, rather than videotaping, will continue to be the logical choice sometimes, especially when a camera operator is unavailable or interviewees, for whatever reasons of privacy or vanity, refuse to have their pictures taken. But if the opportunities are available, the funds are forthcoming, and the subjects are willing, then future researchers and users of oral history may ask why we failed to capture the historical picture as well as the words.[41]

6

PRESERVING ORAL HISTORY IN ARCHIVES AND LIBRARIES

Why are oral history projects so often associated with archives and libraries?

The oral history movement in the United States traces its roots to the archival collections at such prestigious universities as Columbia, Cornell, Berkeley, and UCLA. These collections were started not as individual projects, or to produce books, but as a means of gathering reminiscences for general research use. At many of these "founding" programs, the staff conducted most of the interviews and still do. Since then, archives and libraries have provided the institutional home for many oral history projects, offering space, services, and sometimes—although not always—salaries for the project staff. Once interviews have been conducted, archives and libraries process and preserve them, prepare catalogs and other finding aids, and make them accessible for research.

This early identification with archives profoundly shaped the conduct of oral history in the United States. By contrast, individual researchers—or sometimes smaller centers of scholars conducting interviews for specific projects—were responsible for the advent of oral history in Europe. Over time, the Europeans increasingly acknowledged what Ronald J. Grele, director of the Columbia Oral History Research Office, has called a "sense of collective responsibility that these are documents made for public use, not just private documents for private research or those connected with a particular center." American archivists identified oral history as another way of supplementing the letters, diaries, and memoranda in their collections. They sought interviews with the same prominent people who donated manuscripts to their archives, thereby giving oral history its initially "elitist" bent.

Archival oral historians also promoted the ideal of the interviewer as a neutral, objective observer, free from any compulsion to prove a particular thesis. Philip Brooks, director of the Truman Library, described the "pure" oral historian as someone who was "accumulating a stock of evidence for the use of other researchers, any and all researchers, as we do in an archival agency." Such an archival oral historian was "almost by definition likely to be doing a more objective job than the one who is writing his own book, especially the one that has a case to prove." Given their preference for paper, archival oral history projects championed the transcript rather than the tape as the primary record and ultimate product of an oral history interview. Although oral history has remained closely associated with archives, each of these preconceptions has undergone significant modification over the years, just as archives themselves have changed.[1]

With archives filled to capacity with paper records, why should they bother collecting oral history?

Some archivists and researchers are convinced that archives have higher priorities than conducting oral history. The popular historian Barbara Tuchman protested that "over-documentation" was causing those who write contemporary history to drown in "unneeded information," a problem she believed oral history adds to rather than alleviates. Tuchman charged oral history with producing "trivia of appalling proportions . . . with all sorts of people being invited merely to open their mouths, and ramble effortlessly and endlessly into a tape recorder."[2] In a similar vein, archivists have argued that with paper records expanding (despite the increased use of electronic records) and budgets shrinking, they must set priorities and determine the cost-effectiveness of their various functions. Oral history, being expensive, is therefore more often deemed expendable. Both views are regrettably shortsighted.

Although Tuchman aptly labeled the explosion of modern paperwork "over-documentation," she neglected to address the declining qualitative value of that documentation. As the records of government agencies, corporations, and other institutions have multiplied, their worth has decreased. Mass mailings tell less about their authors than did the handwritten correspondence of the past. Memoranda often disguise what actually happened or try to shift responsibility. Telephones, fax machines, electronic mail, and other modern means of communication have reduced the reliance on traditional written documentation. As researchers gain access to modern records, they often discover them to be unrevealing and uninformative.

Oral history can be as useful when there is too much documentation as when there is too little. Every presidential administration leaves behind more paperwork than did its predecessor; the National Archives estimates that every four months the federal government now generates as many records as all those produced between the administrations of George Washington and Woodrow Wilson combined. Scholars trying to trace the development of modern federal policymaking are confronted with more material than they could possibly read in a lifetime. Yet it is nearly impossible to know what documents an official actually wrote or ever saw. A researcher who plowed through the papers of a recent senator complained that the collection consisted almost exclusively of routine correspondence and mass mailings and that he had found almost nothing from the presidents with whom the senator had been closely identified.[3]

Faced with hundreds or thousands of cubic feet of records, usually with limited finding aids, researchers need guidance. Oral history interviews with the principal figures can serve as road maps, suggesting which individuals and what issues should be followed through the manuscript collection. Researchers with limited resources want to make maximum use of a collection in a minimum amount of time. Smart researchers have learned to look first for oral histories; unfortunately, others still leave oral histories to the last.

Being well aware of the limitations of the written record, many archivists have recognized the need for "auxiliary documentation." Oral history is more than a supplement and less than a substitute for other archival materials. As one more type of research tool among many, oral history can be especially helpful in filling the gaps that often obscure the motivations behind individual and institutional actions. Gaps also may exist in what written records can contribute to our understanding of the actions of whole groups of people who, perhaps because of gender, race, class, or ethnicity, have not been represented in the archival collections. The challenge for archivists, James Fogerty has written, "is to go beyond their collections to individuals not represented, who have no personal papers or records to donate. This is an unusual activity for an archives but is one way in which the gap between collections and subject areas can be bridged."[4]

Surely it is not an archivist's job to create records?

The reason pained expressions sometimes appear on the faces of archivists when they talk about oral history is that its practice breaks so many of their rules and customs. Archivists have had difficulty agreeing on a terminology for oral history and refer to "collecting oral history" as if interviews, like manuscript collections, were out there waiting to be acquired. But the information exists only in the interviewee's mind, and someone must first record and preserve it in tangible form. In doing oral history, archivists find themselves creating, not just collecting, a new resource.[5]

Many archivists feel uncomfortable being both curator and creator of primary documents. Oral history is an entirely different type of record from those they normally handle, since it is not an artifact preserved from the past but a present record that attempts to re-create the past and is subject to memory failures and reinterpretation through intervening events. When archivists serve as the interviewers who draw out these memories, they also step out of character to become something of a player in the events. The demands of this new role have raised fears that archivists may become advocates of one form of documentation over another, instead of maintaining professional detachment and neutrality. Of course, whenever archivists choose to accession one collection over another, oral history or not, they put their supposed neutrality on the line. Some archivists consider oral history a secondary form of documentation and regard all the planning, conducting, and processing of interviews a diversion from their primary responsibilities. These concerns most likely reflect the increasing identification of archivists not so much as historians as information specialists, records managers, and computer specialists.[6]

Despite these objections, oral history has become an increasingly standard addition to modern archival collections. As a growing number of librarians and archivists handle oral history collections, it is essential that they become familiar with the theory and techniques of oral history research, interviewing, and processing.

How does funding shape an archival oral history collection?

Funding has a major impact on oral history, just as it does on other archival activities. Conducting and processing interviews can be expensive. Although housed in university libraries, some of the most prestigious oral history archives—such as the Regional Oral History Office at Berkeley—are not directly subsidized by their host university and must raise their own operating funds to finance interviewing and processing. As a result, many projects have been conducted with specific individuals, families, corporations, and associations that actually underwrote their own interviews. This fact of fiscal life can produce some outstanding research resources that might not otherwise exist, but it can also skew a collection toward those who can afford to be patrons. Oral history archivists need to seek alternative sources of funding to ensure that their collections contain a wide representation of voices, and scholarly researchers need to support such broad-based oral history collecting.[7]

Oral history archives have had to be financially creative and flexible. In 1960 the U.S. Navy engaged the Columbia Oral History Research Office to interview high-ranking naval officers. An interviewer was dispatched to Washington to begin a lengthy series of interviews when Columbia discovered that navy regulations prohibited a flat sum payment for a year's worth of interviews. Rather than allow the bureaucracy to defeat them, they instead arranged for the navy to purchase each interview when completed, each payment helping to underwrite the rest of the program.[8]

Grants from such funding agencies as the National Endowment for the Humanities, the state humanities councils, the Ford, Rockefeller, and Doris Duke foundations, and Pew Memorial Trust have launched and supported oral history projects. But the priorities of granting agencies go through periodic shifts. During the 1970s funding agencies were generous to oral history of all sorts. In a spirit of democratization, the agencies funded well-intentioned but unprepared projects that consumed their grants without producing anything more than boxes of tapes that were untranscribed, undocumented, undeeded, unidentified, and consequently unusable. Concerned funding agencies encouraged the Oral History Association to establish standards by which they could judge oral history proposals and completed projects. At an appropriately grant-funded meeting at the Wingspread Center in Racine, Wisconsin, OHA established its first evaluation guidelines in 1979.[9]

Ronald Reagan's election as president in 1980 dramatically reduced the funding sources for oral history. NEH, which had enthusiastically supported oral history under previous administrations, abruptly changed its priorities. Other funding agencies cut grants for archival oral history programs, on the grounds that they were not cost-effective, and concentrated instead on assisting individual research. Funding agencies would underwrite the costs of a researcher's interviews, but they did not always stipulate that the interviews be deposited in an appropriate archives.

As federal funds became scarcer, oral history projects turned to state humanities councils. Although more limited in the amounts they could grant, state councils remained convinced of the benefits of oral history interviewing. State humanities councils helped underwrite transcriptions of interviews that had already been conducted, a way of marshaling their resources to produce a tangible product—the transcript—for deposit in an archives and possibly for further use in publications and exhibits. The state of Kentucky went a step further in 1976 when it established the Kentucky Oral History Commission specifically to fund interviewing and transcription of Kentucky-related subjects. Kentucky remains unique in this respect, but legislatures in California, Hawaii, Texas, and Illinois have officially funded oral history projects within their states.[10]

By the 1990s NEH had regained its interest in oral history and given support to projects at such organizations as the Lincoln Center for the Performing Arts, the Museum of Modern Art, and the Women's Press Club Foundation. Competition for federal funds has grown intense, however, and applicants must weigh the limited chances of being funded against the time-consuming application process. Private foundations, corporations, and state and local agencies remain better avenues for support.[11]

Is it appropriate for oral history archives to charge fees for publication use of their interviews?

Although archives do not, and should not, charge for research access to oral histories, publishing lengthy excerpts from those interviews is another matter. Many library-based oral history collections have enough institutional support to be able to forgo fees of any type, but other oral history archives run on shoestring budgets and are constantly looking for ways to raise funds. One source of funds has been charging users for any reproduction that goes beyond "fair use." In setting costs, archives need to be reasonable and flexible. If their goal is to disseminate information, then setting fees too high will discourage users. Doctoral dissertation writers are rarely in a position to make a payment. Many publishers will not pay for such costs, which then become the author's responsibility. Some archives that charge reprint fees will usually agree to reduce them and are open to negotiation.

A bigger problem arises when oral history archives sell the reproduction rights to their collections to microfiche publishers and other agents. Such arrangements may initially raise needed funds for the archives, but the terms of these agreements can put unreasonable restrictions on the use of the collection, such as prohibiting researchers from making photocopies. Some archives have sold the literary rights to their interviews to one company, which in turn has sold them to another, which thereafter controls the reproduction fees. In a sense, these archives have lost control of their own collections. Limiting the use of an oral history collection is a disservice to those who gave the interviews.

MANAGING ORAL HISTORY COLLECTIONS

Is there any difference between accessioning oral histories and written documents?

In accessioning any form of documentation, an archives determines whether the material is appropriate for its collection, takes legal and managerial control over it, and decides how soon and under what conditions it can be used. Except in the case of "exit interviews" or "debriefings" that are done as a requirement of a job, military assignment, or completion of a project for which someone has been paid, most oral history interviews are voluntary efforts and interviewees retain the copyright until they have deeded it to the archives or to the public domain. Like manuscript collections, donors may set conditions on the oral histories they give to an archives. It is the responsibility of the archives to ascertain the donor's wishes, negotiate any mutual concerns, and honor any restrictions the donor has set.

Deeds of gift and contracts can vary widely, from simple to very complex, depending on the legal advice sought. Attorneys naturally want to protect an archives from any contingency, but some interviewees may blanch at the sight of an overly complicated deed. A brief, straightforward agreement engenders less reluctance to sign. On the other extreme, more prominent interviewees may insist on adding stipulations about permission to quote and other potential uses of their interviews. Whenever possible, archives should adopt a simple release form that indicates what restrictions have been set and when those restrictions will expire. Without such releases, archival oral histories are unpublishable beyond "fair use," since publishers will not take the risk of printing material whose copyright is in question. Sometimes scholars who have recorded verbal agreements with their interviewees, giving them control of the interviews, sign an agreement with the library or archives to deposit the collection as a whole, establishing its copyright and making provision for its research use and reproduction.[12]

What kind of data should be kept on each interview?

Archivists want to know the "provenance" of records, by which they mean the circumstances under which the records were created and originally maintained. For oral histories, they want to know who conducted the interview, with whom, when, where, and for what purpose. In addition to the tapes and transcripts, archives retain copies of legal agreements, correspondence with the interviewee, background information used for the interview, photographs of the interviewee, and indexes to the tapes.

Label your tapes and tape containers with the interviewee's name and the date of the interview. On the container, also indicate the sequence of tapes if more than one was used; the location of the interview; the length of the interview; and the project title (if there are multiple projects within a collection). For some projects, such information is also recorded on separate data sheets.

Archives often ask interviewers to prepare summary sheets on their interviews, recording their impressions of the interviewee and anything significant that happened during the interview. Since the interview itself is an event in the interviewee's life, researchers will be curious about its context. If the interview was never completed or did not deal with certain significant events in the interviewee's life, researchers will want to know why. Did the interviewee cancel sessions? Was the interview terminated earlier than expected? Did the interviewee set ground rules about not answering certain questions? Without some explanation of omissions, the documents will leave the impression that the interviewer neglected important areas of inquiry. Although such administrative files do not require release forms, oral historians should keep interviewees informed as to what sort of material will be made accessible to researchers.

As an oral history archives grows, the need for a general log quickly becomes apparent. Whether done as a file, in a book, or on a computer, the log should contain basic accessioning and labeling information for every interview and collection. By keeping a record of the interviewer's notes and correspondence, from letters setting up the interview to thank-you letters at the end, an archives also has a record of interviewees being kept fully informed of their rights, which is useful if their heirs question or object to the opening of the interview for research or its publication.

It is fairly common for oral history projects to include introductions to individual interviews, summarizing the person's life and providing other background information. Oral historians in general, however, have not been as diligent as anthropologists and ethnographers in noting their personal observations of the interview's circumstances, and not every oral history collection keeps all of this data. Each archives determines what types of records will best serve its researchers. Whatever decisions archives make, consistency is key: archivists should think through the process at the outset to avoid having to go back to re-create information and fill in gaps later.[13]

How should interviews be arranged in a collection?

A government attorney, in all seriousness, once advised a federal historical office against arranging its oral history files alphabetically by name and recommended that the office keep its interviews "in a box at random." The attorney worried that an alphabetical file would constitute a system of records, as defined by the Privacy Act, and would therefore be an invasion of privacy. However seriously offered, the advice was ridiculous. All the interviewees had participated willingly, with full knowledge that they were creating resources for future research. Almost any other system of arrangement would make more sense.

Oral histories are most often filed by name of interviewee, individually or as part of a larger collection. Some archives create an alphabetical or numerical accession system for arranging all interviews and accompanying materials. Others divide the interviews according to the specific projects for which they were done. The interviews conducted around a specific community, event, or group of individuals can be filed according to that project name, though arranging by subject becomes more complex unless the project titles were clearly subject-oriented. Specific subjects can be located through indexes and other retrieval systems.

What types of finding aids are most useful for oral history?

Oral history collections may begin with just a few interviews but can grow so quickly that even the interviewers have trouble remembering who said what. For the purposes of both internal administration and efficient research use, oral history archives must instigate and establish finding aids, such as catalogs, indexes, and computer retrieval systems. Oral historians need to recognize that doing the interviews is not the end but the beginning of the process. With microfiche editions of their oral histories, catalogs, indexes, and a great deal of communication with their users, archives are better able to attract researchers to use the interviews they have collected.

Researchers, who want to know whether they have seen all the pertinent material on their subject in an archives, have a responsibility to inquire about what records are open, but the institution also has an obligation to ensure that cataloging information about their collections is available. Nothing infuriates researchers more than learning after they have left an archives that they missed important information. When dealing with archival oral histories, researchers face three major retrieval problems: learning the location of an oral history with a particular individual or about a specific subject; determining which interviews to consult; and then finding the information inside a tape or transcript.

The most common finding aid is a simple, alphabetical list of all the individual interviews within a collection by name of interviewee, whether in a publication, card catalog, or computer retrieval system. In addition to the name of the interviewee and the date of the interview, the list might include a biographical sketch of the interviewee and identify key subjects and individuals discussed. Finding aids should indicate whether the tapes have been indexed or transcribed and note whether the interview is open, closed, or otherwise restricted, and when restrictions will end.

Either the tapes or transcripts of interviews should be indexed, ideally by subject as well as by name. From such separate indexes, the archives can construct a cross-reference index. The Columbia Oral History Research Office began a simple card file index for the names of individuals mentioned in its interviews; this index has become an enormous and valuable tool for searching through its thousands of interviews. Creating a cross-reference index is always easier when it is started at the beginning of a project and grows with it than when attempted after the bulk of the material has been collected. Cross-reference indexes uncover fascinating information. (It has often been observed of oral history that the most useful insights come from the least expected sources.) Text-searching computer programs also make it possible to search the entire text of an interview, or a series of interviews, by names and other key words.[14]

What are the prospects for automating oral history materials?

For all their reliance on technology, oral historians tend to be "humanistic, personalistic, and impressionistic" and therefore have been slow to adapt to computers. (Tight budgets also put restraints on the embrace of new technology.) Computers can not only organize, manipulate, and make available oral history material but offer solutions to many of the problems of cataloging and indexing collections. For projects that have been manually indexing and cataloging and have a fairly set system, changing to computer databases involves a considerable investment of funds and staff and raises questions about cost-effectiveness. But for smaller projects, and those just beginning, a computer system provides a faster, cheaper way of cataloging and retrieving a growing collection.[15]

Computers have opened up diverse possibilities for oral history. The word processor has at least halved transcribing time. Previously, many projects typed two entire versions of the transcript: the first a rough version of the transcript, which was edited by the interviewee and retyped into a second, clean copy. Word processors have not only speeded up the initial transcription but eliminated the second retyping. Computer software packages also enable users to search oral histories for key words and to pull up specific names and subjects from any of the interviews scanned into the computer.

Computers provide a new medium for storing oral histories and protecting them from damage. At the University of Alaska at Fairbanks, oral history archivists have experimented with the storage of interviews on compact disks (CDs) that include not only the interview recordings but the transcripts, release forms, and related photographs and maps. As the archivist Will Schneider explained: "An interview with a dog musher may be accompanied by photographs of him racing the dogs, a map showing where he lives, a copy of the release form he signed at the time of the interview, and even a short article about him." CD storage provides greater archival control over their materials and makes the interviews far more accessible for research.

Automated text-search systems permit researchers to locate and listen to the portions of interviews relating to specific subjects. Researchers need not listen to an entire interview but can follow topical themes throughout the collection, with more assurance of having seen all of the information relating to a specific topic and having it made instantly available. At a workstation, researchers can search by individual interviewees or by topics that cut through many interviews. Text-searching computer programs can search and identify lists of all key words on all of the tapes. After selecting a key word from the list, the researcher is presented with a list of the people whose discussions included it, and their tape numbers. The computer then takes the researcher to that part of the transcript where the name or key word occurs. Researchers have the option of reading the transcript or listening to its audio version. The original tapes and transcripts will be preserved in the archives, but the CD copy can be distributed more widely to other research facilities.[16]

The Southwest Oral History Association (SOHA) has developed a database system that offers descriptions of projects and interviews (although not the text of interviews) within its vast region, "for efficient input, organizational storage, and retrieval of up-to-date information." SOHA's experience is a lesson in how critical the accuracy of the data is to the creation of an automated system. Those inputting information must first verify it for accuracy and consistency. Data security also needs to be established, to prevent not only accidental deletions but unauthorized tampering with the data. SOHA recommends that, in choosing a system, an archives or library seek to be compatible with and link into other systems.[17]

Is there a national database on oral history?

Archives have been slow and inconsistent in cataloging their interviews for the national on-line computer databases. Some major oral history collections have reported their interviews on the Research Libraries Information Network (RLIN), and others have adopted the Online Catalog Library Center (OCLC) form of cataloging. Many smaller archives and libraries that lack access to these national databases have not cataloged their collections at all.

The result is that only a small percentage of all archival oral histories are currently included in national computer systems, and researchers must rely on published guides to oral history, which quickly become out-of-date.

The National Historical Publications and Records Commission has funded efforts to develop a standard MARC-AMC (Machine Readable Cataloging-Archival and Management Control) format for cataloging oral history. The new format will provide oral history archivists and special collection catalogers with appropriate descriptive information on how to catalog their interviews consistent with other collections. Once in MARC-AMC format, published guides for these interview citations can be easily generated. The national databases will also encourage interlibrary loans of those oral histories whose tapes and transcripts can be easily copied for such distribution. Putting oral histories and indexes on the Internet system, which would vastly increase their use, is also a possibility. Since many oral histories have been microfilmed, copies can be made available to libraries that do not have their own collections.[18]

Should an archives prepare its own oral history processing guide?

Given how many different staff and volunteers might be involved in conducting, processing, accessioning, cataloging, and retrieving oral history, any archives with a substantial oral history collection should seriously consider preparing its own procedures manual. A guide serves as an introduction for newcomers and assures overall consistency. Starting with a general mission statement, the guide should suggest general areas for investigation through interviews and outline procedures for handling the oral histories, from acquisition to conservation, including samples of all forms used and the rationale of the filing system. For instance, records of the actual interviews, such as transcripts, indexes, and correspondence, may be filed separately from organizational papers such as financial records, internal correspondence, and bills for supplies and equipment. The guide should set standard procedures for cataloging and indexing the interviews to assist ultimately in their retrieval for research.

SOUND RECORDINGS

Do oral histories belong specifically in sound archives?

Most archives divide their collections according to physical types, separating photographs, sound recordings, and computer materials from written documents. This division may be for managerial purposes or for the preservation of the audiovisual and electronic materials under the most appropriate temperature, humidity, and storage conditions. Specialists in sound archives are more concerned than most oral historians with sound quality—and for good reason, given the poor quality of so many of the recorded interviews they receive. Too many oral historians think that they have succeeded so long as the voice on the tape is audible enough to transcribe, but poor recordings eliminate the possibility of any uses that go beyond simply conveying factual information, such as contributions to exhibits and documentaries.

Archives can either disperse oral history interviews among the collections from which they were drawn or centralize both the tapes and transcripts in a special oral history section. Whatever the option chosen, if the interviews are separated from their original agency records, or if the tapes and transcripts are stored in separate areas, then cross-references must exist to alert researchers to these divisions and show where to locate the material. Never underestimate a researcher's ability to misunderstand archival cataloging systems. Unless the signposts are obvious, researchers may devote themselves entirely to manuscripts and neglect oral history and other types of nonprint documentation.

Transcripts, easily skimmed and photocopied, are so often the research tool of choice in the United States that the preservation of original sound recordings has not received its deserved attention. Since archives, especially those in large institutions, often separate audio from printed materials, archivists responsible for preserving sound recordings often work separately from other archivists and tend to be more technologically oriented, belong to different professional associations, and read different literature—all of the ingredients for failures of communication. Although print-oriented archivists have adapted to film and photographic sources, they all too often have ignored sound recordings, as is reflected in the thin literature about sound in archival publications. One sound archivist complained that "the silence of the archival community on the subject is deafening."[19]

Audiovisual archivists deal with musical records, tapes and compact discs, recorded speeches, radio and television broadcasts, and other materials that they often do not distinguish from oral history. An audio archivist once commented, in all sincerity, that if interview tapes were preserved, he could not understand the purpose of also keeping a transcript. To him, the tape and transcript were duplicate copies of the same record. His view is as erroneous as that of those print-oriented archivists who, in their devotion to the transcript, went so far as to record over the tapes once the transcripts were completed. As Louis Starr, then director of the Columbia Oral History Research Office, reported in 1962:

> We erase most of our tapes for re-use. This is largely because we permit our victims to edit their transcripts. While the editing, we urge, should be done with accuracy alone in mind, there is nothing to prevent a man from changing his own words—particularly in view of the fact that we regard the material as his, and ourselves as merely the custodians. Thus if we kept the tapes, we'd be saving a first draft, which would make a lot of our people unhappy.
>
> Cost is another factor, and so is storage—the problem of "feed back" has yet to be solved. Finally, we are inclined to doubt the practicality of saving, for example, 200 hours of Madame Perkins on tape, assuming she permitted us to do so. It would have to be indexed to be of much use, and that in itself would be pretty expensive. Only one scholar among the hundreds who have used the Oral History Collection has ever asked us for a tape, incidentally.

Fortunately, by the late 1960s Columbia had reversed this policy and has since been saving its tapes. Oral historians and archivists began to view both the tape and transcript as "primary" in their own mediums and to deem both worthy of preservation.[20]

Should tapes be preserved any differently from other documentation?

Although there are enough similarities in the preservation of paper and audio documentation to permit their storage together, sound recordings confront archivists with problems unique to their medium. Paper, particularly if low in acidity, can sit unattended for years without much damage, but sound recordings need constant care. Tape, if left unplayed for long periods or not rewound regularly, undergoes a process by which the sound on one layer of tape is imprinted on the next layer, a condition, called "print-through" or "voice-over," that creates an echo on the tape. Fungus can attack certain types of sound recordings, quickening their deterioration. Storage also poses problems, since standard archival shelving designed for paper documents is often inappropriate for sound recordings, especially when it encourages horizontal stacking. Furthermore, tape can be erased accidentally, and records and disks can be damaged and become unplayable. Every time a tape is played, its sound quality is diminished, and the quality of rerecordings is never as high as that of the original.

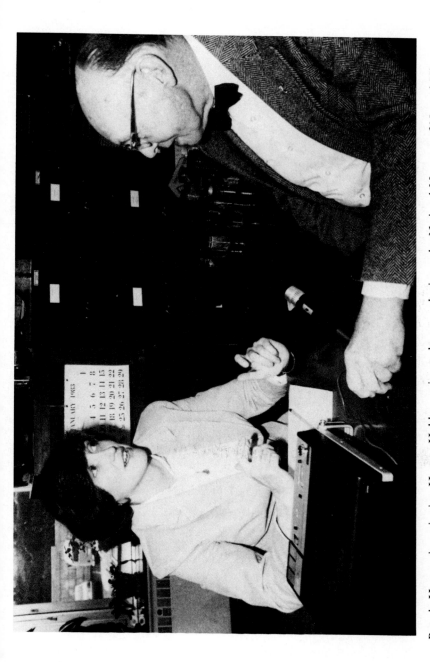

Pamela Henson interviewing Horton Hobbs, an invertebrate zoologist at the National Museum of Natural History. *Courtesy of the Smithsonian Archives.*

Stan Goldberg interviewing a group of participants in the Manhattan Project. *Courtesy of the Smithsonian Archives.*

Albert Boggess, instrumental in the design and development of the International Ultraviolet Explorer, being interviewed. Brien Williams, producer of the videotape, standing. *Courtesy of the Smithsonian Archives.*

A videotaped oral history. *Courtesy of the Smithsonian Archives.*

Ted Robinson interviewing African American aviators. *Courtesy of the Smithsonian Archives.*

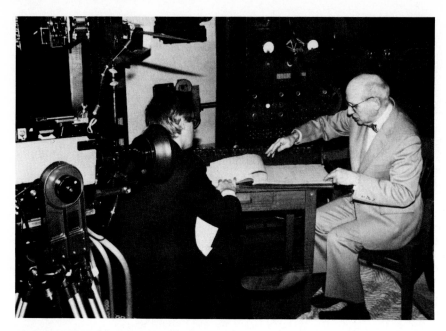

Presper Eckert, developer of ENIAC, the first computer, being interviewed by David Allison. *Courtesy of the Smithsonian Archives.*

Interviewer audio-editing a tape recording. *Courtesy of the Smithsonian Archives.*

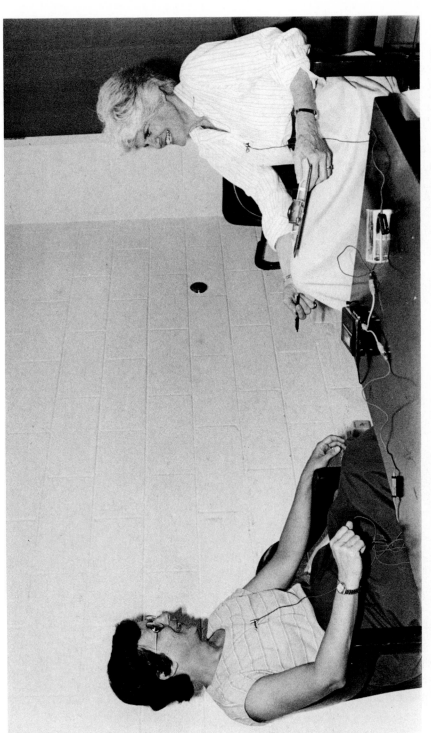

Jewell Fenzi interviewing Casey Peltier, seven-times great-granddaughter of Abigail Adams, for the Foreign Service Spouse Oral History Program. *Courtesy of State magazine.*

A videotaped interview with Jack Ruttger on location at Ruttger's Bay Lake Lodge, Minnesota. *Photograph by Michael Thompson, courtesy of the Minnesota Historical Society.*

Context:

Walter Akpik -- Tapes
00038 &00039 (H87-101
C & D)

These recordings were made with William Schneider and Wendy Arundale. The research was funded by the North Slope Borough, Commission on History, Language, and Culture and its purpose was to document historic sites in the Meade River.

Tape Numbers:

00085
00038 (H87-101C)
00039 (H87-101D)

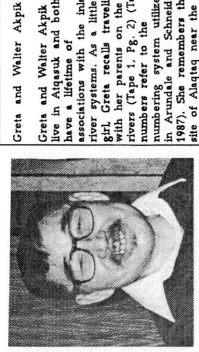

Biography:

Greta and Walter Akpik

Greta and Walter Akpik live in Atqasuk and both have a lifetime of associations with the inland river systems. As a little girl, Greta recalls traveling with her parents on the rivers (Tape 1, Pg. 2) (Tape numbers refer to the numbering system utilized in Arundale and Schneider, 1987). She remembers the site of Alaqtaq near the

Click on a tape number to view a summary of the transcript and the associated keywords.

Return to Elders screen

Return to main menu

A computer screen from a jukebox entitled the Chipp-Ikpikpuk and Meade Rivers Oral History Project. *Courtesy of the University of Alaska Fairbanks.*

Demonstrating an oral history program on computer that reproduces the experience of flipping through a photo album while hearing elders describe the images. Fort Yukon, Alaska. Clockwise, from bottom: Myra Francis, Elizabeth Cook, Betty Flitt, Hannah J. Solomon, Kathy Carroll, Abel Tritt. *Photograph by James H. Barker, courtesy of the University of Alaska Fairbanks.*

The same technology that makes oral history possible can make its preservation almost impossible. Interviews that were recorded on machines that no longer exist outside of museums, such as wax cylinders, wire recorders, and belt recorders, must be copied onto new media. One archives has a set of interviews done on an obsolete belt-type recorder from the 1950s, but being unable to locate such a machine, even from its manufacturer, the archives cannot play back the tapes. More recently, reel-to-reel recorders have become harder to find even as they remain the recommended form of tape for long-term archival preservation. The catalog of horrors is enough to suggest that oral history archives that are not regularly caring for their tapes and making transcripts are playing Russian roulette with their interviews.[21]

What literature exists on the preservation of sound recordings is alarming—but may also be alarmist. Archivists have reported receiving tapes that had been stored in people's attics and basements under the worst possible conditions for decades and yet were still playable, at least enough to be rerecorded. But no tape is permanent. Oral history archivists cannot afford to allow technological problems to tie their hands and make them quit the enterprise, any more than they can go about blindly ignoring the problems. We search for a responsible middle ground.

How long will most audiotapes last?

The type of magnetic tape used for most oral history interviews has an approximate shelf life of 25 years. But estimates vary widely and have become progressively more pessimistic. Magnetic tape has existed only for the past half-century, and experts can only speculate about how well it will maintain its sound quality into the future. With each new development in recording, whether magnetic tape, videotape, or digital audiotape (DAT), the initial predictions of longevity always have been more confident than justified by later assessments. Older oral historians have encountered some real crises with tape preservation. The George C. Marshall Research Foundation in Lexington, Virginia, discovered that the wire recordings Forrest C. Pogue conducted with General Marshall in the early 1950s had deteriorated badly. With the help of an NEH grant, these wire recordings were copied onto cassettes, transcribed, and published, so that both the sound and the substance have been saved.[22]

If kept under hot and dry conditions, standard audiotape will become brittle and crack after a decade of storage. Some tape has begun to stick between layers or to separate its coating from its backing after 15 years in storage. On the other hand, if stored under proper conditions, decades-old tape has sounded very near the original recording quality. To ensure that an oral history archives has enduring value, that its interviews are accessible so that researchers can listen to them in later years, and that the recorded voices can be used for future exhibits and documentaries, the tapes must be processed and maintained carefully.

What's the best way to preserve tapes?

Start by conducting interviews on good-quality tape, with a good microphone and as little background noise as possible. Folklorists, anthropologists, and ethnomusicologists prefer to capture ambient noises, but even they must be careful not to let the background obscure the interview. Most interviewers now record on 60-minute cassette tapes—certainly on nothing longer than 90 minutes. (Anything longer than 90 minutes is too thin and likely to stretch, twist, or break.) Archives generally accept cassette tapes, although for longer preservation they may require that cassettes be copied onto reel-to-reel tape.

To avoid the problem of erasure from accidental rerecording, remove the two small square tabs on the back of the cassette case. When using reel-to-reel and other equipment for playing back tapes for transcription and research, disengage the recording mechanisms.

Magnetic tape is coated with millions of magnetic particles that can change their magnetic strength under the influence of heat, humidity, magnetic fields, radiation, and physical stress. Keep magnetic tape away from exposure to such magnetic fields as power lines, motors, generators, and transformers, and store them on nonconductive shelves and containers.[23]

Tapes generally survive well under "people conditions," that is, with air conditioning and air filtering at a constant temperature of around 70 degrees Fahrenheit and a constant humidity of about 45 percent. Some archives file their tapes, transcripts, notes, clippings, and deed of gift for each interviewee in a single, acid-free archival storage box. If adopting this filing system, make sure that any documents in the container are also on acid-free paper. For instance, save photocopies of newspaper articles rather than the original clippings, since newsprint will deteriorate and adversely affect the rest of the contents of the box. Transcripts should always be printed on acid-free paper. Remember that storing all records in the same location runs the risk of having everything damaged or lost together should a fire or tornado or similar disaster occur. Keep tapes away from windows and heat sources. Be careful of insects, rodents, mold, and other elements that can damage tape as well as paper. Archivists admit that they cannot eliminate the causes of decay, but they can slow down the deterioration.

"Constant" is the key word for preserving tapes. Archives need to avoid wide fluctuations in heat and humidity because, at different temperatures, air holds different amounts of moisture that in turn affect tapes. Moisture from the air is absorbed into the tape binder (which holds the magnetic particles to the tape), causing the tape to lose its strength and break down. High temperatures and humidity will cause irreversible damage to the tape, as anyone who has heard the sound distortion caused by leaving a music tape inside a car during hot weather can testify.

The original tape is kept as the master copy (or even better, the original cassette may be copied onto reel-to-reel tape, which then becomes the master copy). For transcribing and research, always use copies of the tape rather than the master. Avoid eating, drinking, or smoking around tapes. (Ashes are the chief contaminant from smoking.) Oils from fingers can damage tapes, which should not be handled directly. Store tapes in their original containers or their equivalents. Some archives seal master tapes in polyethylene bags. Given all the potential dangers to tapes from fires, floods, and other hazards, it is advisable to store the master tape and its copies in separate places.

To avoid print-through, tapes must be rewound at play speed every year or two. This is a time-consuming and expensive procedure that large collections often follow less than diligently. But rewinding is essential to maintain distinct sound on the tapes and is all the more important for interviews that have not been transcribed.

Technological advances, including the development of compact disks and digital audiotape, may allow for better sound preservation in the future. But as equipment becomes outdated, archivists must decide whether to maintain obsolete equipment or convert their collection to the newer technology; either course can be expensive. Approach new technology warily until it has been assessed for its usefulness in long-term preservation. Whatever equipment you choose, make sure that it can be serviced conveniently and replaced if necessary.[24]

How reliable are digital audiotapes and CD-ROMs?

Audio specialists have mixed opinions about these new recording media. The advantages of digital audiotape are that the machines are compact in size and fast in retrieval, the tapes are inexpensive, and the recordings are clear and free from distortion. Because the sound is represented by a series of digits, the tapes do not run the risk of print-through or echoes. Each copy of a DAT should sound as good as the previous one, suggesting that the original sound on digital recordings could theoretically last forever so long as it was routinely copied. But there are troubling signs as well. Even a small particle of dust can throw the DAT out of line. Some engineers have speculated that the DAT's "usable life" may be limited to a few years, requiring frequent copying.

Similar questions have been raised about optical storage media (CD-ROM). Since optical disks employ a laser reading mechanism, there is no wear on them during use and no degrading of the sound. But archivists have raised concerns about the quality of compact disks, about "disk rot," and about occasional obstructions that impede access to portions of the disk, similar to the type of glitches that owners of CD players have experienced listening to music. The life span of a CD-ROM is estimated at 10 to 20 years.[25]

What if the tapes are damaged?

Archivists always have to be prepared for fire, flood, and other natural disasters. Damaged tapes need to be copied onto clean tapes, but they may not initially be copiable. In 1989, when Hurricane Hugo struck the South Carolina coast, among the many items submerged under water were the tapes of the interviews Theodore Rosengarten conducted for his award-winning book *All God's Dangers*. Forty-eight reels of magnetic tape were soaked in water and caked with mud and sand. After a month's delay, the tapes were turned over to the Southern Folklife Collection at the University of North Carolina at Chapel Hill, where each tape was wound by hand through a bath of distilled water and then up in a cardboard tube filled with air warmed by a hair dryer. The dried tapes were then wound onto new reels and were playable enough to be copied onto new master tapes. This procedure was funded by a grant from the North Carolina Arts Council. Rosengarten deposited his tapes with the Southern Folklife Center so that "the voices and experience of Ned Cobb ["Nate Shaw" in the book] and his family . . . will be heard again."[26]

Is it appropriate to edit tapes?

For preservation reasons, the master tape should never be spliced, and for ethical and methodological reasons, the master tape should never be edited. What was said was said and should not be altered to make it seem different. Although tapes are edited and condensed for documentary purposes, the original must remain true to the actual circumstances of the interview so that researchers can use the material in the confidence that it has not been tampered with. Interviewees' restrictions must always be honored, but if either the interviewee or the project decides—for reasons of privacy or to avoid a libel action—to close portions of the interview for a period of time, then a copy of the tape can be made with the portions in question deleted, to be used for research until the entire tape can be opened safely. Even though the transcript has been edited to improve the meaning of the interview, the spoken word, with all its imprecisions, should remain intact as a primary record or document.

If an archives does not transcribe its tapes, what alternatives are available?

The problems of preserving tape of unknown durability, deterioration of sound quality, and potential obsolescence of equipment all reinforce the value of transcribing tapes for long-term preservation of oral history interviews. But transcribing is expensive and time-consuming. If an archives lacks the funds to transcribe, plans to transcribe only selectively, or anticipates long delays before it can transcribe, then it needs to index its tapes to identify the major subjects discussed on them. Researchers need guidance and should not have to listen to entire tapes to locate specific information. A tape index may be a simple list of topics in the order that they are mentioned on the tape, or it may offer a schedule of the playing time of the tape indicating the approximate location of each name or subject discussed.[27]

Archivists should keep in mind, however, that if transcripts are not made, they must maintain adequate equipment for researchers to play back the tapes while making notes, and enough equipment that several researchers can listen to tapes at the same time. Just as archives need to consider whether to allow researchers to photocopy all of an interview, they should have a policy on making copies of all or portions of their tapes and establish requirements for copying, quoting, and publishing excerpts.[28]

DONATED INTERVIEWS

If an archives does not conduct oral history itself, is it likely to receive donated interviews?

Yes, even without seeking them out, archives are likely to receive oral histories as part of a larger accession of corporate, associational, or government agency records, or as donations by individual researchers. The oral history may be a random transcript filed away with other records, or it may be part of a larger collection focusing on an individual or institution. There are so many forms and conditions in which donated oral histories may arrive that, to exercise any archival control, an archives cannot afford to be a passive recipient. Instead, an archives should establish its own standards and work with oral historians—whether individuals or representatives of an agency—to meet those standards.

The likelihood of all archives receiving oral history donations increased exponentially in 1989 when the American Historical Association (AHA) adopted its statement of principles on oral history interviewing, stipulating that "interviewers should arrange to deposit their interviews in an archival repository that is capable of both preserving the interviews and making them available for general research. Additionally, the interviewer should work with the repository in determining the necessary legal arrangements."[29]

The historical profession was responding to the laxity with which many authors had been treating oral sources. When books include citations to "interviews in author's possession," other historians want the opportunity to examine them for verification and further research use. Through their professional association, historians also wanted to create a greater awareness among researchers that they may have the only interview with individuals who have died. And even if the interviewee was also interviewed by another oral history project, each interviewer's questions shed a different light on the interviewee's experiences. Other scholars who examine an author's oral source material may draw different conclusions from those of the original interviewer, just as researchers disagree over the meaning of written documentation.

Many academics, freelance writers, graduate advisers, and graduate students had simply never considered giving their interviews to an archives before the AHA promulgated its standards. The historian David Oshinsky had conducted many interviews for his biography of Sen. Joseph R. McCarthy, particularly for information on McCarthy's early life, about which little had been published. Although he taped most of his interviews, he did not use any release forms because it never occurred to him to deposit them in an archives. After reading the AHA rules, Oshinsky became determined to adopt archival-quality standards. For his next book, he taped all of his interviews, obtained releases, produced written transcripts, and deposited tapes and transcripts in his university library, where they have already been used by other researchers.[30]

The Columbia Oral History Research Office both conducts its own interviews and regularly receives interviews from writers who have published their books. The Walt Disney Archives has no formal oral history program of its own but contains an extensive collection of interviews with Disney, his family, studio animators, park planners, and other employees, donated by various authors who did the interviews in the course of their research. The University of Kentucky archives estimated that nearly 80 percent of the 200 interviews added annually to the university's oral history collection are generated outside the archives by faculty from history, political science, anthropology, and sociology and by graduate students and freelance researchers. The archives also found that, however valuable the contributions of these "associate interviewers," their interviews often arrived untranscribed, unindexed, unabstracted, and with no legal release forms. The University of Kentucky archivist Terry Birdwhistell has noted that "the preservation of personal interviews generated by historians is a two-way street. For every historian who for one reason or another fails to place his or her interviews in an archives, there is likely an archivist who does not want to add an historian's recorded interviews and transcripts to his collections. Overcoming these biases will take the cooperation of both historians and archivists."[31]

Archives must avoid even the appearance of favoritism when dealing with researchers. When offered donations of interviews from a researcher, they must balance what they do against what the researcher is giving. It would be questionable for an archives to invest large amounts of its staff time and financial resources in transcribing and preserving an oral history collection if it was to be closed for an excessively long period of time to all but the original researcher. If an archives provides equipment and invests its resources in the collection of oral histories, then it should avoid open-ended agreements and seek to negotiate with the donor a reasonable time for releasing the materials for general research.

What should archives do to get control over donated interview tapes and transcripts?

Ideally, archivists work with researchers from the outset of an oral history project, rather than coming in at the end. But when researchers appear at the archives' door at the end of a project, carrying their interview tapes and no release forms—or having followed other guidelines—the archives needs to determine whether the material meets its standards. If the archives agrees to accession the interviews, it can provide the researcher with deeds of gift to take back to interviewees for their signatures. Again, the interviews can be restricted until the book is published.

Archivists need to publicize their willingness to serve as repositories for individual and group oral history projects, whether conducted at their university, in their community, or on subjects complementary to their larger collections. By attracting such donations, they can build their oral history holdings in the most cost-effective manner. But even more important, interviews will be "out of the desk drawers, closets, and basements" of the interviewers and made available to scholarship in general.[32]

Should an archives treat donated oral histories the same as those it commissions or conducts itself?

Donated interviews can be treated like those sponsored by the archives in terms of paperwork and filing arrangements. Once archivists receive donated tapes, they should immediately make a security copy and store the original tapes in an environmentally controlled and secure area. In anticipation of receiving oral history donations, archives should establish guidelines for accession of oral documentation, including sample legal releases, recommended tape for long-term preservation, and other processing standards. A good model is the guideline that the National Archives and Records Administration issued for accessioning federal oral history projects.[33]

LEGAL CONSIDERATIONS

If only portions of an interview are restricted, can the rest of the interview be made available for research?

Emphatically yes. There is no reason to hold back the bulk of an interview for the sake of a few pages of restricted material. Remove the restricted pages and place them in a sealed envelope identified with the name of the interviewee and the date the restriction will be lifted. Insert a note in the transcript: "Pages *x* to *y* have been restricted until [date]." Or, "A portion of the interview at this point in the transcript has been restricted."

Some archives do not announce that they even possess an oral history until the restriction has passed, in part to avoid legal challenges. But researchers want to know if they have seen all the relevant material and what lies beyond their research. Some will delay publication of their own work if they know that the restriction is to be lifted soon. By not announcing the existence of closed interviews, the archives favors those who happen to be present when the records open, a circumstance that too often has made researchers suspicious that favoritism was being shown.

If an archives does not advertise that it has a certain interview, even though restricted, then another oral history project may interview the same person and duplicate the information. One flattered interviewee never bothered to tell the second interviewer that he had already given a lengthy life review interview. If an interview is closed, researchers may seek to interview that person themselves and would be entirely within their rights to do so. But when the interviewee is deceased, only the archival oral history will be available.

In the government, are oral histories official public records?

They can be, but not necessarily. If an interview is done as a job requirement of a government employee, such as a debriefing, it is clearly an official record and should be treated like other government records. But simply because interviewees work for the government does not mean that they automatically waive rights to their interviews. Under federal copyright law, anyone whose words are recorded and reproduced retains copyright over the recording. If a private citizen or government employee voluntarily gives an interview to a government oral history project, they should be asked, like anyone else, to sign a deed of gift assigning their copyright in the interview to the agency's repository and stipulating any restrictions on its use. The federal government recognizes the gift of restricted oral histories as an exemption to the Freedom of Information Act (FOIA). That is, researchers' FOIA requests for transcripts do not supersede interviewees' stipulated restrictions.[34]

Oral history is under way throughout the three branches of the federal government. Every military service conducts oral history, as do historians at the Energy and Labor departments, the Nuclear Regulatory Commission, the National Park Service, NASA, the CIA, and the FBI. Over the decades, they have produced oral histories in the tens of thousands, most of which are open for research. The Smithsonian Institution is an outstanding example of the diversity of oral history. The Air and Space Museum has interviewed aviation pioneers; on the occasion of its fiftieth anniversary, the National Gallery of Art interviewed those who built and operated the gallery; the Natural History Museum has interviewed early curators who brought back specimens; the American History Museum has interviewed African-Americans who migrated "from field to factory." The Smithsonian Archives also has conducted video interviews with old-time curators throughout the Smithsonian's many museums.[35]

Is an archives liable for any potentially libelous or defamatory remarks in an oral history?

Libel and defamation are false statements that can injure a person's reputation, holding them up to public ridicule and contempt. Fortunately, the dead cannot be defamed, or else history could not be written. But should an interviewee defame a living person in an oral history, then the interviewee, interviewer, and archives could share liability for the statements. A defamatory statement would have to mention a person specifically by name, be published, and damage the person's reputation. Courts have been more protective of average citizens than of public figures in defamation cases.

Generally, libel and defamation cases have involved mass-circulation books, newspapers, and magazines rather than archival oral histories. Although there is no body of case law specifically involving oral history, no oral history archives relishes the possibility of becoming the first case, and most of them recognize that discretion is the better part of valor. Since most oral history projects cannot afford to have a lawyer read every interview for potentially libelous statements, they have used their common sense instead. Confronted with a potentially libelous portion, an archives can delete the specific names or close that portion of the interview for a period of time, perhaps 10 or 20 years, until the remarks are no longer controversial.[36]

If interviews or other records are closed for a seemingly vague reason, researchers may well challenge why and by whose authority such restrictions have been made. In anticipation of such questions, most archives list their own institutional restrictions in a document that researchers can read when they arrive at the archives. Such information sheets establish that the archivist has the authority to impose restrictions, if needed, to protect privacy, to guard against libel, and to meet other general criteria set by the archives' governing board.

Should an archives release restricted interviews that have been subpoenaed?

Archivists are responsible for honoring and protecting donor restrictions. The premature release of an oral history interview not only could embarrass the individual but could have a "chilling effect" on other interviewees, making them more reluctant to speak candidly on tape. Archivists therefore are faced with a legal and ethical dilemma when restricted oral histories are subpoenaed for use in a court proceeding. The few cases that have arisen have not been focused specifically on oral history but have been blanket requests, or "fishing expeditions," for any and all archival materials regarding an individual, organization, or issue. Archivists and their attorneys have been able to negotiate a more limited release of subpoenaed materials, arguing that the type of information sought can be obtained from sources other than the closed oral histories. Submitting the deeds of gift under which interviewees donated restricted interviews, archives can also attempt to invoke their "fiduciary responsibility" to protect such sealed materials they hold in trust. Archives that are open and consistent in their treatment of restricted materials stand a good chance of having the subpoena invalidated.[37]

PUBLIC PROGRAMS

How can an archives use oral history for public outreach?

Public programs sometimes get lost in the archival shuffle of accessioning, maintaining, and preserving collections and dealing with researchers and reference questions. But outreach is an important function that can heighten the public's interest in and appreciation for historical records and increase public support for libraries and archives. Oral history offers unique opportunities for reaching members of a community who might not otherwise use a library or archives. After the first contacts have been made by conducting interviews in the community, the connection is reinforced through public programs that display the finished product.[38]

In California, the San Joaquin Valley library system sponsored an oral history with first- and second-generation Japanese-Americans in the valley who had lived through the Second World War. The project aimed not only to create a resource for scholars but to influence the community's thinking about its ethnic heritage. The collected oral histories enabled the library system to publish three volumes and create a videotape (*Success through Perseverance*) and a slide-tape show (*Improving Library Services to Japanese-Americans in the Valley*), which they publicized broadly on radio and television and in newspapers. Librarians rated the programs a great public relations success and noted that they resulted in greater utilization of the local libraries by Japanese-American patrons.[39]

Archivists also have found public outreach benefits closer to home. Many archives are housed in universities and other institutions and are supervised by a board of trustees or executive board that determines whether the archives gets more space, staff, and equipment. The members of these governing boards can be directly involved in an oral history program, making recommendations about potential interviewees, getting copies of the interviews, discussing their use in public relations, and even being interviewed themselves. This contact helps make the work of the archives more tangible and immediate to those who influence its policies and budget. Similar public outreach can be directed toward the administrators, staff, faculty, students, and alumni of a university and toward management and workers in a corporation.

Another return of such community awareness are the donations of photographs, manuscripts, and other memorabilia from those who have given oral histories or who have attended the public programs. Archives should not hesitate to ask oral history interviewees to consider making such gifts; most will be honored by the request and will be pleased to have family keepsakes preserved. A word of caution, however: libraries and archives need to establish and communicate their collecting policies to ensure that their public programs do not generate inappropriate gifts.

Oral histories make good subjects for press releases. Local newspapers have reprinted portions of interviews, as single articles, running features, or special supplements. Consider also using oral history tapes to create public service announcements for local radio and television stations. Some archives have used oral history interviews in curriculum packets for schools.[40]

Such public programs are fine for larger, well-funded archives, historical societies, and library systems, but how could a local library afford to do that kind of outreach?

Some oral history has been well funded, but a lot more has operated on a shoestring, using volunteers, borrowing equipment, and surviving on modest donations. The local library often houses a local history collection, which is not only the local repository for community oral histories but the best research source for those conducting the interviews. Local librarians know the community and have a sense of who uses the facility and who does not. The librarian may not have the time to do the interviews but can coordinate volunteer interviewers, indexers, and transcribers. The librarian can also work with local students or with the state or local historical society, which may be eager to conduct oral history interviews. The library can serve as the sole repository for the interviews, or copies of the tapes and transcripts can be shared with the cooperating schools and historical societies. If guided, volunteers from the community often enjoy doing interviews and making a contribution to preserving community history. Remind them that creating the oral documentation is not an end in itself but just a first step toward the use of local oral histories in research, publications, and public programs. The best reward for volunteers is to include them in public exhibits, performances, and receptions, where they can see the product of their labor.[41]

The Martin Luther King, Jr. Public Library in Washington, D.C., sought to enhance its Washingtoniana collection with oral histories of the people, neighborhoods, institutions, and events that had fostered public understanding of the history of the District of Columbia. Interviewers were invited to register their ongoing projects with the library so that others could be informed of their activities. Registrants were asked for the name of their project, the name, address, and telephone number of their project director, a brief description of their project's focus, and an estimated date for completion. The library also agreed to accept donations of tapes and transcripts so long as they were accompanied by formal legal agreements between interviewers and interviewees releasing the donated materials to unrestricted public use, were recorded with good sound quality, and were time-indexed or transcribed. The library provided copies of sample legal release forms; promised periodic workshops and seminars on oral history for those who requested them; offered to make referrals to university oral history classes in the metropolitan area; and promoted itself as a clearinghouse for local oral history projects and bibliographic references to oral history materials that were part of its collection. This Washington library's efforts exemplify the mutually beneficial relationship that can be established between libraries, archives, and interviewers to preserve the oral history of our time for the future.

7

TEACHING ORAL HISTORY

How extensively has oral history been used in the classroom?

Teachers have implemented oral history at every level from grade school to graduate school and in continuing and community education programs, including workshops for senior citizens. Interviewing techniques can be taught to students of all levels of ability. In secondary schools, oral history more often has been directed toward honors, gifted and talented, and advanced-placement students. But oral history has demonstrated that it can motivate slow learners and otherwise indifferent students as well. Doing oral history helps students break loose from their textbooks and become their own collectors of information—and students learn best from what they have researched themselves.

Oral history works for teachers who, frankly, have grown tired of lecturing and want to engage their students more actively in learning. Instead of teachers telling students what is important, oral history projects require students to find out for themselves, by interviewing people and then by processing and analyzing the information gathered. Students often prove innately able to establish the necessary rapport, since many older interviewees feel a special need to make young people understand the events of their past. In many ways, the ideal oral history relationship occurs when the interviewer plays student to the interviewee as teacher.[1]

It sounds too good to be true. What's the catch?

School oral history projects frequently encounter a lack of funds and equipment, school boards that are unsympathetic to new student electives, and department chairs and colleagues who are dubious about anything outside the standard curriculum. A teacher can grow discouraged over the time and commitment that oral history requires. Some lack training and personal experience in using oral history and have no mentor to turn to for advice.

Teachers complain about the difficulty of completing oral history projects within the limited confines of a semester; others complain about students who do not prepare adequately for their interviews. Teachers also recognize the need for more structured assistance to help student projects succeed.

Admittedly, oral history is hardly a panacea for all that ails modern education, and not every student readily adapts to it. But those teachers who have used oral history offer enthusiastic assessments of its pedagogical advantages and attest that the rewards are worth the effort.[2]

Does oral history work in other classes besides history?

With "history" in its name, oral history has shown up most often in history and social studies programs; teachers can use it to study family, culture, community, and government. But interviewing has also flourished in English, journalism, drama, folklore, science, and many other disciplines. The innovative *Foxfire* program sprang from an English composition course designed to get students to develop content and grammar skills by writing about what they saw and did. A composition or language skills class can assign students not only to conduct interviews and to write descriptions of the experience but to do tape transcription, which is an exercise that calls for language skills in sentence structure, syntax, and punctuation.[3]

Students may never have associated their own everyday language with the standard English of textbooks and classroom assignments. One English teacher was surprised when her inner-city black students complained that Alice Walker's novel *The Color Purple* (1982) sounded odd and was hard to read, despite the teacher's observation that Walker's prose perfectly captured her students' own "black English." None of them, she concluded, "had ever learned how to read and write their own verbal system of communication." An oral history project that had students recording and transcribing their own speech patterns would offer rare opportunities for self-revelation. Interview transcriptions similarly provide students with a means of examining regional dialects, colloquialisms, and jargon.[4]

What is Foxfire?

Familiar to mass audiences through the stage play, television movie, and series of best-selling books, *Foxfire* is the pioneering secondary school project that combined oral history and folklore as instructional devices. It began in 1966 when a teacher at the Rabun Gap-Nacoochee High School, in an Appalachian community in Georgia, realized that his lectures just were not getting through to his students, who were deficient in language skills and uncomfortable expressing themselves in writing. "How would you like to throw away the text and start a magazine?" he asked them. Soon, *Foxfire* proved so effective in motivating students that it spawned countless other school interviewing and journal-writing projects across the country.[5]

A typical *Foxfire* class lasts one semester. Before students begin interviewing, they listen to a short story read aloud and try to write down everything they hear. A sample reading of these papers easily demonstrates why the original is richer and fuller than any of the remembered versions. Then the same story is read again, slowly, with the students trying to take it down as dictation—a task they quickly find impossible. These exercises demonstrate the problems involved in listening and also make clear the need for tape-recording interviews. But this leaves the question of how to get the story off the tape, a discussion that in turn leads to an explanation of transcribing, followed by students attempting practice transcripts. Other class sessions cover the varying sound quality of different tape recorders, tapes, and microphones, with demonstrations on how to set up equipment properly. *Foxfire* classes include sessions on cameras as well, since students are encouraged to take photographs of the people they interview and to collect other items related to the subject matter.

Foxfire seeks to involve students in all phases of the oral history project. The class picks the theme of the project, whom to interview, and what questions to ask. Before going out to conduct interviews, students watch a practice in-class interview in which someone—perhaps another teacher, a school administrator, a cafeteria worker, a parent—is invited to the class to be interviewed. The in-class interview is not a drill but an actual interview designed to impress on the students the seriousness of their responsibilities as interviewers.

In-class interviews give students the chance to analyze not only the interviewing process but also the transcription and the effects of different transcription styles on the content of the interview. Students begin to realize how easily a careless transcriber can alter the meaning of an interview. With all this in-class experience and discussion absorbed, the students finally go out to interview for themselves.[6]

Foxfire spread its message to other schools, recommending a "fieldwork enterprise" that mixes research, interviewing training, and community-school relationships. A term's project might be a slide-tape show or a video, but quite often it has resulted in publication of a school journal. Since the publication of the first *Foxfire Book* in 1972, numerous schools have produced similar magazines combining oral history, folklore, and local history. Two of its offspring, in Kennebunkport, Maine, and Lebanon, Missouri, similarly made the transition from local school magazines to nationally published books: *The Salt Book* (1977) and *Bittersweet County* (1978). Students with learning disabilities in Littleton, Colorado, published the journal *Aspen Glow*, and the children of migrant farmworkers in Boulder produced *El Aguila. Bloodlines* is a student oral history journal in Holmes County, Mississippi, one of the poorest counties in the nation.

Many school oral history magazines have not lasted long. Some were identified with a particular teacher who moved on, and others were eliminated by school budget cuts. One well-regarded publication was canceled when its budget allotment went to pay for the school's heating oil. Its director bemoaned the project's death from "administrative ineptitude." Yet new oral history journals and newsletters in schools continue to appear, made increasingly possible by the availability of school computers for desktop publishing.[7]

Where can a teacher get personal training in oral history?

If a teacher did not have an opportunity to take an oral history course in graduate school, courses and workshops are regularly available at universities and community colleges and in adult education programs. Between school years, summer institutes and weeklong oral history workshops are conducted around the country. State historical societies whose collections contain oral history interviews often can be enlisted to help.

The Oral History Association and its several affiliated state and regional oral history associations regularly run workshops and offer sessions for teachers. They publish a practical-minded pamphlet, *Oral History in the Secondary School Classroom*, which outlines instructional units for teaching oral history in periods of two weeks, eight- to ten weeks, or a full year; topics that can be studied using oral history; ways in which students can use information collected through interviews; and suggestions on how to raise funds to support a school oral history project. The National Council for the Social Studies offers its own pamphlet, *Oral History in the Classroom*, in its "How to Do It" series.[8]

A number of these organizations have recognized that overworked teachers are too busy preparing lessons, grading papers, and dealing with their supervisors to attend many extracurricular programs. Some have made their oral history workshops more attractive by offering certificates or by qualifying as "in-service" teacher training during scheduled release time. Although these occasional workshops are usually brief and unable to cover much ground, they provide teachers with basic models for their own classroom projects. Teachers have also recognized oral history as a highly positive way of meeting state mandates and performance evaluations of students' advancement.

Where can a school get oral history equipment?

It was the availability of low-cost, lightweight, easy-to-operate cassette tape recorders that made oral history feasible as a teaching device in the first place, but acquiring equipment on limited school budgets still calls for creativity. Some school audiovisual departments have tape recorders, microphones, video cameras, and computers, but in general teachers can expect anything from a complete lack of equipment to severe limitations on its availability. Poll your students to see how many can use their own tape recorders. Some have access to family camcorders. Local merchants have cooperated with school projects by lending equipment. One California camera store annually lends a local high school all the equipment it needs for filming and editing its History Day media entries. Local support groups, from parent-teacher associations to alumni, should also be tapped for funds and equipment. With its objective of publishing a magazine of its interviews, the *Foxfire* program sent its students out to solicit contributions from local merchants and towns-folk. They listed gifts of any amount in the magazine, and each donor received a copy signed by all of the students.[9]

What is the single most important ingredient for starting an oral history project in a school?

Every classroom oral history project needs a teacher who is sincerely committed to it. "It's not all fun and games," as Barbara Gallant, a high school teacher in Gainesville, Florida, reported. "It has to be part of the curriculum and not something extra. I don't think you need the money to start, because I think that can be found. I do think there has to be a person who cares and wants to do it, who feels that there is some real value in it." Gallant began supervising an oral history project at a time when federal courts had ordered racial integration of her school system. Teachers and administrators at her school felt it was essential to get white and black students communicating with each other and to build stronger ties with the community. Using borrowed tape recorders, she assigned students to interview family members about how the county had changed over the past 50 years and brought local historians and anthropologists into class to talk to the students. The project worked well—although she discovered that after a while her students grew bored with using school integration as the only subject. She subsequently allowed her classes to branch out into other areas. Still, the interviews they conducted helped the students through a time of dramatic change and created a useful resource for future research on their school.[10]

ORAL HISTORY IN ELEMENTARY AND SECONDARY SCHOOLS

Can oral history be tried in elementary school classes?

At the elementary school level, oral history is used not for teaching subject matter but for helping students become more aware of their surroundings. Recognizing that children wonder about themselves before they begin to appreciate others, elementary school teachers have had students interview their parents on the theme, "What was I like when I was younger?" Elementary school students have collected anecdotes about their families and learned about their neighborhoods. Educators note that children "grow socially" when they interview adults.[11]

In one elementary school project, students were asked to describe the route they typically took to school. They recorded what types of buildings they passed, such as businesses, churches, and other schools. Accompanied by an adult, students interviewed someone identified with one of the buildings on their daily route. They asked shop owners why they chose the location, how long they had been doing business there, and whether most of their customers came from the local community. Drawing from such programs, the District of Columbia school system published *Earth Waves*, a newsletter that reported on oral history in elementary schools, offered sample projects and questions, and reproduced portions of student interviews. Fourth-graders in Middlebury, Vermont, have published a similar journal, called *Village Green*.[12]

Young children can focus their interviews on what their parents and grandparents did when they were children. What types of games did they play when they were young? What did they ever do before television? Was their schooling different? What types of songs were popular then? Children seem most comfortable interviewing grandparents—perhaps, as has been said, because they share a common enemy.

Do the objectives change when using oral history with middle and junior high school students?

Both the objectives and levels of sophistication in oral history advance as students move toward adolescence. For middle and junior high school students, oral history has been used more for dealing with the "affective domain," that is, issues pertaining to emotions and feelings. Since adolescents are struggling with their personal identity, oral history helps to refocus their attention from themselves to their families and communities. Middle and junior high school social studies curricula often emphasize local history and provide local history texts that can be the basis for doing a local oral history project in which students get to practice social studies, "almost without realizing it." Local history can further be compared and contrasted to national trends, rather than seen in isolation. Many middle schools have also embraced an interdisciplinary approach to learning by combining English and social studies, and using oral history as a bridge between these fields.[13]

Schools in Quincy, Massachusetts, involved sixth-, seventh-, and eighth-grade students in the Family Ties program. Students visited the Quincy Museum and studied Eliza Susan Quincy, who throughout the nineteenth century had recorded all of the furnishings and objects in the Quincy family home and had collected reminiscences of other family members. Returning home, students were asked to list what items their own families counted as "treasures" and to prepare their own family inventories in album form. The albums documented the students' families, homes, and times, with the idea that the albums could someday be passed along to their own children.

As part of this project, the museum staff helped train the students to interview family members. The interviews assisted in creating the family inventories by helping students understand not only what the items were but their emotional significance. Little-noticed bric-a-brac took on new meaning as mementos of the past. For students who were first- or second-generation immigrants, family treasures were cherished reminders of a former life in a different culture. The experiment helped students learn to use primary source materials, gave them experience in different kinds of writing, and raised their curiosity about local historical resources. Students completed the project with a stronger sense of being "rooted in the past" as well as an "active part of the present." An unexpected by-product of the class discussions, students' increased consciousness of the different backgrounds of their classmates, was one the project directors trusted would foster greater tolerance in a multicultural environment.[14]

Would an oral history project be any different at the high school level?

In high school, oral history tends to be more closely connected to the subject matter being taught in the classroom. Students learn the same oral history techniques but apply them to a wide range of subjects. Often the interview subjects are particularly relevant to the local region but have national significance as well and fit into a curriculum that includes world and U.S. history. Topics that high school students have tackled include native villages of the Aleutian Islands, Japanese-American relocation during the Second World War, the Buffalo Soldiers, the Three Mile Island incident, the Baltimore Air Show of 1910, multiculturalism in Hawaii, and the changing Lower East Side of Manhattan. One high school student evaluating an oral history course reported: "It helped me understand the human causes, not just 'the war began because'. . . but why it began, who was involved and most importantly—how they felt."[15]

How should you prepare high school students to do oral histories?

A good way to begin is to have students read other oral histories before they begin doing their own interviews. If previous classes at the school have done interviews that are available in the school library, students can read a sampling of the best ones. Since the spoken word is less formal than written text, published oral histories are usually easy to read and their stories can be gripping. Reading these oral histories stimulates classroom discussion, engages students' interest, and gives them some of the needed background to conduct their own interviews. By reading other oral histories, students get a better idea of the type of information that interviewing can elicit, and they see that interviewees often present contradictory accounts.[16]

The class textbook can also become a research tool; it provides the broad outline and some of the specifics for the subject being studied, and sometimes bibliographies suggesting further reading. When interviewees cover information outside the scope of the text or contradict something in the text, students must weigh the conflicting evidence and consider the complexity of the issue. Old magazines, newspapers, memoirs, and histories are all standard research sources, but research can also include photographs, music, physical artifacts, and any number of other sources. There is a story behind almost every photograph in a family photo album. The same items that provide inspiration for doing the interviews can also serve as illustrations for the transcripts, publications, videos, exhibits, and other projects that grow out of the interviews.[17]

Preinterview research is absolutely essential. An unprepared student is likely to conduct a poor interview and will miss most of the learning experience that oral history offers. If student interviewers have not done their homework, they will not know all the questions to ask, will not be able to assist interviewees with faulty memories, will not recognize new leads that require follow-up questions, and will neither fully understand nor appreciate what they are hearing.

Whom should students interview?

Students generally start with their own families. Oral history gives them a chance to collect more systematically the many stories they have already heard at the dinner table or at family reunions. They can interview one person in-depth as a full life history, or several members of the same family in a family history. Their interviews can cover many generations, since grandparents can tell stories about their own parents and grandparents. Questions can include: When did their families immigrate to America? When did they move to the state they are now living in? How long have they lived in their community? What wars have family members fought in (or against)? What types of jobs have they held?

But the oral history experience is enhanced when students use it to interview people they normally would not have met and talked with. Working with the students, teachers can suggest likely places to seek interviewees. A class working on a group project can contact the local historical society for advice about potential interviewees. Local newspapers and involved citizens, nearby colleges, senior citizens' centers, veterans' hospitals, and such national organizations as the Veterans of Foreign Wars (VFW) and the American Legion are all potential sources of interviewees.[18]

Whether they interview their family, neighbors, or members of the community at large, students will discover how historical events have affected people like themselves, a revelation that will expand their historical consciousness and make their classwork more meaningful. A school oral history project can also lead students to reexamine their own communities and to break down the walls between the classroom and the "real world" outside.[19]

Student oral history projects can examine great national and international events and their impact on the local community—events of the magnitude of the Great Depression, the war in Vietnam, the 1970s energy crisis, the environmental movement, the civil rights movement, and the women's rights movement. Churches and other religious centers in the community, a housing development, a manufacturing plant, an event like a flood or tornado, can be documented through oral history.

The humorist Garrison Keillor once wrote a spoof about students living in a development so new that it had no cultural heritage to document. The only craft to document was that of placing boards across stacks of bricks to make bookcases. But most communities have existed long enough to have a history. Possible subjects are neighborhood organizations, civil rights groups, local charities, newspapers, radio and television stations and their personnel, as well as local entertainers. Students can even document their own school by interviewing current and past administrators, teachers, and graduates. Student oral histories have recorded local folklore, crafts, skills, trades, occupations, and customs. Students have studied local government by interviewing political candidates, office holders, and civic associations. The purpose of these interviews is to record what people and organizations did (and why), and how people, events, and practices have changed over time.

The result will not be simply a snapshot of how things are today but a record of how they used to be, and how and why they evolved.[20]

Students can be quite unpredictable in choosing whom to interview. One student noticed an elderly man at her local library. After introducing herself, she asked him to give her an interview for her oral history project. The man replied, "I'm honored by so charming a young lady, but . . . no! I don't like publicity." Undeterred, the student approached her subject again a week later and persuaded him to give an interview about how different their city was during his childhood.[21]

Some students have no hesitation in going to the source. They will read a name in the newspaper or a book and call or write for an interview without any trepidation. In 1993 a group of high school students from North Carolina interviewed the eminent historian John Hope Franklin for the documentary they produced on slave spirituals as a History Day project. When asked how they came to interview Professor Franklin, they explained, "Oh, Coretta Scott King recommended that we call him."

Other students will be too shy to go next door and interview a neighbor. To help them overcome their shyness, teachers should encourage students to interview someone they feel comfortable with, a family member or a friend. Students may also feel more at ease if someone else, a family member or fellow student, accompanies them. There is no reason why students should not work in teams, with one asking the questions and the other operating the tape recorder and perhaps taking photographs, an arrangement that helps to maximize the use of the equipment. Sometimes team interviewing works when each student handles a specific set of questions, although it requires a certain degree of practice and coordination to keep the interviewers from interrupting each other. Instead of interviewing, other students prefer preparing and editing transcripts or writing up the results. Even veteran interviewers get butterflies before starting a new interview, but the experience of doing interviews can help students build their self-confidence.[22]

What can oral history teach students about historical research in general?

There is a good deal of historical detective work involved in doing oral history that can help students identify the ways in which historians operate. Interviewing turns students into the primary historical investigators; they must learn how to choose a topic, find people to interview, do the research, and prepare the questions. The more students prepare, the more they recognize what they do not know, as well as how much more they need to learn in order to ask meaningful questions—and understand the answers. Student interviewers are likely to be confronted with contradictory evidence: different people give different versions of the same event, and an interviewee's story can differ noticeably from the textbook and other sources of information. In short, students begin to appreciate how history is collected and interpreted and perhaps even begin to think like historians themselves.[23]

Once they have done their interviews, students, in class discussions or in written papers, analyze the varying responses and inevitably realize that historical events do not affect all people the same way. Seeing pictures of breadlines and widespread poverty during the Great Depression, for instance, students might assume that everyone suffered equally. But interviews with family members reveal that, although one grandfather was unemployed, the other kept his job and saw his real income rise as prices fell.

Oral history teaches students about cause-and-effect relationships, communication skills, and historical concepts. Interviewing also may give them a greater political awareness as they listen to interviewees discuss the role of the government and political issues in their lives. Could the unemployed grandfather have gotten work through the Works Progress Administration (WPA), or was he barred from the federal relief rolls in his local jurisdiction because of his political affiliation?

Doing oral history helps students not only to see firsthand what historians do but to appreciate the jobs of journalists and other professional interviewers. Educators have found that oral history teaches students "how to learn" as well as what to learn. Students develop problem-solving skills and come away with an understanding "that history is risky, as is any enterprise that attempts to arrive at the truth." Writing papers about oral history experiences further sharpens analytical and composition skills.[24]

Oral history fits the modern trend in teaching away from an emphasis on political history and toward social history. More than ever before, schools study everyday life over time, looking at several past generations of immigrants, ethnics, racial minorities, and women. Textbook publishers have struggled to keep up with these new trends, and teachers incorporate more outside materials into their classes. The historian Peter Stearns noted that high school experiments with social history had "generated enthusiasm among students who were intrigued with issues also familiar in their own lives, and some teachers, extending these same experiments, were able to move toward more sophisticated analytical training on issues of periodization or causation." But Stearns concluded that too many school assignments continue to require merely factual research. In family history projects, students gather information about their own families but rarely analyze the material or try to relate their families to larger generalizations about family behavior in different time periods. Stearns wants high school students to go beyond the recording of facts and discover not only "how it happened" but "what is the meaning of what happened?" They can do this only by learning how to handle various types of primary evidence, from documents and statistics to oral sources, to compare the activities, beliefs, and behaviors of their own lifetime with those of past eras.[25]

Oral history can deal with families and communities, but can it also be used to study the issues that are covered in the social studies curriculum?

Teachers who use oral history report that it is an especially powerful tool for addressing such social issues as the nuclear arms race, racism, the civil rights movement, human rights, war, and environmental issues. As a teaching device, it allows students to meet, hear from, and engage in discussion with people who have played a personal role in these social issues; it also presents students with different points of view and demonstrates the individual beliefs, opinions, and experiences that underlie people's social concerns.

Students—and other researchers—can be impressed and swayed by a single strong-minded interviewee. But they need to be made aware that social issues are inherently complex, and that the opinions from a single interview will not represent all sides of the issues. To obtain as complete a picture as possible, they must interview a variety of people representing different, conflicting points of view.[26]

Is oral history primarily an engaging extracurricular activity, or can it help improve students' learning skills?

Oral history is certainly no more than an educational accessory, but studies have shown that students respond more positively to it than to traditional methods of learning, and take more away from it. One analysis of the entire eleventh grade in a Baltimore County, Maryland, high school—including honors, average, and basic-ability students—compared oral history and traditional methods of instruction. Half the students considered immigration and black history using oral history, the other half explored these subjects using regular teaching methods. Tests given at the beginning and end of the four-week curriculum revealed that the oral history students at all levels of ability showed greater instructional gains than students taught by the traditional methods.

Those students using oral history felt that it had made their historical instruction more realistic. Particularly in the honors program, oral history students were more motivated to continue their learning about a topic even after the unit of study had been completed. Students appreciated oral history as a change of pace; as a highly creative activity; for making history more believable by associating real people with historical events; as an activity open to a great deal of student input; and as a project with "a real purpose." They also showed an appreciation for learning from fellow students rather than from their teachers.[27]

Does an oral history project have to be done by the whole class?

Definite benefits accrue from having all the students experience and discuss oral history, but interviewing also can be done by a single student, or a small group, as part of their own project. With the increasing popularity of cooperative learning, oral history offers ideal strategies for getting students to work together in teams (and many state performance assessments are concerned with cooperative efforts). Oral history can be a onetime project or an ongoing series of projects. Many individual students and groups of students use oral histories as part of their History Day projects.

Should a practice interview be conducted in class before students do their own interviews?

In-class interviews are a good way to demystify oral history for students. The teacher can conduct an in-class interview, or one or more students can serve as the interviewers. Invite someone connected with the school, an administrator, another teacher, a support staff member, or a parent, to be interviewed. Be sure to conduct the interview as seriously as possible. To be most effective, the in-class interview should be a real experience rather than playacting. Although adolescents adapt more easily than adults to using the technology of oral history, they still need experience in setting up the tape recorder and microphone to ensure the best sound quality—and a reminder that there is no third side on a cassette tape. (Many a good interview has been recorded over by a nervous interviewer.)

Before conducting the in-class interview, have the class as a whole plan the questions. Teachers find that students have more interest in the interview when their own questions will be asked. After the interview is finished, the class can discuss the effectiveness of different questions. Which questions encouraged the interviewee to open up and talk? Which questions gathered new information? Which questions proved to be dead ends or were poorly phrased? Did the interviewer follow up on unexpected leads? Tape-record the in-class interview so that portions can be replayed in the discussion.[28]

As the class scrutinizes the in-class interview, it should consider whether the interviewer interrupted the answers or failed either to pay attention or to follow up on information. The hardest thing to teach a student, or any interviewer for that matter, is to sit and listen to the interviewee's answers and not be too quick to ask the next question. Too many student interviews become a long string of questions followed by short, sometimes one-sentence answers, suggesting that the questions are too narrow, not open-ended, or that the interviewer has moved to the next question too quickly.[29]

What is the teacher's responsibility for the student's actual conduct of the interview?

Even though they probably will not accompany students to the interviews, teachers need to impress upon students the responsibilities and ethics of conducting interviews, especially in someone's home or office. Like any other interviewer, students need to schedule an appointment in advance and then keep it. Interviewers must appear on time, act courteously, and be careful not to damage people's property. Interviewers have an obligation to explain to their interviewees the purpose of the interviews and to respect any wish they may express not to talk about certain subjects. Students should have their interviewees sign release forms. Finally, they need to remember to thank interviewees for their cooperation, either verbally or in writing, and should give them a copy of any transcript that might be made. If the school produces a magazine, exhibit, slide-tape show, video documentary, or stage production based on the interview, invite the interviewees to the performances or functions; doing so ties the student, the project, and the school more firmly to the community and makes for good public relations.

Writing for the National Educational Association, John A. Neuen-schwander strongly recommended that students be made to realize that oral history interviewees "are not simply talking books" but require special handling. "The interviewer must always be sensitive to the interviewee's personal stake in the interview and avoid any psychological harm." Students, of all people, should not make their oral histories a test of older people's memories. The interviewee may not be able to recall specific names and dates or answer other detailed factual questions, and the experience may leave them feeling depressed.[30]

Should students process the interviews as well as conduct them?

Interviewing is only one step in teaching thorough oral history. While the interview is still fresh in their minds, students should review the entire tape to make sure it recorded properly and to prepare a summary of the remarks. Students can distribute these summaries to the class, relating their experiences and playing a portion of their tape. The class can analyze the sound quality of the tape, the types of questions asked, the quality of the content, the way the student opened and closed the interview, any distorted or slanted material, and how engaged the interviewer and the interviewee were in the interview. Some teachers ask students to review and evaluate each other's interviews.[31]

Transcription is arduous work, but it is not beyond the capabilities of most high school students. Students should attempt to transcribe at least a portion of their interviews, an exercise that will allow them to consider the amount of interpretation involved in converting spoken words into written form. Do people speak in full sentences or fragments? How do they determine punctuation and paragraphs? Does the transcript accurately reflect both what was spoken and the way it was spoken? How do transcripts deal with words that are spoken differently from the way they are written? What meanings are expressed when people use slang and street talk? The decisions that go into creating a transcript will force students to reexamine both the spoken and written word and will also help them develop their own writing skills. The completed transcripts can be included in student portfolios—in those schools that assess and grade portfolios of students' writings as a substitute for examinations.

How closely should the teacher monitor each student's interviews?

Teachers need to supervise individual students closely as they begin their projects. As useful and motivating an experience as oral history can be, without appropriate preparation it can be a total failure. Even well-prepared students feel apprehensive about conducting interviews. Throughout the course, the teacher should return to discussions of interviewing techniques, to keep students' minds focused, provide useful suggestions, and reinforce the lessons. After the students have done their first interviews, the teacher should try to meet with each one individually to review at least a portion of their interviews. Students will be anxious to know how well they performed and will need guidance on what they did right, and what needs improvement, before they do their next interviews.[32]

How should student interviews be evaluated?

No two interviews will be alike, but most interviews depend on the interviewer's skills, which can be graded. In monitoring the interviews, consider whether the student engaged in an informed dialogue or merely read scripted questions. Did the questions pursue thoughtful rather than perfunctory lines of inquiry? Did the interview collect useful information? It becomes clear after listening to a few tapes or reviewing a few transcripts how much the student's preparation, interview technique, and demeanor invoked a responsive chord in the interviewee.

From long experience in using oral history in the classroom, Frank Fonsino devised criteria that teachers can use to evaluate student interviews. These include:

1. What was the topic or focus of the interview?
2. Does the introduction to the tape provide sufficient information for the listener?
3. Does the interviewer use leading questions or make biased comments?
4. How capable was the interviewing style?
5. How good was the sound quality of the tape?
6. What is the historical value of the interview?[33]

When the class is over, what should we do with the completed oral histories?

Give the tapes and any transcripts to the school library. If the interviews are of particularly good quality and deal with the community, consider giving copies to the local public library as well. Collected oral histories in a nearby library will provide a valuable resource not only for future students preparing to do their own interviews but for researchers interested in the community's history. Since oral history often is conducted with the elderly, they may no longer be alive when others seek to interview them, and your students' interviews could be the only record they leave. The librarian may prefer not to receive the poorer collections, but students will value their work all the more if they know it will be permanently preserved in a library collection.[34]

Many high school students participate in state and national History Day contests. How have they used oral history in their entries?

National History Day (not a specific date, but a series of contests held on the local, state, and national level) provides an opportunity to see what students from schools across the nation are capable of doing. Modeled after science fairs, History Day contests are held in most states and several territories for students in grades 6 through 12. Annually, some 400,000 students and 20,000 teachers participate in local and state contests, and the winners advance to national competition. Students do projects, media presentations, papers, and dramatic performances based on a common theme ("Change and Continuity," "Turning Points in History," "Communication in History"). About one-third of the entries each year contain some use of oral history interviews.

Judges at History Day competitions have viewed some memorable projects based on oral history. Students from Asheville, North Carolina, videotaped an interview with the survivor of a Nazi concentration camp who was living in their community. Students in El Dorado, Kansas, discovered that their town had once housed a camp for German prisoners during the Second World War, and they interviewed one of the former prisoners, who had returned to live in the town after the war. Elementary and secondary school students in Toms River, New Jersey, interviewed shopkeepers to document the rise and fall of their Main Street. One junior high school student from Philadelphia studied the history of a chemical plant where his father worked, basing much of his information on interviews. The student made an appointment with the company vice president for public relations but told the man he seemed "too young" to be interviewed for a history project. The vice president located a 90-year-old retired employee who agreed to be interviewed, and whose answers indeed gave the project a long historical perspective.

Two students from Billings, Missouri, produced a slide-tape show, "Like Losing a Member of the Family," recounting the story of a century-old general store, The Mercantile, which had been demolished to make way for a convenience store. The students conducted a dozen interviews with people who had worked or shopped in the store, collecting their memories of Saturday shopping days, fires, depressions, bankruptcies, celebrations, and other memories to produce a touching tribute to a small-town institution that had fallen victim to the forces of modernization. They used photographs, newspaper ads, and other items submitted by their interviewees that captured the store as a patriotically decorated backdrop for parades from World Wars I and II and other town celebrations; indeed, the store had long been witness to all the town's daily business. The project won first prize in the senior media division, and the town's public library planned to accession the slide-tape show into its local history collection. "Our media presentation began as a local library project, hopefully to leave some record of the building when it was gone," the students reported. "But between our project's beginning and ending we have made so many new friends among the elderly in our town, and learned so much more about the history of the community that our research has seemed more fun than chore."[35]

History Day students have interviewed Japanese-Americans who were relocated and interned during World War II, farm protesters from the 1930s, and civil rights demonstrators of the 1950s and 1960s. They most often interview people in their own communities but have also interviewed over the phone, compensating for their lack of travel funds. A high school student in South Carolina sought to interview Rosa Parks about her role in the Montgomery bus boycott. Parks agreed but stipulated that the student and other members of his school history club read her autobiography before the interview.[36]

Using the following criteria, the Oral History Association presents annual awards to the students who make the best use of oral history in their History Day projects:

1. Were the interviews tape-recorded and/or videotaped?

2. Were the recordings of high quality (cassette and videotape)? Were the excerpts used of high quality?

3. Were the interviews transcribed, abstracted, and/or summarized?

4. How wide a range of interviews were selected? More than the immediate family? People on both sides of the controversy? etc.

5. Did the interviewer ask meaningful questions?

6. Did the interview elicit meaningful information?

7. Did the oral history interviews significantly influence the conclusions of the project/performance, etc.?

8. How was the oral history material incorporated into the project/performance (structure, analysis, and creativity)? Was it summarized, quoted, etc.?

9. Was the factual information verified for validity and accuracy?

10. Were the interviews properly cited?

The judges also consider the creativity and challenge of the topic.[37]

How supportive of oral history projects are school administrators?

Since oral history lies outside the standard curriculum, some administrators look upon it with suspicion, questioning the amount of class time necessary to prepare for, conduct, and process the interviews. It is advisable to submit a proposal to the school administration before starting an oral history project. The proposal should detail the project's objectives and methods of evaluation and indicate how oral history supports the regular curriculum and how it develops skills and teaches computer literacy. Buttress your case with manuals and published articles on oral history in the classroom. School administrators also are attracted by the argument that oral history projects can benefit the school's public relations with the community, both through the collection and the exhibition of the collected interviews and memorabilia.[38]

ORAL HISTORY IN UNDERGRADUATE AND GRADUATE EDUCATION

How widely is oral history taught in colleges and universities?

The number of college-level oral history methodology courses is difficult to measure, since course offerings have fluctuated and appear in different departments. Oral history may be dealt with not as a separate course but as part of a larger historiography course on conducting research and analyzing historical sources. Anthropology and other social sciences offer their own forms of instruction in fieldwork interviewing; oral history is also as likely to appear in the course offerings of the library school, the journalism department, or the American studies program as in history departments.

Oral history courses are offered more consistently at colleges and universities that have established oral history archives. Directors of the oral history archives often teach the courses, and class projects contribute to the larger oral history collection. In schools with no oral history archives, finding departments and teachers interested in oral history is usually more difficult than signing up students.

Oral history has also proved attractive within many community colleges, whether for adult-education or transitional studies between secondary school and the university. Conducting and processing interviews can develop and tap skills at all levels, even for those students approaching English as a second language. Classroom discussions can draw not only from the substance of the interview, but from the many styles of speaking.

Are methods courses in interviewing really necessary? Isn't it better for students to learn simply by going out and doing interviews?

Disciplines that employ fieldwork periodically have debated whether to teach interviewing as a methods course or to just send students out to experiment for themselves. Some argue that, since all field situations are different, students need to learn on their own and the only methods necessary are "sensitivity and creativity." Others concede that fieldwork requires more than simply mastering a textbook but contend that students still have to prepare themselves to do it right. Even though oral history interviewing is best learned by doing, students can learn much in the classroom, both before and after conducting their interviews.

The anthropologist John Forrest believes that before students go out to interview, they need to learn about the complexity of human interaction. In his methods course, he stipulated that "students had to *care* about what they were documenting" because their projects would take them into other people's lives. "If they were insensitive they knew that at best they would end up with no data, and at worst they would have hurt a fellow human." Finding subjects that genuinely mattered to them also helped motivate the students and made it less necessary for the instructor to "drone on about why fieldwork and data collection are important, or to show how good data leads on to appropriate social theory."[39]

The social sciences have been more consistent than the humanities in teaching fieldwork methodology. It undoubtedly is safe to assume that the majority of history undergraduates and graduate students who use interviews as part of their research have never taken an oral history course. Interviews are done seat-of-the-pants style—sometimes tape-recorded, more often captured in handwritten notes only; usually devoid of deeds of gift; and almost never conducted with the intention of depositing the completed interviews in an archive. Such interviews can still generate valuable information, despite needless mistakes, improper planning, and unnecessarily limiting procedures. The chief problem is that few graduate advisers have had any training themselves in oral history; they assume that anyone can interview and do not hold their students' oral sources to the same documentation standards as their written ones.

Graduate-level courses in oral history deal more with theory and methodology than do undergraduate courses. The growing literature in the field has increased the amount of background reading for these courses; although most students do interviews, some classes have permitted graduate students to write papers on theory and interpretation in lieu of interviewing. Some theoretical literature could also be introduced into undergraduate courses; the historian James Hoopes has observed that college students "should have a more ambitious goal than the *Foxfire* students' objectives of merely collecting information on customs, folklore, and habits." College students should be better able to interpret the material they collect, to place it in historical context, and to apply theory to their fieldwork interviewing.[40]

What problems are encountered in teaching oral history in undergraduate college classes?

Instructors find that their biggest problem is the uneven abilities and prior experience of their students. Although it is true that students of every ability level can benefit from doing oral history, teachers who seek to develop an oral history as a research methodology prefer students with some training in a particular area of study, such as ethnic, labor, cultural, or economic history or the social sciences. Students who lack such backgrounds often feel frustrated over the demands placed on them. They discover that oral history is a tool for study, not an end in itself, and that there is more to the process than just interviewing someone. In both the research before the interview and the interpretation afterwards, they must be able to place the material in its larger social or historical context. Some instructors have recommended offering oral history classes only as advanced electives—or, at the minimum, requiring students to have taken the basic survey classes in history—to ensure some control over students' levels of preparation.[41]

How should a college course on oral history be structured?

Structure and objectives will depend on the department in which the oral history is being taught and on whether it is an undergraduate or graduate level course. Library science courses, for instance, will focus more on the use of interviews in research libraries and archives, on developing standards for the acquisition and preservation of oral history materials, on integrating oral history materials into library and archival collections, and on using automated databases for the storage, retrieval, and cataloging of interviews. In other departments, oral history courses may concentrate more on the methodological literature of oral history, on designing and running oral history projects, or on the techniques of interviewing and the content and analysis of the interviews.

Since much supervision and review of students' work in oral history is required, it is advisable to keep classes small and manageable. Students may need help in finding people to interview, especially if the campus is geographically or culturally detached from the surrounding community. Because they operate best in a practical, "hands-on" environment, oral history classes should be taught as seminars or laboratories rather than in lecture halls.

Consider having the students monitor their own progress by maintaining a log in which they make regular notes on their impressions of the course, their readings, their interview objectives and preparations, and their observations of actual interview situations. What unexpected leads and information developed? Did the interviews differ from what they expected? How did they rate themselves as interviewers, and did they feel they improved over time? Students might submit these logs at the end of the term for extra credit.

Regardless of the discipline in which oral history or fieldwork interviewing is taught, students should be introduced to the use of oral techniques in other fields, from folklore to anthropology and social psychology. They should understand the different interview standards and objectives in different fields. Consider inviting to class guest lecturers from other disciplines to discuss how they use interviews in their research. Similarly, oral history courses often study the common forms of interviews that students have watched on television or read in newspapers and magazines, requiring them to monitor and critique the interviewing style of media interviewers.

Review the literature in the field—particularly that dealing with the ethical responsibilities of interviewing—familiarize the students with the equipment, and plan for practice interview sessions in the classroom. If the students plan to interview around a common theme, have them discuss the questions that might be asked of all interviewees, to provide for comparisons and to balance the detail and complexity of individual stories with generalizations about the historical experience. Since experiences vary so widely from interview to interview, students should be required to interview more than one person. (When one instructor discovered that his students were conducting short interviews as a means of reducing the amount of transcribing they had to do, he set a three-hour minimum for interviews.)[42]

After students have conducted their interviews, they should compose a brief paper not only about the interview, and the subject covered, but about the interviewee's place in local, regional, and national events. Students also should be required to transcribe at least portions of their interviews. Students are necessarily interested in the interview itself and impatient about learning the techniques of interviewing and processing interviews. It is imperative, however, to stress that poorly conducted interviews seriously undermine the end product—the information gathered by interview that the students hope to use themselves and to leave behind as an archival legacy.[43]

Finally, students should be encouraged to analyze and critique the type of information generated by oral history, the interviewer-interviewee relationship, and the validity of oral versus written sources. They should consider the ways in which oral history can be integrated into the larger historiographies of the subject matter, as well as the ultimate uses of oral history in research, publication, and public presentation. More and more oral history classes also include discussion of video interviews.

Can oral history be incorporated into classes other than methodology?

In addition to its value as a teaching tool, the content of oral history interviews is also important for classroom use. As historians increasingly investigate issues of race, ethnicity, and gender, oral history has become a means of having students collect information not covered in the older textbooks. History courses, for instance, instead of focusing entirely on the public sphere, are now using oral history to examine the activities in the private sphere of family and community.

Women's studies programs early adopted oral history in their curricula. At the University of Massachusetts at Boston, for instance, the women's studies program has had students conduct interviews with individuals outside the university about sex-role stereotyping, women's roles in the workplace, family relationships, and women's movement organizations. Summaries of these interviews form the basis of class discussions. Many of the students had known surprisingly little about their mothers' lives and began to reexamine and appreciate the strength of other "unnoticed, unrewarded female relatives." Women's history programs at Boston University and Simmons College have also provided useful generational studies, requiring students to interview two or more women in the same family, such as mother and daughter or aunt and niece. These interviews show cultural change over time, most notably in immigrant families. One student was astonished to learn that her Irish-Catholic grandmother had been a vociferous supporter of the birth-control advocate Margaret Sanger. In another set of interviews, a father stated that he and his wife had as many children as "God had sent them," while the mother admitted using a diaphragm. Women students reported seeing the source of many of their own ideas and beliefs when they interviewed family members.[44]

College oral history classes have seized on developing events in their own communities as subjects for student projects. When school integration became an issue in suburban Montgomery County, Maryland, nearby George Washington University launched an oral history project. The first stage in the project was compiling newspaper clippings on the issue, to prepare students to interview school officials, parents, and teachers. As it developed, the project uncovered a story that was far more complex than the newspaper reports had suggested. The students discovered, for instance, that the initiative for the most original element in the integration plan had come from teachers at the school rather than from the school board. Their interviews also revealed that, although men held most of the formal leadership positions in the various organizations involved, women had been most active in the grass-roots movement, "ringing doorbells, making phone calls, and using their organizational know-how to promote their respective causes." The transcripts of the interviews were deposited at the university library, where they became instructional material for courses in political science and education.[45]

Would a college itself be a suitable subject for an oral history?

Students, faculty, and alumni have participated in recording the histories of their schools, often in connection with school anniversaries. For the University of Kentucky oral history program, students have interviewed former and current presidents, administrators, faculty, and graduates. Interviews on the

181

subject of campus life and history conducted by students from Bryn Mawr to Stanford have been compiled not only as archival collections but as highly profitable books and videos marketed to alumni.[46]

When Northern Virginia Community College reached 20 years of age, 5 historians in the system began interviewing those who had started the community college system, built it, taught in it, and attended its first classes. They published 27 interviews with these "prime movers" and pioneers. "At the end of our labors as oral historians, some of us working within the methods of this subdiscipline for the first time, we have come to feel great pride in what we have been privileged to compile—this history of our college—as well as renewed pride in the college itself," they concluded. "We often felt ourselves in the presence of that admixture of pragmatism and idealism characteristic of so many of our once and current colleagues who have stamped these traits onto our colleges." The tapes and transcripts were deposited at one of the college system's libraries, where they form the nucleus of a research collection on the institution's beginnings.[47]

Doing oral history of one's own college or university is not always a celebratory practice. In May 1968, when student demonstrators took over Columbia University, the Columbia Oral History Research Office hired three advanced fellows from the School of Journalism to interview students, faculty, administrators, and mediators. Within a month's time, they had collected more than 1,500 pages of testimony. Interviewers from Cornell University conducted oral histories connected with the killings of two Jackson State University students by Mississippi state police very shortly after the incident. Cornell similarly conducted interviews related to the dramatic 1968 demonstrations on its own campus.[48]

Ultimately, what do undergraduates get out of taking oral history courses?

Undergraduates take oral history courses for any number of reasons, usually because they sound interesting and easy. Once enrolled, they find the subject much more complex than they had imagined. Oral history challenges their preconceived notions and makes them rethink how they research and analyze.

One prelaw student in an oral history class chose the topic of the impact of judges on the law, assuming that it was "a very easy way to get a good grade." Nothing came easy, however. The busy lawyers he interviewed kept taking phone calls, disrupting their answers, and straining his efforts to build rapport. Some answered precisely and briefly, quibbled over words, or evaded his questions. A circuit judge insisted on having his three rather obnoxious law clerks sit in on the interview. Despite these obstacles, the student collected valuable perspectives. What surprised him most was how often their answers disagreed with his written research. From his interviews, the student concluded that "the way a practitioner looks at the corpus of law differs greatly from the way a scholar investigates the law," a finding he suspected was true of other fields as well.[49]

Willa Baum, director of the Regional Oral History Office at the University of California at Berkeley, has observed that even in graduate school oral history helps students learn "to go and ask people for information." She noted that graduate students excel at doing library research and using transcripts of Berkeley's oral history interviews, "but they are appalled when we suggest that they should just go out and ask a person for information we don't have on our tapes or transcripts."[50]

What is the difference between an oral history class and a workshop?

Time, essentially. A class might extend over a 14-week semester; a workshop might last for only a single day. Many state and regional oral history organizations hold annual and semiannual workshops to serve as introductions for those just beginning and as refresher courses for those in midcareer. When oral history projects begin, they often seek an experienced oral historian to conduct a workshop to train volunteer interviewers and processors to ensure consistency in their product.

What role does oral history play in continuing education programs?

Oral history courses are offered in adult education programs and as summer institutes. People take such continuing education courses to aid them in changing careers, refreshing their knowledge, doing freelance interviewing, or interviewing family members or longtime community residents. A variety of such courses are publicized in the newsletters of the Oral History Association and its many state and regional affiliates.

Some of the most active oral historians are those who came to the field as a second career, often after raising families or retiring early, sometimes simply because they were looking for something interesting to do. Some study interviewing techniques and return to conduct oral histories within their previous profession. Others shift within a profession, such as librarians and archivists seeking training to start or continue an oral history collection in their institutions. If you want to do oral history, it is never too late to get some formal training.

8

PRESENTING ORAL HISTORY

After the interviewing is done, how can oral histories best be put to use?

After taking their interviews from the community, oral historians have an obligation to return the information, to share their findings with the community. The options for using oral history interviews are remarkably varied, limited only by imagination and financial resources. Previous chapters have discussed creating oral history archives, using oral history in published articles and books, and producing video documentaries. What follows are examples of additional uses that recognize the accessibility of oral history—literally, the words of the people—and the ease with which oral history interviews can be used in a number of arenas: in public presentations, in community and family history projects, in exhibits, on radio broadcasts, in stage productions, in interactive videos, and even in therapeutic settings.[1]

COMMUNITY HISTORY

What exactly is "community history," and how does oral history apply to it?

A community can be defined loosely as any group of people who share a common identity, whether based on location, racial or ethnic group, religious identity, organizational affiliation, or occupation. Obviously, communities differ considerably. One group may be fiercely proud of its collective identity, and another needs to be convinced that it is even a community or that its heritage is worth preserving. Oral historians have helped to broaden traditional notions of what constitutes a community's history by looking not only at its political and institutional structures but at its economic development and the ethnic and occupational composition of its population. Some oral history projects have tried to preserve lost communities, conducting interviews about buildings that were demolished or institutions that disappeared in all respects except in people's memories.[2]

In Philadelphia, Temple University developed the Discovering Community History Project, which encouraged residents of different neighborhoods to document their pasts through oral history, manuscripts, and photographs. The project staff wanted to aid and encourage the neighborhoods rather than do the work themselves. They started with a slide show to introduce the project to the community but discovered that merely stating the importance of the community's heritage was not very convincing. Neighbors initially hesitated to share memories and photographs they believed outsiders would consider commonplace. Slowly over time, and after repeated staff visits, residents eventually came to realize how their community looked to the outside, and how they could contribute to recording its history.

Temple's experience demonstrated that such projects cannot expect the same response from every community. The most significant differences in neighborhood response to the project were based on neither race nor class but on the neighborhood's recent history and demographics—that is, on whether it was stable, declining, or undergoing gentrification. The project achieved its greatest successes in those neighborhoods with strong community organizations—civic associations, clubs, churches and synagogues, especially those that cared for the elderly—that were willing to take charge of contacting potential interviewers and interviewees, "assigning tasks, checking up, and following through." Communities that lacked organizations with such clout, or where community associations were distracted by more pressing concerns, proved the hardest to convince of the merits of oral history.[3]

Noting that people who live in the same area can actually be quite distant from each other, the D.C. Community Humanities Council sponsored the City Lights Program to bring scholars, storytellers, and other performers to senior citizens living in public housing to talk about their common culture and history. At the predominantly African-American Potomac Gardens, these discussions focused on religious traditions, migration from the South to the city, work as domestics, living through the Depression, and the Washington riots of 1968. The elderly residents of Potomac Gardens had attended school at a time when, except for references to slavery, black people did not exist in the history textbooks, which gave them little sense of having contributed anything worthwhile to society. The City Lights Program emphasized how important their experiences were, and how much they had in common with each other. "We were strangers before," Thelma Russell, a member of the community, asserted. "Now we understand that our common ground is the African-American heritage that we share."

Senior citizens at Potomac Gardens collected the stories of their struggles and accomplishments to leave as a record for their children and grandchildren. Supported by a Humanities Council grant, they conducted a door-to-door survey in their building and collected data about the residents. Drawing from this information, they scheduled weekly meetings, focusing each week on a different birthplace and encouraging the residents to share their personal memorabilia and stories of home and migration. With the assistance of the local historical society, the seniors learned how to interview each other. A local video production company videotaped the interviews, from which they produced a documentary video, *In Search of Common Ground* (1993). A curator from the Anacostia Neighborhood Museum helped residents develop an exhibit from their project. Both the video and the exhibit were displayed at schools, public housing sites, and other neighborhood organizations throughout the city and will be preserved as a legacy for the future. "We may not be rich," Thelma Russell concluded, "but we are rich in history."[4]

Can oral history be used to aid historic preservation?

Preservationists have tapped the memories of still-living informants to reconstruct the material culture of the past—furnishings, tools, structures, vehicles, and many other physical objects—and to determine how these items were used, by whom, and how they fit into the broader social and economic patterns of the community. Oral history has helped gather the details of day-to-day life in historic buildings—to re-create period furnishings and decorations—through interviews with those who visited the house during the era in question, often when it was associated with a particular family or prominent individual. Their memories bring color to the black-and-white photographs of the past and provide context for otherwise sketchy and incomplete documentary evidence.

In seeking to save San Diego's older architecture during a period of massive redevelopment, the Downtown San Diego Project found gaps in the official records that only oral history could fill. Project members interviewed construction crews and demolition company employees to determine the extent to which bulldozers and backhoes had penetrated certain areas. The California Office of Historic Preservation called for interviews with the state's architects and engineers and advocated interviews with those in the building trades, those who established the utility networks, transportation planners, bridge builders, and officials of the development agencies in local government.[5]

On a national level, the National Historical Preservation Act of 1966 has required federal agencies to consider how such federally funded projects as highway construction, dams, reservoirs, airports, and parks affect local cultural resources. To carry out this mandate, cultural resource management (CRM) teams have applied the insights of archaeology, architectural history, folklore, and oral history to urban planning, resource conservation, public works projects, and commercial development. While archaeologists were working on a CRM crew in Irion County, Texas, they uncovered hundreds of what first appeared to be prehistorical petroglyphs in a limestone outcropping. But they also found the carved name of Burt Smalley, dated 1921; by then, Smalley was deceased. The mystery was solved through oral history interviews with surviving family members and old-timers in the community. These interviews developed a portrait of a recluse who spent his time carving petroglyphs in the rocks near his ranch.

Oral history interviews have helped CRM projects locate unmarked gravesites and abandoned farmsteads, as well as the otherwise unrecorded names of sharecroppers. Interviews have helped reconstruct farmers' living patterns, including the layout of yards and houses, gardens, fields, wells, barns, and privies. "Oral history can turn a prairie foundation into Hansford County's one-room Palo Duro Schoolhouse," noted Dan Utley, an oral historian who works with CRM teams. "Oral history can transform seemingly unrelated artifacts—a Model T transmission, a scatter of bricks, and welded metal barrels—into an irrigation system used to pump Concho River water up a steep bank and across a ravine to what was a parched cotton field in the 1950s."[6]

Does it matter whether the interviewer on a community project is an "outsider"?

Just as the race and gender of the interviewer and interviewee may affect the interview, whether the interviewer comes from the subject community will influence what is said. The Temple Discovering Community History Project found that its best interviews often came from enthusiastic amateurs in the community. Because "spontaneity and candor naturally extended between friends, neighbors and people of the same background," it was easier for these insiders to establish rapport. But with thorough research, persistent effort, and the right personality, interviewers from outside a community can also build the kind of rapport that facilitates interviewing. In fact, all oral historians constantly find themselves shifting between the roles of "insider-outsider, historian-listener, participant-observer, minority-majority, student-teacher, apprentice-mentor." What is important is that interviewers become conscious of these varying relationships and how they influence their interviews. Those who have engaged in extensive fieldwork interviewing in communities in which they are outsiders strongly recommend that interviewers keep a journal of their impressions of the community and their changing relations within it.[7]

Won't a community only volunteer information that will make it look good?

Communities naturally seek to preserve and present their best image. Interviewers often find themselves being steered toward those who tell the "success" stories; they must attempt to record the dissatisfied as well. Interviewers also need to avoid being seduced by the democratic impulse of oral history to just "let people speak for themselves." Unquestioned and unchallenged memory can veer toward the nostalgic. The oral historian's job is not to celebrate the past but to explore and document its diversity and complexities.

At the same time, people's privacy becomes an issue when recording a community's oral history. Interviewers must consider what right they have to raise questions that embarrass the community, especially if they are outsiders who will not remain there to live with the consequences. When dealing with a community's denial of a difficult or traumatic event or issue, interviewers ask challenging questions and then give people an opportunity to respond, but they must also honor interviewees' refusal to address certain issues. Clearly, it is essential to interview as broadly as possible. Some people cannot or will not reflect on painful issues of the past, but others have just as strong an impulse to bring the same issues out into the open.

Stories and opinions within a community will probably vary widely. When oral historians try to determine which versions are more reliable, they seek patterns—another reason to interview more than one type of person in a community. Rather than simplifying the past, oral historians complicate the history by collecting counterevidence and challenging simple answers. The picture of the community that emerges from the interviews is thus most likely to be neither all good nor all bad.

What if the community will not cooperate at all?

Interviewers usually assume that the community will be pleased, flattered, and empowered by being the focus of an oral history project, but some communities want no attention and consider any project suspicious and intrusive.

In New York City, the public historian Joe Doyle studied the Chelsea neighborhood on Manhattan's West Side. Situated along the Hudson River docks, Chelsea had a history as a longshoremen's and seamen's community. During the 1940s the Longshoremen's Union had expelled its Communist members, badly splitting the neighborhood. Then, during the 1950s, newspapers had published lurid exposés of organized crime on the waterfront. A "code of silence" developed in the neighborhood, and Chelsea residents would not talk to the police or to outsiders. In later years the neighborhood residents had no desire to reminisce about those troubled times. "As for talking at the present time to young historians eager for 'oral history,' it still does not quite sit right with old-timers," Doyle concluded. Uncomfortable with its history, the National Maritime Union destroyed all its noncurrent records; nor were its members interested in re-creating those records through oral testimony. Far more willing to talk about the past were the members of the Marine Workers Historical Association, many of them battle-scarred "Reds" who had been ejected from the union. Pragmatically aiming his project toward the most cooperative segment of the community, Doyle shifted the focus of his interviews to the Communist party on the waterfront. But even that subject was still so sensitive that people had second thoughts about speaking for the record. When Doyle organized an "oral history day" for residents, none of the invited speakers appeared. Doyle then gave the oral history a "breathing space" of two years, after which he opened a second round of public meetings. By that time some of the tensions and opposition to studying waterfront history had begun to decrease. His persistence even encouraged local Longshoremen's Union officials to speak more openly. Doyle's experiences suggest that interviewers facing uncooperative communities need to give them time rather than to give up their projects.[8]

How do you return community oral histories to the community?

A project's immediate goal may simply be to record the recollections of key members of a community, but it should consider long-term objectives as well. The ultimate goal may be a book, play, exhibit, videotape, or other public presentation that depicts the patterns and themes of importance to the community.

Excerpts from oral histories can be published in local newspapers or broadcast over local radio stations or community-access television channels. The oral historian Charles Hardy produced a series of five radio programs, "Goin' North: Tales of the Great Migration," based on interviews with African-Americans who left their homes in the South to relocate in the City of Brotherly Love. The *Philadelphia Inquirer* ran a special education supplement to serve as a companion to the series and to encourage listeners—particularly students—to collect similar information about their own families.[9]

Community oral historians have found outlets for their work in brochures distributed by the local chamber of commerce to promote the area and as source material for secondary social studies classes studying local history. Oral history has been incorporated into exhibits, walking tours, and dramatic productions. The key to public presentation of a community history is always to display the material where people will actually see it. A local history society or museum may be eager to participate but may not attract many viewers. Instead, consider displaying the exhibit at a shopping mall, senior citizens' center, public library, school, union hall, church, or civic organization to reach a broader cross-section of the community. Find out where people congregate in the community and put your exhibit there. Hold a reception to show the exhibit, invite the interviewees, make a formal presentation of their interviews, and allow the rest of the community to view the product.

In Idaho a county museum director used oral history to catch the attention of the area's schoolchildren and to attract them to the museum. She conducted interviews on women's rural life and roles in the county during the early decades of the twentieth century and turned the interviews into a 45-minute presentation that combined a slide show, period music, museum props, and a narration by a character in costume. The production traveled to every school in the county, as well as to many senior citizens' organizations.[10]

The Montana Historical Society encouraged the collection of historical materials on Montana's many women's clubs by producing a booklet, *Molders and Shapers: Montana Women as Community Builders: An Oral History Sampler and Guide* (1987) that detailed how clubs could collect their histories through club records, minute books, financial records, yearbooks, luncheon programs, newspaper clippings, and craftwork. From these archives, interviewers from the clubs could gain a better sense of what topics to cover and what questions to ask in club oral histories. *Molders and Shakers* urged club members to be imaginative in getting the stories generated from the oral histories back to the community, recommending that the clubs consider publishing newspaper articles drawn from the interviews, creating a booklet on the club's history featuring excerpts from the interviews and accompanying photographs, or producing slide-tape shows with interview excerpts as narration. The oral histories were incorporated into lesson plans on women's experience for local history classes. Transcripts also provided scripts for readers' theaters—club members presenting dramatic readings of the interviews. *Molders and Shakers* reminded women's club members that the results of oral history can be shared with the club's own membership or made more widely available as a public program at a local library or community center.[11]

How have folklife festivals used oral histories?

A staple of folklife festivals, oral histories have been conducted before audiences: interviewees tell their story, play their music, or demonstrate their craft. In 1981, with little in the way of funds, staff, or publicity, the Center for Southern Folklore turned a previously commercial crafts festival, the Sorghum Days Folk Festival, into a folklife festival by arranging for people to demonstrate their techniques and talk about their lives and work. The festival brought together white and black crafts workers and presented the differences and similarities in their heritage; it drew large and appreciative audiences of local residents and out-of-town visitors. Similarly, the Mid-South Folklife Festival invited blues musicians to perform and then to participate in oral history workshops by being interviewed by professional historians and discussing how the conditions of the rural, segregated South influenced their music.

Oral history has been prominently featured at the Smithsonian Institution's annual folklife festivals on the Mall. One event in the mid 1980s blended generations as well as races and genders by bringing together sleeping-car porters and airline stewardesses to compare the similarities and differences in their jobs before an audience that had never before fully appreciated what went into their work. The 1992 festival celebrated the bicentennial of the White House by inviting White House workers, from stone cutters to table setters, to reflect on their careers and on the many occupants of the White House whom they had served. Their behind-the-scenes testimony was supported by photographs, menus, and other memorabilia.[12]

FAMILY INTERVIEWING

Can oral history be used to collect family history?

There always seems to be at least one relative who retains the family lore, who can identify every obscure photo in the family album, and who corresponds with far-flung kin. Or there is a family member with an interesting past that we have always wanted to ask about. They make logical candidates to interview, but somehow no one has gotten around to it. Suddenly they are gone, taking with them all that unrecorded family history. Christopher Columbus's son Fernando admitted to a hazy knowledge of his father's early life and voyages, "for he died before I made so bold as to ask him about such things; or to speak more truly, at the time such ideas were farthest from my boyish mind."[13]

The traditional means of tracing one's family tree through census reports, city directories, and ship manifests can be supplemented with the recorded memories of living relatives. Older family members are repositories of stories about their childhood and of stories their parents and grandparents told them about the family's past, about immigration, about former residences, and about changes in the family name over time. They often feel a responsibility for passing along the family traditions to the following generations—who are not always appreciative or responsive. Grandparents are usually willing to talk, but their children and grandchildren, feeling they have heard these stories too often before, have never taken the trouble to record them. Then, too, it is hard to admit that older relatives will not always be around to be interviewed later.

Families can do their own interviews—a number of useful guidebooks include sample questions—or they can hire professional interviewers. Many family interviewing services have developed; they conduct interviews and produce tapes, transcripts, videotapes, and book-length family histories. The interviews become family keepsakes to be passed along, and copies can be given to alma maters, church libraries, or local public libraries.[14]

Is doing a family oral history any different from doing other oral histories?

To get a good interview, family oral histories should follow the same standards and procedures that apply to any other oral history. Prepare a family history questionnaire that includes some standard questions to ask all the family members to be interviewed as well as specific questions for each interviewee. Even for a family interview a legal release is advisable, so that the tapes and transcripts might someday be deposited in a suitable library.

Family oral histories need not be just a series of anecdotes. They can tell not only the "who" and "what" in a family but the "why" as well—the motives and attitudes that research in traditional genealogical sources would not necessarily bring to light. Sometimes the interviews provide clues that lead the interested family researcher to other sources of family documentation, such as the name of a town where family members once lived, or the location of a cemetery where birth and death dates appear on tombstones, dates that in turn help in locating newspaper obituaries. Traditional sources of family history provide preliminary research for the interviews. Family Bibles often contain dates of births, deaths, and marriages. In addition, school diplomas, letters, and local newspaper clippings provide basic information about family members.

Families reflect their times and communities. Questions can be directed at family life during the Great Depression, the Second World War, the cold war, the turbulent 1960s, the civil rights movement, the women's rights movement, and other sociohistorical periods. Family interviewers pursuing such questions should familiarize themselves with some of the history of these larger events, perhaps through reading basic history textbooks; such preparation generates questions to ask and frames the interviewee's story against a larger backdrop.

But do not limit your family oral history to a simple collection of pleasant memories. Family pasts may include stories of feuds or deaths that may be painful to revisit but are important for understanding family relationships. Some family members may be reluctant to dredge up unhappy memories, and others will want to use the interviews to settle a few scores.[15]

When Corinne Krause interviewed three generations of ethnic American women in Pittsburgh, she found that grandmothers, mothers, and daughters offered dissimilar versions of the same family's shared history. Their stories suggest how family members experience the same events and react to the same individuals in different ways, depending on their age, attitudes, and expectations. Krause recorded the conflicts between the generations, but she also tracked their deep bonds and persistent values. She conducted her initial round of interviews during the 1970s, a time when the granddaughters were in open rebellion against old traditional family ways. When she returned a decade later, most of the grandmothers had died and their granddaughters had married and had their own children, in whom they were trying to instill the traditional values of their families.[16]

Bill Fletcher, whose book *Recording Your Family History* (1986) offers a multitude of sample questions to ask family members, has noted that the geographic spread and mobility of modern society has led to less frequent interaction between the generations of many families. Families often see each other only on holidays or during vacations and other limited encounters. Fletcher views taping an oral history as an excuse "to talk across the generational lines." Similarly, Linda Shopes has argued that doing family oral history "can be the impetus for developing or deepening relationships with other family members. Even more important, it can enhance one's own sense of identity."[17]

Will my family oral history be of any use to anyone outside my family?

Yes, because family history is part of popular culture and has become a subject of scholarly study. Researchers are increasingly interested in the lives of everyday people and open to looking at family oral histories for valuable information. The information a family wants from oral history interviews—treasured stories, information on births, deaths, weddings, divorces, graduations, jobs, and trips—are the same subjects that social historians now study.

Oral history can record a family's daily patterns of living, how the household was organized, how the family spent money, who sat where at the dining table, and what types of meals were served. Since these topics are common to all families, researchers use data from one family to compare with data on others as they compile aggregates from which to make generalizations about social patterns. "From classroom projects for family efforts to large research projects, the possibilities for such family history are endless," the historian Carl Ryant noted. "What is required is a greater scholarly sensitivity to the possibilities of oral history and family history. This should result not only in more extensive scholarly analysis of existing data but also better quality data being generated for future analysis."[18]

THERAPEUTIC USES OF ORAL HISTORY

What therapeutic value do the elderly get from recording their oral histories?

Near the end of his life, the journalist Henry Fairlie commented that "in growing old, one has a stocked attic in which to rummage and the still passing show and pageant of life to observe, not only at a more leisurely pace, but with the convincing satisfaction and interest of having lived through many of the changes, even from their beginnings, that have brought us from there to here." The object of oral history interviews with elderly people is to collect their recollections for the record, but the elderly themselves also gain something from the process. Aristotle observed that the elderly "are continually talking of the past, because they enjoy remembering." Some in a family may scoff that their older relatives are "living in the past," but as the gerontologist Robert Butler noted, elderly people naturally pass through a period of life review. As people take stock of their lives, they may reveal information that they have long suppressed, even from their families.[19]

Oral historians often comment on the eagerness with which many older people agree to be interviewed. The elderly seem to return to their youth while talking about it. They act more animated and treat the knowledgeable interviewer as a contemporary. Their children and grandchildren have heard snatches of these stories for so long that they no longer ask about them; the interviewee's friends and other contemporaries may be deceased. The folklorist Patrick Mullen thought that it was "as if elderly persons are waiting for someone to come along and ask for their stories, and the folklorist had better be a good listener." Henry Glassie also noted that "old tellers of tales are not astray in a wilderness of nostalgia. . . . They fill a crucial role in their community. They preserve its wisdom, settle its disputes, create its entertainment, speak its culture. Without them, local people would have no way to discover themselves."[20]

Nursing homes have encouraged and sometimes hired oral historians to record the reminiscences of their residents. The Parker Jewish Geriatric Institute in New Hyde Park, New York, videotaped interviews with its residents. These interviews provided families with "a lasting record of treasured stories" but also had therapeutic value for the storytellers, who came away from the experience feeling more positive about themselves and their lives. "It reaffirms for them that their lives were valuable and productive," concluded Edith Shapiro, the institute's director of therapeutic recreation.

For others, the experience of being interviewed for an oral history stimulates a cathartic release of long-pent-up emotions. Ronald Marcello has interviewed hundreds of Americans who were prisoners of war during the Second World War. "One byproduct has been some therapeutic value for the men," said Marcello. Many had been encouraged by their wives and children to participate in the taping. "Some say to me, 'I wouldn't have talked to you about this in 1946. The scars were too recent.' " Yet oral historians should keep in mind that the recall of painful memories can have traumatic as well as therapeutic effects. Those who have interviewed Holocaust victims, for instance, report that some interviewees express a felt duty to leave a record for future generations, but that doing the interviews triggered recurring nightmares.[21]

Are there any special considerations for interviewing in nursing homes?

Nursing homes have been described as places "where biography ends," since the residents so often have no knowledge of their neighbors' past lives before they became old and infirm. Yet when Tracy Kidder researched his book *Old Friends* (1993), he was always welcomed because older people enjoyed having someone to talk with. "Old people have nothing to do but try to make meaning out of their lives," he concluded.[22]

A video interviewer who works in nursing homes has suggested that the interviewer try to put the person in a comfortable setting, "preferably a favorite place—with soft, flattering light." As a starting place for her interviews, she usually asks about such enjoyable family occasions as weddings and bar mitzvahs to give the interviewee a chance to introduce all the characters of the story "in a celebratory manner."

Those working with the elderly recommend asking about a particular event or occasion more than once. The chances are that the second time the question is asked it will receive a more thorough answer, since the interviewee will have had time to remember it more vividly. Memory cues become increasingly useful with older interviewees. Sometimes an old photograph or song will bring back the past to them. Photo albums are even more helpful, since they are generally arranged in chronological order. A company in Madison, Wisconsin, called Bi-Folkal Productions sells "reminiscence resources" to nursing homes and libraries. The company produces a dozen different kits that use slides, tapes of sing-alongs, poetry, and photographs and are based on topics like pets, summertime, train rides, and the Depression. The company reasoned, for instance, that playing radio clips from a particular time would elicit memories that no question could ever tap.

The American Association of Retired People (AARP) has acknowledged the therapeutic value of oral history and storytelling among the elderly and established its own reminiscences program to train interviewers. AARP also publishes a guide to help volunteers elicit life stories. In Minneapolis, the Retired Senior Volunteers Program did oral histories of local senior citizens on such subjects as desegregating hotels and restaurants in the city, wartime experiences, and caring for the hungry and homeless. The project was cosponsored by a local radio station, which edited the tapes for weekly broadcast and then deposited them at the Minnesota Historical Society.[23]

Is there therapeutic value in oral history for anyone other than the elderly?

Any group that has gone through a troublesome common experience can benefit from documenting impressions and memories through oral history interviews. The Women Miners History Project has recorded the lives of women coal miners, many of whom are still young or middle-aged women. They began collecting interviews during the 1980s, a period of crisis for women miners because jobs were disappearing rapidly and the miners' union was battling for survival. Many of the women had been thrown into indefinite unemployment and faced a bleak economic future.

During a particularly difficult period, the women miners were able to use the oral history program "as a means of emotional support." The project developed an exhibit out of the personal collections, writings, artwork, and other historical materials related to women miners and conducted videotaped interviews. According to Marat Moore, the project's director, the interviews helped establish "an affirming context" for the women miners: "Our questions involve how we have fared, do we go on from here, and whatever happened to affirmative action in mining and other high-skilled, high-paying industries."[24]

In another example, Northwestern University Medical School instituted an oral history of AIDS patients to learn how hospital personnel could care for them more effectively. Interviews with nurses and other AIDS caregivers at the medical school and associated clinics identified the characteristics, values, training, and behavior needed to treat AIDS patients. Interviewers reported that interviewees frequently commented that the project made them stop and reflect for the first time on what they do in response to having AIDS.[25]

MUSEUM EXHIBITS

Has the use of oral history changed museum exhibits?

Historical museums were once dimly lit halls, seemingly designed for nothing more than the veneration of objects, which were grouped together without much sense of how people had once used them. Lights could be low since there were few captions to be read. Museums are better illuminated now, allowing visitors to read longer, more informative captions for items that are woven together to tell a story of a time, place, event, or people. "History is not the old walking plow but the person who walked behind it," as one museum curator asserted. Many historical museums have incorporated oral history tapes and excerpts from transcripts into their exhibits, which allow visitors to hear the voices of the people who used the objects on display or lived through the events depicted. Interviews not only enhance a museum's displays and exhibits but provide material for public talks and media presentations.[26]

The deindustrialization of the American Rust Belt has generated a number of industrial heritage museums that use oral histories to capture the memories of workers, whether of the preunion era or the heyday of unionization. The labor historian James B. Lane recommended that interviews focus on a wide range of attitudinal studies "about such matters as safety conditions and ecological standards, labor organizing and union-management relations, workplace folktales and corporate customs, and the bureaucratization process in both unions and businesses." Oral historians need to interview not only employees and employers but competitors and customers, and the topics covered should include the machinery, the foremen, and the relationships between workers, especially in industries that have grown obsolete.[27]

Nearly every museum in the vast Smithsonian complex has collected oral history interviews and integrated them into their exhibits. From the Smithsonian's Anacostia Neighborhood Museum to the National Air and Space Museum, interviews are displayed to visitors in audio and visual form and as part of the text of exhibits. The National Museum of American History has long collected and displayed artifacts of American advertising. In the 1980s it realized that its collection consisted of newspaper advertisements, trade cards, tearsheets, and other static objects, but that it had no representations from modern multimedia advertising or from the advertising agencies that created and implemented modern advertising campaigns. The Smithsonian did oral histories with executives of BBD&O (Batten, Barton, Durstine &

Osborn) to collect memories and obtain films of television advertisements, jingles, and other memorabilia relating to its "Pepsi Generation" ad campaign—interviews that revealed how much of the campaign was spontaneous, not planned. Created as an archival collection, with descriptive brochures and finding aids, the taped interviews and television advertisements became part of an audiovisual exhibit at the museum. Historians, archivists, and curators working on the project discovered that they had not only created new material for scholarly research and museum use but had "established a healthy working relationship between a private corporation and a public research institution. This relationship went beyond financial support, in that employees of the company identified and contacted potential interviewees and encouraged their cooperation."[28]

What are the problems of using oral history in museum displays?

Museum curators use oral history to connect objects with the people who used them, in an attempt to "bridge the gap between representation and reality." Oral history can be inserted as sound or video played at stations throughout an exhibit, or transcripts can be excerpted in captions and other text to inform visitors. Some exhibits incorporate interviews in documentaries shown in small theaters, usually before or after the exhibit; others intersperse the oral history material throughout the collection on various monitors and interactive videos. Since usually only a fraction of the interviews can be used, selection, editing, and brevity of remarks are all-important. As David Lance has noted, such display tapes are "most effective when they combine a variety of speakers and a range of subject content in short and pithy juxtaposition."

The extensive use of audio and visual playback machines can escalate the costs of mounting an exhibit, and there is always the risk that the machines will break down. It can be a depressing experience to walk through an exhibit with darkened gaps in its presentation owing to malfunctioning machines. Too often the equipment has been "adapted for exhibition purposes rather than designed for it" and breaks down because of the strain of continuous playback. Showing documentary films and videos with sound or having audio broadcasts requires a careful positioning of speakers "and a fairly elaborate arrangement of equipment and wiring that takes careful planning and craftsmanship to conceal." Using loudspeakers so that all may hear can be distracting; listening to repeated playback of the same tape becomes unnerving, and many museums have opted to use headsets for individual listening. Tape-recorded tours that are played individually can also include oral history excerpts.[29]

RADIO AND ORAL HISTORY

How has oral history been used in radio broadcasts?

Since both involve recorded human speech, oral history is "custom built for radio," according to David Dunaway, an oral historian who has produced radio documentaries. Radio production is less costly than producing video documentaries, and radio studios operate in all kinds of communities throughout the nation, from inner cities to rural counties, and on the campuses of many universities. The growth of national and local public radio stations has especially stimulated interest in producing and broadcasting historical documentaries over the radio, and funding agencies have underwritten some ambitious projects. "The craft of radio production rises to art in the hands of someone fashioning a program from disparate interviews, ambient noise, and historical recordings such as speeches and old radio broadcasts," Dunaway notes. "By juxtaposing these elements the expert producer creates a textured tapestry of sound, complete with the built-in punctuation of pauses and music."[30]

Oral history–based radio broadcasts have included "Living Atlanta," an urban history of Atlanta, Georgia; "First-Person America," reminiscences of the Great Depression; and the life and times of New York City's colorful mayor Fiorello LaGuardia. The University of Alabama funded an oral history of Alabama blacks who worked as coal and iron ore miners, sharecroppers, union organizers, domestics, teachers, ministers, lawyers, and small-business operators. Focusing on Birmingham, Alabama, which in the 1920s had the largest black population of any major U.S. city, the project resulted in a dozen half-hour radio programs, "Working Lives," that was broadcast on National Public Radio (NPR).[31]

The Blues Archives at the University of Mississippi worked with Media Production International of Memphis, Tennessee, to produce "The Original Down Home Blues Show," a regular NPR series. The program combines blues music with interviews with the musicians. Each interviewee is asked to select the records played on the show, a practice that the producers feel reveals "a deeper insight into their sense of memory of place and time." Recognizing that music is their livelihood, and that blues is a particularly marketable form of oral history, the producers feel a moral obligation not only to secure the rights of interviewees for their copyrighted material but to pay them a fee for their contributions to the show. In return, such programs provide outstanding publicity for oral history archives and stimulate use of its collections.[32]

If radio and oral history are so compatible, why has there not been more oral history on the radio?

Oral history archivists often feel frustrated that radio producers do not make greater use of their collections as raw material for documentaries. More often trained as journalists than historians, and working under tight deadlines and budget constraints, radio producers are often loath to spend the time needed to review long archival tapes. Too often they find the sound quality of archival tapes inadequate for broadcast use. Radio documentary producers may find it easier simply to do their own interviewing, using broadcast studio equipment and asking questions specific to their project—an alternative that is possible, of course, only if there are survivors left to interview.[33]

To expand use of their collections, oral historians need to recognize the differences between their type of interviewing and radio interviewing and to try, when possible, to accommodate radio's needs. "Radio producers work with action, sensation, emotion, and audio presence as their palette, the oral historian with objectivity and verisimilitude," Dunaway argued. "Both pursue truth, on different roads." Oral historians must improve the sound quality of their recordings and preserve them under optimal archival conditions for future use. Radio producers pick and choose from many different interviews, editing and rearranging them, adding music and sound effects, and rarely using more than a fraction of a single interview. Interviews therefore need to be abstracted or indexed for easy retrieval. Oral historians can work with radio producers to identify the most colorful dialogue, revealing anecdotes, emotional interludes, and those moments of verbal eloquence that can give spark to a documentary. Interviewers can also explain the themes and historical framework of the interviews. They need to take some care that the rights of the interviewees are protected, and that in the editing and excerpting of the interviews for broadcast, the meaning is not distorted and the interviewees are not held up to ridicule.[34]

ORAL HISTORY ON STAGE

If an oral history project has already resulted in an archival collection or a book, what is the advantage of trying to turn it into a stage production?

Taking their material from the community, oral historians want to return it to the community, but they recognize that the community may never read their books and articles. The six authors who collaborated on the highly acclaimed book *Like a Family: The Making of a Southern Cotton Mill World* (1987) recognized that, as a university press publication, it reached a predominantly academic audience. They had collected the life stories of the mill workers, then processed, edited, interpreted, and published them, but the authors wanted to do even more to "keep the stories alive and keep history ongoing." Recognizing how much interviews involve storytelling, and that these stories were already in a sense a performance, the speech communications department at the University of North Carolina at Chapel Hill offered an independent study course in which 11 undergraduates read through the interview transcripts and pulled characters and dialogue from the book to produce a script. In 1988 they took the play to many mill towns throughout North and South Carolina. The producers observed that audiences, seeing their own lives performed on stage, responded instinctively, "imitating what was going on and talking to each other about it." At the end of each performance, the cast would remain to talk with the audience, who contributed additional stories and argued with cast over interpretation, keeping alive the collaborative process between history and performance.[35]

In Baltimore and St. Paul, groups have used oral histories to produce stage plays about local history for local audiences. The Baltimore Voices oral history project was initiated in 1978 to explore and present in popular forms the social history of Baltimore's six oldest neighborhoods. A team of professional historians, graduate students, and community historians interviewed over 200 people, transcribed the interviews, and divided them into such common topics as family, neighborhoods, ethnicity, religion, work and labor, income, wages and expenditures, education, immigration and migration, race, prejudice, and the Great Depression. From these, they produced hundreds of one-page stories, with different ethnic groups, broken down by neighborhoods. The Baltimore Theatre Project organized these excerpts into a play, also named *Baltimore Voices* (1981), which was presented in the various Baltimore neighborhoods and videotaped as a documentary. The same year the Baltimore Voices project started, the St. Paul History Theatre produced the first in a series of oral history–based plays. In the 1970s and 1980s its repertoire included *The Deadly Decades*, dealing with the effects of Prohibition on the city; *You Can't Get to Heaven through the U.S.A.*, about Swedish and Italian immigrants; *We Win or Bust*, about a railroad strike; and *Nina! Madam to a Saintly City*, the story of police corruption and a famous operator of a local bordello. The playwright Arthur Miller turned Studs Terkel's oral history *Working* into the stage play *An American Clock* (1982).[36]

In the 1990s students at Cuyahoga Community College conducted oral histories in ethnic and minority neighborhoods in Cleveland, Ohio, from which *The People of Cleveland: Building Community* was drawn. Accompanying dialogue from the life histories were slides and music and dance performances. *The People of Cleveland* played to more than 100 audiences in churches, schools, and neighborhood organizations. Another play, *Growing up and Growing Old*, drew from interviews about life cycles and sought to overcome negative stereotypes of the elderly.[37]

COMPUTERS AND INTERACTIVE VIDEO

Computers have been a boon to transcribing oral histories, but can they be used for presenting the material as well?

Oral historians are just beginning to utilize computer technology for the public presentation of interviews. Archives are using computer text-searching programs for indexing and retrieving information from their interviews. Oral history tapes and transcripts have been put on CD-ROM, along with videos and other illustrations, and programs have been devised to enable students to interact with the material they are seeing.[38]

Roy Rosenzweig, Steve Brier, and Josh Brown incorporated oral history reminiscences into a CD-ROM "electronic book," *Who Built America? From the Centennial Celebration of 1876 to the Great War of 1914* (1993). The audio and film clips, 600 pictures, and 5,000 pages of text are combined with computer-based search features to help students see and hear the history they are studying. The project begins with the late nineteenth century, since Rosenzweig and his colleagues discovered that many of the earliest oral histories were conducted with people who grew up in the 1880s and 1890s. Although some projects did not save their tapes, and the sound quality of other tapes was not reproducible, the authors of *Who Built America?* nevertheless were able to collect first-person recollections to accompany the photographs and written documentation. "Readers" of their electronic book can actually hear the voices of history, since oral history interviews are incorporated, along with sound recordings, music, and newsreels. "Our larger motivation in experimenting with this new technology has been toward democratizing historical understanding," the authors explained.

Interactive technology offers a broad range of users the kind of primary resources that are usually more available somewhere like the Library of Congress than at local libraries. Students can use the computer technology "to move at their own pace and make decisions about what direction they want to take, about what byways they want to investigate." The electronic book turns users into "active participants in the process of constructing historical interpretations rather than merely passive consumers of historical 'facts.' "[39]

In the summer of 1992 the National Park Service installed Project Jukebox as a workstation at the Yukon-Charley National Preserve in Alaska. A system of stacked compact disks that allows computer searching and retrieval of information, Project Jukebox combines oral histories of people who lived, fished, hunted, and worked in the Yukon-Charley Preserve. It provides recordings on historical themes about the Yukon River, the administrative history of the preserve, and experiences of people who settled there. Visitors to the park, local students, and new park rangers use the workstation to select topics and pull up recordings, transcripts, and illustrations at their own speed and are able to follow their own interests. The system permits listening to portions of the interviews relating to specific subjects and sites. Many interviewees speak in their native languages, but the computer can provide an English translation. Users can access the material from a list of individual interviewees, from lists of key words, and from lists of locations within the preserve. The project's director, William Schneider, explained:

> The opening screen is a general map of the Yukon-Charley National Preserve with key points indicated by triangles for historic sites and small rectangles with water symbols for bodies of water. Along the left of the screen is a list of locations marked on the map. Clicking on the name of a place highlights the location, and clicking on the location highlights the name. You have the option of looking at the map in greater detail. The "greater detail" section zooms you to an inch-to-the-mile U.S. Geological Survey map of the area. This screen also lists all audio recordings with information about the place. . . . Clicking on an audio section will take you eventually to a discussion of the place.[40]

From the Yukon to the inner-city neighborhoods of Philadelphia, on audio- and videotape and computers, over the radio, on the stage, in museums and community centers, oral history has proven to be a multifaceted tool, usable in a seemingly limitless number of ways, in many disciplines. Beyond their immediate purposes, oral historians seek to leave a better historical record, to preserve what would otherwise be lost or more obscure. In a sense, oral history has turned upside down George Santayana's famous dictum that "those who cannot remember the past are condemned to repeat it." Now oral historians are making sure that those who *can* remember the past must repeat it—on tape and for the record.[41]

Appendix 1: Principles and Standards of the Oral History Association

The Oral History Association promotes oral history as a method of gathering and preserving historical information through recorded interviews with participants in past events and ways of life. It encourages those who produce and use oral history to recognize certain principles, rights, and obligations for the creation of source material that is authentic, useful, and reliable. These include obligations to the interviewee, to the profession, and to the public, as well as mutual obligations between sponsoring organizations and interviewers.

Oral history interviews are conducted by people with a range of affiliations and sponsorship for a variety of purposes: to create archival records, for individual research, for community and institutional projects, and for publications and media productions. While these principles and standards provide a general framework for guiding professional conduct, their application may vary according to the nature of specific oral history projects. Regardless of the purpose of the interviews, oral history should be conducted in the spirit of critical inquiry and social responsibility, and with a recognition of the interactive and subjective nature of the enterprise.

Responsibility to Interviewees

1. Interviewees should be informed of the purposes and procedures of oral history in general and of the aims and anticipated uses of the particular projects to which they are making their contribution.

2. Interviewees should be informed of the mutual rights in the oral history process, such as editing, access restrictions, copyrights, prior use, royalties, and the expected disposition and dissemination of all forms of the record.

3. Interviewees should be informed that they will be asked to sign a legal release. Interviews should remain confidential until interviewees have given permission for their use.

4. Interviewers should guard against making promises to interviewees that they may not be able to fulfill, such as guarantees of publication and control over future uses of interviews after they have been made public.

5. Interviews should be conducted in accord with any prior agreements made with the interviewee, and such preferences and agreements should be documented for the record.

6. Interviewers should work to achieve a balance between the objectives of the project and the perspectives of the interviewees. They should be sensitive to the diversity of social and cultural experiences, and to the implications of race, gender, class, ethnicity, age, religion, and sexual orientation. They should encourage interviewees to respond in their own style and language, and to address issues that reflect their concerns. Interviewers should fully explore all appropriate areas of inquiry with the interviewee and not be satisfied with superficial responses.

7. Interviewers should guard against possible exploitation of interviewees and be sensitive to the ways in which their interviews might be used. Interviewers must respect the right of the interviewee to refuse to discuss certain subjects, to restrict access to the interview, or under extreme circumstances even to choose anonymity. Interviewers should clearly explain these options to all interviewees.

Responsibility to the Public and to the Profession

1. Oral historians have a responsibility to maintain the highest professional standards in the conduct of their work and to uphold the standards of the various disciplines and professions with which they are affiliated.

2. In recognition of the importance of oral history to an understanding of the past and of the cost and effort involved, interviewers and interviewees should mutually strive to record candid information of lasting value and to make that information accessible.

3. Interviewees should be selected on the basis of the relevance of their experiences to the subject at hand.

4. Interviewers should possess interviewing skills as well as professional competence or experience with the subject at hand.

5. Regardless of the specific interests of the project, interviewers should attempt to extend the inquiry beyond the specific focus of the project to create as complete a record as possible for the benefit of others.

6. Interviewers should strive to prompt informative dialogue through challenging and perceptive inquiry. They should be grounded in the background of the person being interviewed and, when possible, should carefully research appropriate documents and secondary sources related to subjects about which the interviewee can speak.

7. Interviewers should make every effort to record their interviews. They should provide complete documentation of their preparation and methods, including the

circumstances of the interview. Interviewers, and when possible interviewees, should review and evaluate their interviews and any transcriptions made from them.

8. With the permission of the interviewees, interviewers should arrange to deposit their interviews in an archival repository that is capable of both preserving the interviews and of eventually making them available for general use. Interviewers should provide basic information about the interviews, including project goals, sponsorship, and funding. Preferably, interviewers should work with repositories prior to the project to determine necessary legal arrangements. If interviewers arrange to retain first use of the interviews, it should be only for a reasonable time prior to public use.

9. Interviewers should be sensitive to the communities from which they have collected their oral histories, taking care not to reinforce thoughtless stereotypes or to bring undue notoriety to the community. They should take every effort to make the interviews accessible to the community.

10. Oral history interviews should be used and cited with the same care and standards applied to other historical sources. Users have a responsibility to retain the integrity of the interviewee's voice, neither misrepresenting the interviewee's words nor taking them out of context.

11. Sources of funding or sponsorship of oral history projects should be made public in all exhibits, media presentations, or publications that the projects produce.

12. Interviewers and oral history programs should conscientiously consider how they might share with interviewees and their communities the rewards and recognition that might result from their work.

Responsibility of Sponsoring and Archival Institutions

1. Institutions sponsoring and maintaining oral history archives have a responsibility to interviewees, interviewers, the profession, and the public to maintain the highest professional and ethical standards in the creation and archival preservation of oral history interviews.

2. Subject to conditions that interviewees set, sponsoring institutions (or individual collectors) have an obligation to prepare and preserve easily usable records, to keep accurate records of the creation and processing of each interview, to identify, index, and catalog interviews, and to make known the existence of the interviews when they are open for research.

3. Within the parameters of their missions and resources, archival institutions should collect interviews generated by independent researchers and assist interviewers with the necessary legal agreements.

4. Sponsoring institutions should train interviewers, explaining the objectives of the program to them, informing them of all ethical and legal considerations governing an interview, and making clear to interviewers what their obligations are to the program and to the interviewees.

5. Interviewers and interviewees should receive appropriate acknowledgment for their work in all forms of citation or usage.

Appendix 2: Sample Legal Release Forms

[From John A. Neuenschwander, *Oral History and the Law* (1993)]

Contractual Agreement

In consideration of the tape (video) recording and preservation of my oral history memoir by _____, consisting of _____, I, _____ (name of interviewee), of _____ (address), City of _____, County of _____, State of _____, herein relinquish and transfer to the _____, for such historical and scholarly purposes as they see fit, the following rights:

1. All legal title and literary property rights which I have or may be deemed to have in said work.

2. All my rights, title and interest in copyright which I have or may be deemed to have in said work and more particularly the exclusive rights or reproduction, distribution, preparation of derivative works, public performance and display.

I herein warrant that I have not assigned or in any manner encumbered or impaired any of the aforementioned rights in my oral memoir.

The _____ in turn agrees to:

1. Allow me to copy, use, and publish my oral memoir in part or in full until the earlier of my death or _____, 19_____.

2.

3.

IN WITNESS WHEREOF, we have hereunto set our hand(s) and seal(s) this _____ day of _____, 19_____.

_____
(Signature of Interviewee)

_____
(Signature of Authorized Agent)

Deed of Gift Agreement

I, _____ , (name of donor), of _____ (address), City of _____ , County of _____ , State of _____ , hereby give, convey, and assign to _____ , which is currently in possession of my oral memoir consisting of _____ , to have and to hold the same absolutely and forever. I understand that _____ will use my oral memoir for such historical and scholarly purposes as they see fit and that by this conveyance I relinquish:

1. All legal title and literary property rights which I have or may be deemed to have in said work.

2. All my rights, title and interest in copyright which I have or may be deemed to have in said work and more particularly the exclusive rights of reproduction, distribution, preparation of derivative works, public performance, and display.

I herein warrant that I have not assigned or in any manner encumbered or impaired any of the aforementioned rights in my oral memoir. The only conditions which I place on this unrestricted gift are:

1. The right to copy, use, and publish my oral memoir in part of in full until the earlier of my death or _____ 19_____ .

2.

3.

I, _____ (as agent for or as the duly appointed representative of) _____ , accept the oral memoir of _____ for inclusion in the _____ .

Dated _____ , 19_____ .

_____   _____
(Signature of Donor)   (Signature of Authorized Agent)

[Senate Historical Office]

Deed of Gift to the Public Domain]

I, _____ , do hereby give to the
_____ (archives or organization) the tape recordings
and transcripts of my interviews conducted on _____ .

I authorize the _____ (archive or organization) to
use the tapes and transcripts in such a manner as may best serve the educational
and historical objectives of their oral history program.

In making this gift, I voluntarily convey ownership of the tapes and transcripts to the public domain.

_____   _____

(Agent of Receiving Organization)   (Donor)

_____

(Date)

[From Plum Borough High School, Pittsburgh, Pennsylvania]

_____ School
Oral History Program
Interviewee Agreement
You have been asked to participate in the _____ School Oral History Program. The purpose of this program is to gather and preserve information for historical and scholarly use.
A tape recording of your interview will be made by the interviewer and will be kept and used at _____ School. If a transcript is made of the tape, you will receive a copy. Other institutions or persons may obtain copies of the interview. These materials may be made available for purposes of research, instructional use, publication, or other related purposes.

I, _____ (name of interviewee), hereby give the copyright of my interview to _____ School, to be used for whatever educational and scholarly purposes that the school shall determine.

Interviewee Signature	Interviewer Signature

Date	Date

[from Barry A. Lanman and George L. Mehaffy,
Oral History in the Secondary School Classroom (1988)]

I, _____ (name of donor), of _____
(address), hereby give, convey, and assign copyright in my oral history memoir to _____ (school), which is currently in possession
of my oral history memoir consisting of tapes and/or transcripts to have
and to hold the same absolutely and forever. I understand that
_____ (school) will use my oral memoir for such historical
and scholarly purposes as they see fit and that by this conveyance I relinquish:

1. All legal title and literary property rights which I have or may be deemed to
have in said work.

2. All my right, title and interest in copyright which I have or may be deemed
to have in said work and more particularly the exclusive rights of reproduction,
distribution, preparation of derivative works, public performance, and display.

I herein warrant that I have not assigned or in any manner encumbered
or impaired any of the aforementioned rights in my oral memoir. The only
conditions which I place on this unrestricted gift are:

1.
2.
3.

I, _____ (as agent for or the duly appointed
representative of) _____ (school), accept the
oral memoirs of _____ for inclusion in the
_____ .

Dated _____

_____   _____
(Signature)   (Signature)

215

Notes and References

Chapter 1

1. Charles T. Morrissey has grappled persuasively with the definition of oral history in his essays "Why Call It 'Oral History'? Searching for Early Usage of a Generic Term," *Oral History Review* 8 (1980): 20–48; "Introduction," in *Oral History: An Interdisciplinary Anthology*, ed. David K. Dunaway and Willa K. Baum (Nashville: American Association for State and Local History, 1984), xix–xxiii; and "Beyond Oral Evidence: Speaking (Con)structively about Oral History," *Archival Issues* (forthcoming).

2. See Oral History Association, *Evaluation Guidelines* (Los Angeles: Oral History Association, 1992). The principles and standards are reprinted as appendix 1 in this volume.

3. William W. Moss, "Oral History: What Is It and Where Did It Come From?" in *The Past Meets the Present: Essays on Oral History*, ed. David Stricklin and Rebecca Sharpless (Lanham, Md.: University Press of America, 1988), 5; Thucydides, *History of the Peloponnesian War* (New York: Penguin, 1972), 48. See also William W. Moss and Peter C. Mazikana, *Archives, Oral History, and Oral Tradition: A RAMP [Records and Archives Management Programme] Study* (Paris: UNESCO, 1986), 2.

4. Paul Thompson, "Britain Strikes Back: Two Hundred Years of 'Oral History,'" *Oral History Association Newsletter* 15 (Summer 1981): 4–5; Paul Thompson, *The Voice of the Past: Oral History* (New York: Oxford University Press, 1978), 19, 25–26; Fritz Stern, ed., *The Varieties of History: From Voltaire to the Present* (New York: Vintage Books, 1973), 39; Dean Albertson, "Remembering Oral History's Beginning," *Annual of the New England Association of Oral History* 1 (1987–88): 2.

5. Thompson, *Voice of the Past*, 46–47; Peter Novick, *That Noble Dream: The "Objectivity Question" and the American Historical Profession* (Cambridge: Cambridge University Press, 1988), 21–46.

6. Donald A. Ritchie, *Press Gallery: Congress and the Washington Correspondents* (Cambridge: Harvard University Press, 1991), 81–83.

7. Donald A. Ritchie, "Oral History in the Federal Government," *Journal of American History* 74 (September 1987): 587–95.

8. Stephen E. Everett, *Oral History Techniques and Procedures* (Washington,

D.C.: Center of Military History, 1992), 5–11; H. Lew Wallace, "Forrest C. Pogue: A Biographical Sketch," *Filson Club Historical Quarterly* 60 (July 1986): 373–402; see also John Douglas Marshall, *Reconciliation Road: A Family Odyssey of War and Honor* (Syracuse, N.Y.: Syracuse University Press, 1993), for some of the controversies concerning Marshall's interviews and the conclusions he drew from them.

9. Joseph L. Mitchell, *Joe Gould's Secret* (New York: Viking Press, 1965), reprints two *New Yorker* essays from 1942 and 1964. Winslow C. Watson referred to "oral history" in an address to the Vermont Historical Society in 1863, but Watson lacked the national audience and notoriety that the *New Yorker* gave to Gould. See Morrissey, "Why Call It 'Oral History'?" 20–48.

10. Allan Nevins, *The Gateway to History* (Boston: Appleton-Century, 1938), iv; Ray Allen Billington, ed., *Allan Nevins on History* (New York: Charles Scribner's Sons, 1975), 209–10, 281–83, 288–93; Elizabeth I. Dixon, et al., "Definitions of Oral History," *Oral History at Arrowhead: The Proceedings of the First National Colloquium on Oral History* (Los Angeles: Oral History Association, 1969), 14.

11. Willa K. Baum, "A Brief History of Oral History," address delivered at California State University, Fullerton, 22 April 1972. "Oral History in the Soviet Union: Filling Gaps in the Collective Memory," *Oral History Association Newsletter* 24 (Fall 1990): 1–2; Thomas L. Charlton, "Scherbakov: 'Only the Memory of Oral History,'" *Oral History Association Newsletter* 25 (Fall 1991): 1–2.

12. Thompson, *Voice of the Past*, 55–59; Studs Terkel, *Hard Times: An Oral History of the Great Depression* (New York: Pantheon, 1970); Studs Terkel, *Working: People Talk about What They Do All Day and How They Feel about What They Do* (New York: Pantheon, 1974); and Studs Terkel, *"The Good War": An Oral History of World War Two* (New York: Pantheon, 1984); Alex Haley, *Roots: The Saga of an American Family* (Garden City, N.Y.: Doubleday, 1976); and Alex Haley, "Black History, Oral History, and Genealogy," in Dunaway and Baum, *Oral History*, 264–87.

13. See Ronald J. Grele, "Why Call It Oral History? Some Ruminations from the Field," *Pennsylvania History* 60 (October 1993): 506–9.

14. Reporting on an oral history project in three Philadelphia neighborhoods, Charles Hardy noted, "We have found that the best interviewes often come from the enthusiastic amateur. . . . The historian generally comes from or has been trained in academic culture and academic style which raises the problem of establishing rapport, particularly when the time with the interviewee is limited." Charles Hardy, "The Urban Archives' 'Discovering Community History Project,'" *Oral History Association Newsletter* 15 (Winter 1981): 4–5.

15. Marc Bloch, *The Historian's Craft* (New York: Alfred A. Knopf, 1953), 10; James MacGregor Burns, "The Truth of the Battlefield," *New York Times Book Review* (6 March 1994): 34.

16. Gore Vidal, *Screening History* (Cambridge: Harvard University Press, 1992), 88. For an example of the blind spots in written history, see Lael Morgan, "Writing Minorities out of History: Black Builders of the Alcan Highway," *Alaska History* 7 (Fall 1992): 1–13.

17. Louise A. Tilly, "People's History and Social Science History," "Between Social Sciences: Responses to Louise A. Tilly by Paul Thompson, Luisa Passerini, Isabell Bertaux-Wiame, and Alessandro Portelli," and "Louise A. Tilly's Response," *International Journal of Oral History* 6 (February 1985): 5–46; David Lodge, *Out of the Shelter* (New York: Penguin, 1989), 185.

18. Dixon, et al, "Definitions of Oral History," 4–8; see also Martha J. Ross, "Interviewer or Intervener: Interpretation in the Oral History Interview," *Maryland Historian* 13 (Fall-Winter 1982): 3–6.

19. Joseph Roddy, "Oral History: Soundings from the Sony Age," *RF* [Rockefeller Foundation] *Illustrated* 3 (May 1977): 4; E. Culpepper Clark, Michael J. Hyde, and Eva M. McMahan, "Communication in the Oral History Interview: Investigating Problems of Interpreting Oral Data," *International Journal of Oral History* 1 (February 1980): 29; Saul Benison, "Oral History: A Personal View," in *Modern Methods in the History of Medicine*, ed. Edward Clark (New York: Oxford, 1971), 291; Ronald J. Grele, "Introduction," in *International Annual of Oral History, 1990: Subjectivity and Multiculturalism in Oral History* (Westport, Conn.: Greenwood Press, 1992), 2; and Ronald J. Grele, ed., *Envelopes of Sound: The Art of Oral History* (New York: Praeger, 1991).

20. Perry Blatz, "Craftsmanshp and Flexibility in Oral History: A Pluralistic Approach to Methodology and Theory," *The Public Historian* 12 (Fall 1990): 7–22; Ross, "Interviewer or Intervener," 3–6; Michael Frisch, *A Shared Authority: Essays on the Craft and Meaning of Oral and Public History* (Albany: State University of New York Press, 1990), xx–xxiii; Donald A. Ritchie, "An Interview with Michael Frisch," *OHMAR Newsletter* 11 (Fall 1988): 4–9.

21. Eva M. McMahan, *Elite Oral History Discourse: A Study of Cooperation and Coherence* (Tuscaloosa: University of Alabama Press, 1989); Sherna Berger Gluck and Daphne Patai, eds., *Women's Words: The Feminist Practice of Oral History* (New York: Routledge, 1991); Alessandro Portelli, *The Death of Luigi Trastulli and Other Stories: Form and Meaning in Oral History* (Albany: State University of New York Press, 1991); and Terry L. Birdwhistell, "Re-Educating an Oral Historian: Putting Practice into Theory" (unpublished, 26 April 1990).

22. Herman Kahn, review, *American Historical Review* 73 (June 1968): 1471.

23. Gluck and Patai, *Women's Words*, 226–27; see also Charles T. Morrissey, "Riding a Mule through the 'Terminological Jungle': Oral History and the Problems of Nomenclature," *Oral History Review* 12 (1984): 13–28.

24. Elizabeth Kolbert, "Memories Wanted for History of Ellis Island," *New York Times*, 24 November 1985.

25. John Neuenschwander, "Oral Historians and Long-Term Memory," in Dunaway and Baum, *Oral History*, 324–32; James W. Lomax and Charles T. Morrissey, "The Interview as Inquiry for Psychiatrists and Oral Historians: Convergence and Divergence in Skills and Goals," *The Public Historian* 11 (Winter 1989): 17–24; William C. Davis, *Jefferson Davis: The Man and His Hour* (New York: HarperCollins, 1991), 687.

26. Robert N. Butler, "The Life Review: An Interpretation of Reminiscence in

the Aged," in *New Thoughts on Old Age*, ed. Robert Kastenbaum (New York: Springer, 1964), 265–80.

27. "Memory has always proven difficult for historians to confront," Michael Frisch noted in his essay "The Memory of History" (*A Shared Authority*, 15–27); see also David Thelen, "Memory and History," *Journal of American History* 75 (March 1989): 1117–29.

28. Diane Manning, *Hill Country Teacher: Oral Histories from the One-Room School and Beyond* (Boston: Twayne, 1990), xx–xxi.

29. Ruth Young Watt, chief clerk of the Senate Permanent Subcommittee on Investigations, interviewed by Donald A. Ritchie, 19 July–9 November 1979, transcripts, Senate Historical Office Oral History Project, Library of Congress, Washington, D.C.

30. On Kirk's memory, the historian Gordon Prange commented, "Pearl Harbor's happening the next day impressed the memory upon him." Gordon Prange, *At Dawn We Slept: The Untold Story of Pearl Harbor* (New York: McGraw-Hill, 1981), 719–20.

31. See Jean Piaget, *Memory and Intelligence* (New York: Basic Books, 1973); and Edmund Blair Bolles, *Remembering and Forgetting: Inquiries into the Nature of Memory* (New York: Walker and Co., 1988).

32. Nigel Hamilton, *JFK: Reckless Youth* (New York: Random House, 1992), 532–33.

33. See Jaclyn Jeffrey and Glenace Edwall, eds., *Memory and History: Essays on Recalling and Interpreting Experience* (Lanham, Md.: University Press of America, 1994).

34. David Brinkley, *Washington Goes to War* (New York: Alfred A. Knopf, 1988); "The Conversation: Arthur Schlesinger, Jr., Interviews David Brinkley," *Washington Post Magazine* (10 April 1988): 29.

35. See Jaclyn L. Jeffrey, "The Waco Tornado of 1953 as Symbol of Modernization and Rite of Initiation," *Sound Historian: Journal of the Texas Oral Association* 1 (Fall 1993): 39.

36. William Allen White, *A Puritan in Babylon: The Story of Calvin Coolidge* (New York: Macmillan, 1938), vii.

37. See, for instance, Charles T. Morrissey, "More Than Embers of Sentiment: Railroad Nostalgia and Oral History Memories of the 1920s and 1930s," *The Public Historian* 15 (Summer 1993): 29–35.

38. Joel Gardner, "An Interview with Linda Shopes," *OHMAR Newsletter* 15 (Fall 1992): 9, 11; Linda Shopes, "Beyond Trivia and Nostalgia: Collaborating in the Construction of a Local History," *International Journal of Oral History* 5 (November 1984): 151–58.

39. Ronald Steel, "Harry of Sunnybrook Farm," *New Republic* 207 (10 August 1992): 34.

40. Jacquelyn Dowd Hall, James Leloudis, Robert Korstad, Mary Murphy, Lu Ann Jones, and Christopher B. Daly, *Like a Family: The Making of a Southern Cotton Mill World* (Chapel Hill: University of North Carolina Press, 1987), xv; see also Selma

Leydesdorff, "The Screen of Nostalgia: Oral History and the Ordeal of Working-Class Jews in Amsterdam," *International Journal of Oral History* 7 (June 1986): 109–15.

41. Rhoda G. Lewin, ed., *Witnesses to the Holocaust: An Oral History* (Boston: Twayne, 1990).

42. Barbara Allen, "Oral History: The Folk Connection," in Stricklin and Sharpless, *The Past Meets the Present*, 15–26; see also William Lynwood Montell, *The Saga of Coe Ridge: A Study in Oral History* (Knoxville: University of Tennessee Press, 1970), vii–xxi.

43. See James Hoopes, *Oral History: An Introduction for Students* (Chapel Hill: University of North Carolina Press, 1979), 33–40.

44. Rick Harmon, "Oral Histories of the Federal Courts: The Oregon Experience," *Western Legal History* 1 (Summer-Fall 1988): 277–84.

45. American Historical Association, "Statement on Interviewing for Historical Documentation," *Statement on Standards of Professional Conduct* (Washington, D.C.: American Historical Association, 1989).

46. See Daniel J. Walkowitz, "On Public History . . . ," *Organization of American Historians Newsletter* 12 (August 1984): 11.

47. See Donald A. Ritchie, "The Oral History/Public History Connection," in *Public History: An Introduction*, ed. Barbara J. Howe and Emory L. Kemp (Malabar, Fla.: Krieger, 1986), 57–69.

48. L. Elisabeth Beattie, "The Advent of Independents: Oral Historians Who Stand Alone," *Oral History Association Newsletter* 26 (Summer 1992): 1.

49. Ibid., 3; Susan Q. Stranahan, "Lending an Ear to Corporate History," *Philadelphia Inquirer*, 21 September 1992.

50. Enid Hart Douglas, "Corporate History—Why?" *The Public Historian* 3 (Summer 1981): 75–80.

51. "Oral History Supports Land Claims in West," *Oral History Association Newsletter* 17 (Fall 1983): 1, 8.

52. Charles T. Morrissey, "Public Historians and Oral History: Problems of Concept and Methods," *The Public Historian* 2 (Winter 1980): 22–29; see also Charles T. Morrissey, "Truman and the Presidency—Records and Oral Recollections," *The American Archivist* 28 (January 1965): 53–61.

53. James Morris, "The Historian's Craft," *Woodrow Wilson Center Report* 4 (September 1992): 4–5.

54. Ritchie, "Oral History/Public History Connection," 57–69.

55. Charles L. Sullivan, *Gathering at the River: South Mississippi's Camp Meetings* (Perkinston, Miss.: Mississippi Gulf Coast Community College Press, 1990), 10–11.

Chapter 2

1. If all else fails, a follow-up session may be conducted by telephone—although it is a poor substitute for a face-to-face oral history.

2. L. Elisabeth Beattie, "The Advent of Independents: Oral Historians Who Stand Alone," *Oral History Association Newsletter* 26 (Summer 1992): 6.

3. See, for instance, Joe Rossi, "Who Was That Masked Interviewer?" *Oral History Recorder: Newsletter of the Center for Oral History, University of Hawaii at Manoa* 8 (Fall 1991): 1.

4. Joyce M. Kornbluh, Brady Mikusko, and Debra Bernhardt, *Working Women-roots: An Oral History Primer* (Ann Arbor, Mich.: Wayne State University, Institute of Labor and Industrial Relations, 1980); Stephen E. Everett, *Oral History Techniques and Procedures* (Washington, D.C.: Center for Military History, 1992); and Blair Hubbard, Heather Huyck, and David Nathanson, *Collecting, Using, and Preserving Oral History in the National Park Service* (Harpers Ferry, W.V.: National Park Service, 1984).

5. "Nuclear History Program Examines Past Policies of Nuclear Arms Management and Explores Assumptions about Nuclear Detente," *Oral History Association Newsletter* 23 (Spring 1989): 1, 8.

6. See, for example, Charles Scribner, Jr., *In the Company of Writers: A Life in Publishing*, based on the oral history by Joel R. Gardner (New York: Maxwell Macmillan, 1990).

7. Dean Albertson, "Remembering Oral History's Beginning," *Annual of the New England Oral History Association* 1 (1987–88): 3.

8. Kevin Mulroy, "Preserving Oral History Interviews on Tape: Curatorial Techniques and Managing Procedures," *International Journal of Oral History* 7 (November 1986): 189–97.

9. For the advantages and disadvantages of group interviewing, see Robert K. Merton, Marjorie Fiske, and Patricia L. Kendall, *The Focused Interview: A Manual of Problems and Procedures* (New York: Free Press, 1990), 135–69.

10. Michael Kenny, "The Patron-Client Relationship in Interviewing: An Anthropological View," *Oral History Review* 15 (Spring 1987): 75.

11. Dale Treleven, *TAPE (Time Access to Pertinent Excerpts) System: A Method For Producing Oral History Interviews and Other Sound Recordings* (Madison: State Historical Society of Wisconsin, 1979).

12. Deborah Reid, "Talk Ain't Cheap: How to Get a Perfect Transcript," Techni-Type brochure.

13. Elliot G. Mishler, *Research Interviewing: Context and Narrative* (Cambridge: Harvard University Press, 1986), 47–51; Henry Glassie, *Passing the Time in Ballymen-one: Culture and History of an Ulster County* (Philadelphia: University of Pennsylvania Press, 1982), 40.

14. David Henige, a specialist in African oral tradition, vehemently dissented on the issue of editing, which he called tampering with the primacy sources and "producing paraphrases disguised as verbatim testimony." Henige believed that any elimination of hesitations or moments of doubt and embarrassment would reduce the transcript to "an amusing or readable vignette," and the status of oral history to dilettantism. David Henige, *Oral Historiography* (New York: Longman, 1982), 107.

15. Carl M. Marcy, interviewed by Donald A. Ritchie, 14 September–16 November 1983, transcripts, Senate Historical Office, 24–25, Library of Congress, Washington, D.C.

16. *The Chicago Manual of Style*, 14th ed. (Chicago: University of Chicago Press, 1993).

17. Katherine R. Martin and Charles E. Martin, "Transcription Style: Choices and Variables at the Appalachian Oral History Project," *International Journal of Oral History* 6 (June 1985): 126–28.

18. Nell Irvin Painter, *The Narrative of Hosea Hudson: His Life as a Negro Communist in the South* (Cambridge: Harvard University Press, 1979), 1–44.

19. See John A. Neuenschwander, *Oral History and the Law*, rev. ed. (Albuquerque, N.M.: Oral History Association, 1993), 16–35.

20. Ibid., 19–22.

21. John Noble Wilford, "Fun and Comradeship," *New York Times Book Review* (7 July 1985): 3; George Tames, *Eye on Washington: The Presidents Who've Known Me* (New York: HarperCollins, 1990).

22. Alben Barkley, *That Reminds Me* (Garden City, N.Y.: Doubleday, 1954); Donald A. Ritchie, "Alben W. Barkley: The President's Man," in *First among Equals: Outstanding Senate Leaders of the Twentieth Century*, ed. Richard A. Baker and Roger H. Davidson (Washington, D.C.: Congressional Quarterly, 1991), 127–62.

23. Neuenschwander, *Oral History and the Law*, 5–12.

Chapter 3

1. Clifford Terry, "The Real Studs," *Chicago Tribune*, 5 April 1992.

2. Ruth Finnegan, "A Note on Oral Tradition and Historical Evidence," in *Oral History: An Interdisciplinary Anthology*, ed. David K. Dunaway and Willa K. Baum (Nashville: American Association for State and Local History, 1984), 113–14; see also Linda Shopes, "Beyond Trivia and Nostalgia: Collaborating in the Construction of a Local History," *International Journal of Oral History* 5 (November 1984): 151–58.

3. Donald A. Ritchie, "Beyond the *Congressional Record*: Congress and Oral History," *Maryland Historian* 13 (Fall-Winter 1982): 7–16.

4. John Brady, *The Craft of Interviewing* (New York: Vintage Books, 1977), 155.

5. Shirley Biagi, *Interviews That Work: A Practical Guide for Journalists* (Belmont, Calif.: Wadsworth, 1986), 56.

6. See Edward D. Ives, *The Tape-Recorded Interview: A Manual for Field Workers in Folklore and Oral History* (Knoxville: University of Tennessee Press, 1980), 33–47; and Cullom Davis, Kathryn Black, and Kay MacLean, *Oral History from Tape to Type* (Chicago: American Library Association, 1977), 9–11.

7. David King Dunaway, "Field Recording Oral History," *Oral History Review* 15 (Spring 1987): 34.

8. Sherna Gluck, "What's So Special about Women? Women's Oral History," in Dunaway and Baum, *Oral History*, 231.

9. Biagi, *Interviews That Work*, 82–85. A useful collection of sample questions for recording family history, and models for other types of interviewing, can be found in William P. Fletcher, *Recording Your Family History: A Guide to Preserving Oral History with Videotape, Audio Tape, Suggested Topics and Questions, Interview Techniques* (New York: Dodd, Mead, 1986.)

10. Charles T. Morrissey, "The Two-Sentence Format as an Interviewing Technique in Oral History Fieldwork," *Oral History Review* 15 (Spring 1987): 43–53.

11. Elliot G. Mishler, *Research Interviewing: Context and Narrative* (Cambridge: Harvard University Press, 1986), 117–35; for the "human element" in fieldwork interviewing, see Robert A. Georges and Michael O. Jones, *People Studying People: The Human Element in Fieldwork* (Berkeley: University of California Press, 1980).

12. William Cutler III, "Accuracy in Oral History Interviewing," in Dunaway and Baum, *Oral History*, 82. Although it is directed at pollsters, anyone asking questions should also consult Stanley L. Payne's classic and oft-reprinted account *The Art of Asking Questions* (Princeton, N.J.: Princeton University Press, 1951).

13. William W. Moss, *Oral History Program Manual* (New York: Praeger, 1974), 43.

14. Studs Terkel, *Talking to Myself: A Memoir of My Times* (New York: Pantheon, 1977), 64–70.

15. Ronald Steel, "The Biographer as Detective: What Walter Lippmann Preferred to Forget," *New York Times Book Review* (21 July 1985): 3.

16. Louis Auchincloss, *The House of the Prophet* (Boston: Houghton Mifflin, 1980), 19.

17. Brady, *The Craft of Interviewing*, 104; Oscar Wilde, *An Ideal Husband*, act 1.

18. Pecora's son, Louis, and nephew, Louis Stephens, recalled his acute memory and persistent reminiscing in interviews that I conducted while writing "The Pecora Wall Street Exposé," in *Congress Investigates: A Documented History, 1792–1974*, ed. Arthur M. Schlesinger, Jr. and Roger Bruns (New York: R. R. Bowker, 1975), 4:2555–732.

19. For a case study, see Mary Elizabeth Aube, "Oral History and the Remembered World: Cultural Determinants from French Canada," *International Journal of Oral History* 10 (February 1989): 31–49.

20. Ives, *The Tape-Recorded Interview*, 74–79.

21. Pete Daniel, *Deep'n as It Come* (New York: Oxford University Press, 1977); Andrea Hammer, "Federal Visions/Regional Revisions: Oral History's Role in Revising FSA Portraits of Southern Maryland" (paper delivered to the Oral History Association meeting, October 1992, Cleveland, Ohio). Another creative merging of oral history and visual imagery is the work of the Alaskan portrait artist Jean Lester, who

interviews her subjects as she paints them to learn more about their personalities and gain a deeper perspective. See Jean Lester, *Faces of Alaska* (Ester, Alaska: Poppies Publishing, 1988), and *Faces of Alaska from Barrow to Wrangell* (Ester, Alaska: Poppies Publishing, 1992).

22. James West Davidson and Mark Hamilton Lytle, *After the Fact: The Art of Historical Detection* (New York: Alfred A. Knopf, 1982), 169–204.

23. Oral History Association, *Evaluation Guidelines* (Los Angeles: Oral History Association, 1992), 2.

24. For an example of this type of strategic planning, see Mary Jo Deering, "Oral History and School Integration Research: A Case Study," *Oral History Review* 7 (1979): 27–41.

25. Marc Pachter, ed., *Telling Lives: The Biographer's Art* (Philadelphia: University of Pennsylvania Press, 1981); see also Theodore Rosengarten, *All God's Dangers: The Life of Nate Shaw* (New York: Alfred A. Knopf, 1974).

26. Donald A. Ritchie, "Learning to Listen," *Southwest Oral History Association Newsletter* 13 (Summer 1987): 1–7.

27. Martha J. Ross, "Interviewer or Intervener: Interpretation in the Oral History Interview," *Maryland Historian* 13 (Fall-Winter 1982): 3–6.

28. Moss, *Oral History Program Manual*, 39–40.

29. Judith Miller, "Erasing the Past: Europe's Amnesia about the Holocaust," *New York Times Magazine* (16 November 1986): 30–36, 40, 109–111.

30. Amelia Fry, correspondence with the author, August 1993.

31. Mike Walters, "Report on 'Siberia' Interviews," *Working Together: A Regional Approach to Community Traditions and History in Idaho* (newsletter) 5 (Fall 1982): 4.

32. Richard F. Fenno, Jr., "Observation, Context, and Sequence in the Study of Politics," *American Political Science Review* 80 (March 1986): 3–15.

33. Ives, *The Tape-Recorded Interview*, 79–81.

34. Walter Liniger, "The Original Down Home Blues Show," *Oral History Association Newsletter* 22 (Spring 1988): 1.

Chapter 4

1. "Statement on Interviewing for Historical Documentation," *Statement on Professional Conduct* (Washington: American Historical Association, 1990), 25–27; *Perspectives: The American Historical Association Newsletter* 27 (October 1989): 8.

2. Barbara Tuchman, "Distinguishing the Significant from the Insignificant," in *Oral History: An Interdisciplinary Anthology*, ed. David K. Dunaway and Willa K. Baum (Nashville: American Association for State and Local History, 1984), 74–78; Shirley Biagi, *Interviews That Work: A Practical Guide for Journalists* (Belmont, Calif.: Wadsworth, 1986), 16–19.

3. Barth Healey, " 'I'm Not One of Those Who Say Kissinger is Paranoid,' Mr. Nixon Said," *New York Times Book Review* (6 September 1992): 20.

4. Martha Ross has cited this incident frequently in oral history workshops.

5. Donald A. Ritchie, Holly Cowan Shulman, Richard S. Kirkendall, and Terry L. Birdwhistell, "Interviews as Historical Evidence: A Discussion of New Standards of Documentation and Access," *The History Teacher* 24 (February 1991): 226–28.

6. The interview with Sen. Hiram Fong was conducted by Michaelyn P. Chou of the University of Hawaii. See Donald A. Ritchie, "Beyond the *Congressional Record: Congress and Oral History,"* *Maryland Historian* 13 (Fall-Winter 1982): 7–16.

7. See Ronald J. Grele, "Why Call It Oral History? Some Ruminations from the Field," *Pennsylvania History* 60 (October 1993): 506–9.

8. Philip Brooks's remarks are included in Elizabeth I. Dixon, et al., "Definitions of Oral History," *Oral History at Arrowhead: The Proceedings of the First National Colloquium on Oral History* (Los Angeles: Oral History Association, 1969), 6–7; see also Ronald J. Grele, "Introduction," *International Annual of Oral History, 1990: Subjectivity and Multiculturalism in Oral History* (Westport, Conn.: Greenwood Press, 1992), 1–8.

9. Emmanuel LeRoy Ladurie, *Montaillou: The Promised Land of Error* (New York: Vintage Books, 1979).

10. John C. Dann, *The Revolution Remembered: Eyewitness Accounts of the War for Independence* (Chicago: University of Chicago Press, 1977), xv–xxi; see also Charles T. Morrissey, "Beyond Oral Evidence: Speaking (Con)structively about Oral History," *Archival Issues* (forthcoming).

11. "Stewart E. McClure, Chief Clerk, Senate Committee on Labor, Education, and Public Welfare," interviewed by Donald A. Ritchie for the Senate Historical Office, December 1982–May 1983, transcripts, Library of Congress, 118.

12. Ritchie, et al., "Interviews as Historical Evidence," 223–38.

13. Dan K. Utley, "From the Ground Up: Oral History and Historical Archaeology," *Sound Historian: Journal of the Texas Oral History Association* 1 (Fall 1993): 24.

14. Donald A. Ritchie, "Learning to Listen," *Southwest Oral History Association Newsletter* (Summer 1987): 1, 3–7.

15. Blair Worden, "Lyrical Historian," *New York Review of Books* 40 (15 July 1993): 12; Johnson quoted in Christopher Matthews, *Hardball: How Politics Is Played—Told by One Who Knows the Game* (New York: Summit Books, 1988), 133.

16. "Southern History and the Politics of Recent Memory: Responses to the C. Vann Woodward Interview," *Radical History Review* 38 (1987): 143–51.

17. Kathleen M. Blee, "Evidence, Empathy, and Ethics: Lessons from Oral Histories of the Klan," *Journal of American History* 80 (September 1993): 596–606.

18. Allan Nevins, "The Uses of Oral History," in Dunaway and Baum, *Oral History,* 33.

19. See Ronald J. Grele, "On Using Oral History Collections: An Introduction,"

Journal of American History 74 (September 1987): 570–78; and Allen Smith, *Directory of Oral History Collections* (Phoenix: Onyx, 1988).

20. Mark A. Stoler, *George C. Marshall: Soldier-Statesman of the American Century* (Boston: Twayne, 1989). Apart from his four-volume biography of Marshall, Pogue's interviews were published in Larry I. Bland, et al., eds., *George C. Marshall Interviews and Reminiscences for Forrest C. Pogue* (Lexington, Va.: George C. Marshall Research Foundation, 1991).

21. Arthur M. Schlesinger, Jr., *Robert Kennedy and His Times* (Boston: Houghton Mifflin, 1979), 1:xv; Lynn A. Bonfield, "Conversations with Arthur M. Schlesinger, Jr.: The Use of Oral History," *The American Archivist* 43 (Fall 1980): 466.

22. Sherna Berger Gluck, " 'We Will Not Be Another Algeria': Women's Mass Organizations, Changing Consciousness, and the Potential for Women's Liberation in a Future Palestinian State," *International Annual of Oral History 1990*, 225.

23. William W. Moss, "Anonymity of Sources in Oral History," *Oral History Association Newsletter* 23 (Fall 1989): 1, 8.

24. Oral History Assocation, *Evaluation Guidelines* (Los Angeles: Oral History Association, 1992), 2.

25. Howard E. McCurdy, *Inside NASA: High Technology and Organizational Change in the U.S. Space Program* (Baltimore: Johns Hopkins University Press, 1993), 189.

26. Joseph Roddy, "Oral History: Soundings from the Sony Age," *RF* [Rockefeller Foundation] *Illustrated* 3 (May 1977); Charles T. Morrissey, "Oral History and the Boundaries of Fiction," *The Public Historian* 7 (Spring 1985): 42.

27. Morrissey, "Oral History and the Boundaries of Fiction," 43. After Miller's death, over seven hours of his recorded interviews with Truman, conducted in 1961–62, and other papers that he used to write *Plain Speaking* were made available for research and verification at the Truman Library.

28. Cullom Davis, "Success and Excess: Oral History at High Tide," in *The Past Meets the Present: Essays on Oral History*, ed. David Stricklin and Rebecca Sharpless (Lanham, Md.: University Press of America, 1988), 77–85.

29. Elizabeth Hardwick, "The Teller and the Tape," *New York Review of Books* (30 May 1985): 3–5.

30. Henry Fairlie, [review of *Robert F. Kennedy and His Times* by Arthur Schlesinger, Jr.], *New Republic* 179 (9 September 1978): 32.

31. Unlike other reviewers who praised *Hard Times*'s uplifting, inspirational spirit, Frisch thought it depressing that even 30 years after a massive breakdown in the American economic system Americans still could not bring themselves to examine their culture and institutions. Reading the other reviews, he decided that most had been more concerned with the celebratory message of the interviews for the dispirited America of the 1970s than with the reality of the 1930s. Donald A. Ritchie, "An Interview with Michael Frisch," *OHMAR* Newsletter, 11 (Fall, 1988), 5; Michael Frisch, *A Shared Authority: Essays on the Craft and Meaning of Oral and Public History* (Albany: State University of New York Press, 1990), 5–13.

32. Bonfield, "Conversations with Schlesinger," 33; Diane Johnson, "I, The Jury: Why This Novelist Can't Resist a Good Book Panel," *New York Times Book Review* (10 April 1994), 14; see also Ina Yalof's rebuttal, "Thinking is Required," *New York Times Book Review* (8 May 1994), 27.

34. Timothy Foote, "Battle Stars: Recollections of the Pacific War," *Washington Post Book World* (18 May 1986): 4–5.

35. Linda Shopes, "Developing a Critical Dialogue about Oral History: Some Notes Based on an Analysis of Book Reviews," *Oral History Review* 14 (1986): 9–25; see also Betty McKeever Key, "Publishing Oral History: Observations and Objections," *Oral History Review* 10 (1982): 145–52.

36. Ritchie, et al., "Interviews as Historical Evidence," 223–24.

37. Kate L. Turabian, *A Manual for Writers of Term Papers, Theses, and Dissertations*, 5th ed., revised and expanded by Bonnie Birtwistel Honigsblum (Chicago: University of Chicago Press, 1987), 196–197.

Chapter 5

1. Henry Glassie, *Passing the Time in Ballymenone: Culture and History of an Ulster County* (Philadelphia: University of Pennsylvania Press, 1982) 40; Richard Sweterlitsch, "Oral History and Myth-Making: Confessions of a Researcher Turned Producer," *Annual of the New England Oral History Association* 1 (1987–88): 10–17.

2. Pamela M. Henson and Terri A. Schorzman, "Videohistory: Focusing on the American Past," *Journal of American History* 78 (September 1991): 620; Joel Gardner, "Oral History and Video in Theory and Practice," *Oral History Review* 12 (1984): 105–11; Brad Jolly, *Videotaping Local History* (Nashville: American Association for State and Local History, 1982), 75–87.

3. See Thomas L. Charlton, "Videotaped Oral Histories: Problems and Prospects," *The American Archivist* 47 (Summer 1984): 228–36.

4. Gardner, "Oral History and Video," 108–9.

5. See "The Mirror with a Memory," in James West Davidson and Mark Hamilton Lytle, *After the Fact: The Art of Historical Detection* (New York: Alfred A. Knopf, 1982), 205–31.

6. L. Elizabeth Beattie, "Video: The Saving Face," *Oral History Association Newsletter* 25 (Winter 1992): 6.

7. W. Richard Whitaker, "Why Not Try Videotaping Oral History?" *Oral History Review* 9 (1981): 120.

8. Charlton, "Videotaped Oral Histories," 235.

9. Joseph Wilson, "The Afro-American Labor Leadership Oral/Video History Series," *Oral History Review* 14 (1986): 27–33.

10. Henson and Schorzman, "Videohistory," 620; Pamela Henson, "Excerpts from an Interview with John Schuchman," *OHMAR Newsletter* 8 (Fall 1990): 6–10.

11. Henson and Schorzman, "Videohistory," 623.

12. Jim Small, "A Visual Recording," *CRM Bulletin* [National Park Service] 13 (1990) 1, 4–5.

13. Henson and Schorzman, "Videohistory," 622; Beattie, "Video: The Saving Face," 6.

14. Jolly, *Videotaping Oral History*, 109–21; this section also draws from a video workshop conducted by the producer Brien Williams, OHMAR meeting, St. Mary's College, St. Mary's City, Md., April 1992.

15. John Shaw, "Public Access Television Opens New Era in Oral History," *MOHC* (Michigan Oral History Council) *Newsletter* (Winter 1989): 2, 7; the Alliance for Community Media is located at 666 Eleventh St., N.W., Washington, D.C. 20001.

16. See "Outline of Useful Information," in Terri A. Schorzman, ed., *A Practical Introduction to Videohistory: The Smithsonian Institution and Alfred P. Sloan Foundation Experiment* (Malabar, Fla.: Krieger, 1993), 176–81.

17. Whitaker, "Why Not Try Videotaping Oral History?" 115–24.

18. David H. Mould, "Composing Visual Images for the Oral History Interview," *International Journal of Oral History* 7 (November 1986): 198–205; Jolly, *Videotaping Local History*, 50–51.

19. Richard Campbell, "Don Hewitt's Durable Hour," *Columbia Journalism Review* (September-October 1993): 26.

20. Schorzman, *Practical Introduction to Videohistory*, 59–65, 210–15.

21. Charlton, "Videotaped Oral Histories," 234.

22. See John A. Neuenschwander, *Oral History and the Law*, rev. ed. (Albuquerque, N.M.: Oral History Association, 1993), 16–34; and Schorzman, *Practical Introduction to Videohistory*, 41–42, 206–8.

23. William W. Moss and Peter C. Mazikana, *Archives, Oral History, and Oral Tradition: A RAMP [Records and Archives Management Programme] Study* (Paris: UNESCO, 1986), 44; Jolly, *Videotaping Local History*, 19–37.

24. Hugh N. Ahmann, "Color Video Not Likely to Fade," *Oral History Association Newsletter* 18 (Summer 1984): 2.

25. William J. Staples, "Videotape Is Dead," *Industrial Photography* (March 1993): 14–15.

26. "The Film and Video Archive Project," *Oral History Recorder* (Newsletter of the Center for Oral History, University of Hawaii at Manoa) 6 (Spring 1989): 2–3, 8.

27. Henson and Schorzman, "Videohistory," 625.

28. E. John B. Allen, "A Sporting Chance: Oral History and Films," *Annual of the New England Oral History Association* 1 (1987–88): 23.

29. Dean Albertson, "Remembering Oral History's Beginnings," *Annual of the New England Oral History Association* 1 (1987–88): 7–8.

30. Michael Frisch, "Oral History, Documentary, and the Mystification of Power: A Critique of *Vietnam: A Television History*," in *A Shared Authority: Essays on the*

Craft and Meaning of Oral and Public History (Albany: State University of New York Press, 1990), 159–78.

31. Sweterlitsch, "Oral History and Myth-Making," 12; see also Brien Williams, "Recording Videohistory: A Perspective," in Schorzman, *Practical Introduction to Videohistory*, 138–54.

32. Daniel Schorr, *Clearing the Air* (New York: Berkeley Books, 1978), 18.

33. Sweterlitsch, "Oral History and Myth-Making," 15–16; Allen, "A Sporting Chance," 19–20.

34. Allen, "A Sporting Chance," 23–24; Robert Brent Toplin, "The Filmmaker as Historian," *American Historical Review* 93 (December 1988): 1219–27.

35. "The Rights and Responsibilities of Historians in Regard to Historical Films and Video," *Perspectives: American Historical Association Newsletter* 30 (September 1992): 15, 17.

36. Jolly, *Videotaping Local History*, 77.

37. Mary Rose Bosewell, [review of "The Boott Cotton Mills Museum"], *Oral History Review* 20 (Spring-Fall 1992): 88–89.

38. Whitaker, "Why Not Try Videotaping Oral History?" 123; Shaw, "Public Access Television," 7.

39. "Oral History and the Arts," plenary session, OHMAR conference, 18 April 1982, transcript, OHMAR Papers, Gallaudet University, Washington, D.C.

40. Lynn A. Bonfield, "Conversation with Arthur M. Schlesinger, Jr.: The Use of Oral History," *The American Archivist* 43 (Fall 1980): 471.

41. Beattie, "Video: The Saving Face," 6; Shaw, "Public Access Television," 7.

Chapter 6

1. Donald A. Ritchie, "A Sense of Collective Responsibility: An Interview with Ronald J. Grele, *OHMAR Newsletter* 16 (Fall 1993), 7; Elizabeth I. Dixon, et al., "Definitions of Oral History," *Oral History at Arrowhead: The Proceedings of the First National Colloquium on Oral History* (Los Angeles: Oral History Association, 1969), 5–7.

2. Barbara Tuchman, "Distinguishing the Significant from the Insignificant," in *Oral History: An Interdisciplinary Anthology*, ed. David K. Dunaway and Willa K. Baum (Nashville: American Association for State and Local History, 1984), 76.

3. Donald A. Ritchie, "Oral Histories May Help Scholars Plow through the Rapidly Accumulating Mass of Federal Paper," *Chronicle of Higher Education* (2 November 1988): A44.

4. James E. Fogerty, "Filling in the Gap: Oral History in the Archives," *The American Archivist* 46 (Spring 1983): 148–57.

5. Ibid., 151; see also Ronald L. Filippelli, "Oral History and the Archives," *The American Archivist* 39 (October 1976): 479–83.

6. Fogerty, "Filling in the Gap," 153–54; William W. Moss and Peter C. Mazi-kana, *Archives, Oral History, and Oral Tradition: A RAMP Study* (Paris: UNESCO, 1986), 4, 25–26, 29.

7. Ritchie, "A Sense of Collective Responsibility," 7.

8. John T. Mason, Jr., interviewed by Benis M. Frank, 16 July 1983, transcripts, Marine Corps Oral History Program, Marine Corps Historical Center, Washington, D.C.

9. Oral History Association, *Evaluation Guidelines* (Los Angeles: Oral History Association, 1992), 4–12.

10. Cary C. Wilkins, ed., *The Guide to Kentucky Oral History Collections* (Frankfort: Kentucky Oral History Commission, 1991); "California Legislature Creates State OH Program," *Oral History Association Newsletter* 20 (Fall 1986): 3.

11. The National Historical Publications and Records Commission has shied away from giving grants for oral histories, with a single exception: the commission concluded that oral traditions were so integral in Native American historical consciousness that efforts to preserve its documentation would be incomplete without oral sources.

12. Moss and Mazikana, *Archives, Oral History, and Oral Tradition*, 60. Federal copyright law stipulates that a transfer of ownership "is not valid unless an instrument of conveyance, or a note or memorandum of the transfer, is in writing and signed by the owner of the rights conveyed." See John A. Neuenschwander, *Oral History and the Law*, rev. ed. (Albuquerque, N.M.: Oral History Association, 1993), 18–19.

13. Ibid., 34–35, 48–49, 56; William W. Moss, *Oral History Program Manual* (New York: Praeger, 1974), 46–49, 64–68.

14. For archival finding aids, see Moss and Mazikana, *Archives, Oral History, and Oral Tradition*, 62–63; for library finding aids, see Cullom Davis, Kathryn Black, and Kay MacLean, *Oral History: From Tape to Type* (Chicago: American Library Association, 1977), 87–101.

15. Roy Rosenzweig, "Automating Your Oral History Program: A Guide to Data Base Management on a Microcomputer," *International Journal of Oral History* 5 (November 1984): 174–87.

16. William Schneider and Daniel Grahek, *Project Jukebox: Where Oral History and Technology Come Together* (Anchorage: Center for Information Technology, University of Anchorage, 1992), 1–8.

17. Cathryn A. Gallacher and Dale E. Treleven, "Developing an Online Database and Printed Directory and Subject Guide to Oral History Collections," *Oral History Review* 16 (Spring 1988): 33–68.

18. Bruce H. Bruemmer, "Access to Oral History: A National Agenda," *The American Archivist* 54 (Fall 1991): 494–501; James Fogerty, "Minnesota Receives Grant to Develop Oral History Cataloging Guidelines," *Oral History Association Newsletter* 27 (Winter 1993): 3.

19. Christopher Ann Paton, "Whispers in the Stacks: The Problem of Sound Recordings in Archives," *The American Archivist* 53 (Spring 1990): 274–80.

20. Louis Starr, letter to David Wallace, 16 February 1962, reprinted in *Oral History Association Newsletter* 24 (Spring 1990): 2.

21. Paton, "Whispers in the Stacks," 276–77; Moss and Mazikana, *Archives, Oral History, and Oral Tradition*, 43–45.

22. Larry I. Bland, ed., *George C. Marshall Interviews and Reminiscences for Forrest C. Pogue* (Lexington, Va.: George C. Marshall Research Foundation, 1991).

23. Stacey Roth, "The Care and Preservation of Sound Recordings," *Conservation Administration News* 23 (October 1985): 5.

24. Moss and Mazikana, *Archives, Oral History, and Oral Tradition*, 43–45; "Magnetic Tape Recording: Forever?" *3M Technical Bulletin* (St. Paul, Minn.: 3M Magnetic Media Division, 1984), 1–3.

25. David H. Mould, "Digital Archival Storage for Oral History," *International Journal of Oral History* 10 (February 1989): 59–63; Schneider and Grahek, *Project Jukebox*, 5; Frederick J. Stielow, "Archival Theory and the Preservation of Electronic Media: Opportunities and Standards below the Cutting Edge," *The American Archivist* 55 (Spring 1992): 332–43.

26. "Nate Shaw Tapes Damaged in Hurricane, Restored by UNC Southern Folklife Collection," *Oral History Association Newsletter* 24 (Fall 1990): 3; Theodore Rosengarten, *All God's Dangers: The Life of Nate Shaw* (New York: Alfred A. Knopf, 1974).

27. The best guide to tape indexing is Dale Treleven, *TAPE (Time Access to Pertinent Excerpts) System: A Method for Producing Oral History Interviews and Other Sound Recordings* (Madison: State Historical Society of Wisconsin, 1979); see also Dale E. Treleven, "Oral History, Audio Technology, and the TAPE System," *International Journal of Oral History* 2 (February 1981): 27–45.

28. Elizabeth P. Jacox, "Making an Oral History Collection Available to the Public," *Idaho Oral History Center Newsletter* 4 (Summer 1982): 3–4.

29. American Historical Association, "Statement on Interviewing for Historical Documentation," *Statement on Standards of Professional Conduct* (Washington, D.C.: American Historical Association, 1990), 25–27; see also "Statement on Interviewing for Historical Documentation," *Perspectives: The American Historical Association Newsletter* 27 (October 1989): 8.

30. David M. Oshinsky, "Oral History: Playing by the Rules," *Journal of American History* 77 (September 1990): 609–14; David M. Oshinsky, *A Conspiracy So Immense: The World of Joe McCarthy* (New York: Free Press, 1983).

31. Jon Wiener, "The Alger Hiss Case, the Archives, and Allen Weinstein," *Perspectives: Newsletter of the American Historical Association* 30 (February 1992): 12; David R. Smith, "Talking Pictures: Oral Histories at the Walt Disney Archives," *SAA* [Society of American Archivists] *Business Archives Newsletter* 10 (Winter 1993): 6; Donald A. Ritchie, "Interviewers and Archivists," *Society of American Archivists Newsletter* (July 1990): 13; Donald A. Ritchie, Holly Cowan Shulman, Richard S. Kirkendall, and Terry L. Birdwhistell, "Interviews as Historical Evidence: A Discussion of New Standards of Documentation and Access," *The History Teacher* 24 (February 1991): 234.

32. Ritchie, et al., "Interviews as Historical Evidence," 235–36.

33. Frederick J. Stielow, *The Management of Oral History Sound Archives* (Westport, Conn.: Greenwood Press, 1986), 36; Ritchie, "Interviewers and Archivists," 13; National Archives and Records Administration, "Procedures for Initiating Cooperative Oral History Projects," typescript report available from the National Archives and Records Administration, Washington, D.C. 20408.

34. "National Archives Adopts Oral History Plan," *The Federalist: Newsletter of the Society for History in the Federal Government* 8 (Fall 1987): 7–8.

35. Pamela Henson, "Smithsonian Leads the Way among Federal Agencies," *Oral History Association Newsletter* 13 (Winter 1979): 1, 6; Terri A. Schorzman, ed., *A Practical Introduction to Videohistory: The Smithsonian Institution and Alfred P. Sloan Foundation Experiment* (Malabar, Fla.: Krieger, 1993).

36. Neuenschwander, *Oral History and the Law*, 5–16.

37. Ibid., 5–7.

38. Ann E. Pederson and Gail Farr Casterline, *Archives and Manuscripts: Public Programs* (Chicago: Society of American Archivists, 1982), 8.

39. Joseph W. Palmer, *Oral History in Public Libraries* (Urbana: University of Illinois Graduate School of Library and Information Service, 1984), 8–9, 10.

40. Pederson and Casterline, *Archives and Manuscripts*, 9, 15, 23–24.

41. Willa K. Baum, "Building Community Identity through Oral History—A New Role for the Local Library," *California Librarian* (October 1970): 271–84.

Chapter 7

1. Richard P. Onderdonk, "Piaget and Oral History: Cognitive Development in the Secondary Studies Class," *Oral History Review* 11 (1983): 77.

2. John A. Neuenschwander, *Oral History as a Teaching Approach* (Washington, D.C.: National Education Association, 1976), 9; John A. Neuenschwander, "Oral History in the High School Classroom," *Oral History Review* 3 (1975): 61; Barry A. Lanman, "The Use of Oral History in the Classroom: A Comparative Analysis of the 1974 and 1987 Oral History Association Surveys," *Oral History Review* 17 (Spring 1989): 223–24.

3. Eliot Wigginton, *Sometimes a Shining Moment: The Foxfire Experience* (Garden City, N.Y.: Doubleday, 1985), 325–86.

4. June Jordan, "Nobody Mean More to Me than You and the Future Life of Willie Jordan," in *From the Hip: Documentary Team Guidebook* (Durham, N.C.: From the Hip, 1993), 14–15.

5. Eliot Wigginton, ed., *The Foxfire Book* (Garden City, N.Y.: Doubleday, 1972), 9–14.

6. Wigginton, *Sometimes a Shining Moment*, 329–30, 343–46, 352, 354; Thad Sitton, "The Descendants of *Foxfire*," *Oral History Review* 6 (1978): 20–35; see also the *Foxfire* series published by Doubleday since 1972.

7. During the 1970s Thad Sitton identified some 80 secondary school oral history magazines in 31 states, the District of Columbia, Guam, Samoa, the Virgin Islands, and the Dominican Republic. See Sitton, "Descendants of *Foxfire*," 20–35; George L. Mehaffy, "Foxfire Comes of Age," *Oral History Review* 13 (1985): 145–49; "Cultural Journalism Shares Oral History through Schoolchildren," *Oral History Association Newsletter* 20 (Summer 1986): 3; Pamela Wood, ed., *The Salt Book* (Garden City, N.Y.: Doubleday, 1977); Ellen G. Massey and Ruth E. Massey, eds., *Bittersweet County* (Garden City, N.Y.: Doubleday, 1978); and Jay MacLeod, et al., "Minds Stayed on Freedom: Movement Veterans Speak to Holmes County Youth," *Bloodlines* 2 (Spring 1990).

8. Barry A. Lanman and George L. Mehaffy, *Oral History in the Secondary School Classroom* (Los Angeles: Oral History Association, 1988); George L. Mehaffy, Thad Sitton, and O. L. Davis, Jr., *Oral History in the Classroom*, "How to Do It" series 2, no. 8 (Washington, D.C.: National Council for the Social Studies, 1979).

9. Lanman and Mehaffy, *Oral History in the Secondary School Classroom*, 11–12; Wigginton, *Foxfire Book*, 12.

10. William Cutler, et al., "Oral History as a Teaching Tool," *Oral History Review* 1 (1973): 38–43.

11. George Mehaffy, "Oral History in Elementary Classrooms," *Social Education* (September-October 1984): 470–73; Stephen Lehane and Richard Goldman, "Oral History: Research and Teaching Tool for Educators," *Elementary School Journal* 77 (January 1977): 173–81.

12. "Cultural Journalism," 3.

13. George Mehaffy and Thad Sitton, "Oral History: A Strategy That Works," *Social Education* 41 (May 1977): 378–82; Barbara A. Levy and Karen Marshall, "Kids Making History," *History News* (March-April 1990): 20.

14. Levy and Marshall, "Kids Making History," 18–20.

15. Lanman and Mehaffy, *Oral History in the Secondary School Classroom*, 1–6, 8; see also Donald A. Ritchie, "Teaching the Cold War through Oral History," *History Teacher* 8 (Winter 1994), 10–12.

16. Samuel Totten, "Using Oral Histories to Address Social Issues in the Social Studies Classroom," *Social Education* 53 (February 1989): 114.

17. Joel R. Gardner, "Using Oral History and Folklore in the Classroom," *New Jersey Folklore Society Review* (special issue) 11 (Spring-Fall 1990): 1–16; Cynthia Stokes Brown, *Like It Was: A Complete Guide to Writing Oral History* (New York: Teachers and Writers Collaborative, 1988), 31–47.

18. Lanman and Mehaffy, *Oral History in the Secondary School Classroom*, 14; Totten, "Using Oral Histories," 115.

19. Neuenschwander, *Oral History as a Teaching Approach*, 11–13.

20. Garrison Keillor, *Happy to Be Here* (New York: Atheneum, 1982), 194–95; Mehaffy, Sitton, and Davis, *Oral History in the Classroom*, 3; Thad Sitton, "Oral History: From Tape Recorder to Typewriter," *The Social Studies* 72 (May-June 1981): 122–23.

21. Interview with G. R. F. Key, *Earth Waves* 3 (1982): 6.

22. Gardner, "Using Oral History and Folklore."

23. Mehaffy and Sitton, "Oral History," 378–82; James West Davidson and Mark Hamilton Lytle offer a valuable case study in *After the Fact: The Art of Historical Detection* (New York: Alfred A. Knopf, 1982), 169–204.

24. Lehane and Goldman, "Oral History," 181; Onderdonk, "Piaget and Oral History," 77–85.

25. Peter N. Stearns, *Meaning over Memory: Recasting the Teaching of Culture and History* (Chapel Hill: University of North Carolina Press, 1993), 15, 63, 155–56, 170, 175–76.

26. Totten, "Using Oral Histories," 114–16, 125.

27. Barry A. Lanman, "Oral History as an Educational Tool for Teaching Immigration and Black History in American High Schools: Findings and Queries," *International Journal of Oral History* 8 (June 1987): 122–35.

28. Totten, "Using Oral Histories," 115.

29. Mehaffy, Sitton, and Davis, *Oral History in the Classroom*; Gardner, "Using Oral History and Folklore," 5.

30. Neuenschwander, *Oral History as a Teaching Approach*, 21.

31. George L. Mehaffy and Thad Sitton, "Oral History Tells Its Own Story: The Development of the Loblolly Project," *The Social Studies* 68 (November/December 1977): 231–35.

32. Neuenschwander, *Oral History as a Teaching Approach*, 9, 22.

33. Frank J. Fonsino, "Criteria for Evaluating Oral History Interviews," *The History Teacher* 2 (1980): 239–43.

34. Mehaffy, Sitton, and Davis, *Oral History in the Classroom*, 1; Willa K. Baum, "Looking at Oral History," *ERIC/CHESS* (Boulder, Colo.: September 1975), 2.

35. "Observations on National History Day," *OHMAR Newsletter* 8 (Fall 1984): 14–15.

36. McGregor McCance, "Learning History from its Source," *Greenville* (South Carolina) *News*, 13 June 1993.

37. The OHA award criteria are distributed each year to all judges at National History Day. See also Barry A. Lanman, "OHA Committee on Teaching Presents First Annual Oral History Award at National History Day," *Oral History Association Newsletter* 20 (Fall 1986), 2.

38. Lanman and Mehaffy, *Oral History in the Secondary School Classroom*, 19.

39. John Forrest and Elisabeth Jackson, "Get Real: Empowering the Student through Oral History," *Oral History Review* 18 (Spring 1990): 29–44.

40. James Hoopes, *Oral History: An Introduction for Students* (Chapel Hill: University of North Carolina Press, 1979), 49; Donald A. Ritchie, "A Sense of Collective Responsibility: An Interview with Ronald J. Grele," *OHMAR Newsletter* 16 (Fall 1993), 6–8.

41. Michael H. Ebner, "Students as Oral Historians," *The History Teacher* 9 (February 1976): 196–201.

42. Edward Ives, untitled subsection of Cutler, et al., "Oral History as a Teaching Tool," 45; see also Louisa Schell Hoberman, "The Immigrant Experience and Student-Centered Learning: An Oral History Video Project, *Perspectives* 32 (March 1994): 1, 13–16.

43. See Ebner, "Students as Oral Historians," 198. Much of the discussion of oral history on the college level is drawn from the course syllabi of Terry L. Birdwhistell at the University of Kentucky, Thomas L. Charlton at Baylor University, and Wendell Wray at the University of Pittsburgh.

44. Jean M. Humenz and Laurie Crumpacker, "Oral History in Teaching Women's Studies," *Oral History Review* 7 (1979): 53–69.

45. Mary Jo Deering, "Oral History and School Integration Research: A Case Study," *Oral History Review* 7 (1979): 27–41.

46. For example, see Dan Riordan, ed., *Reminiscences: An Anthology of Oral History* (Stout: University of Wisconsin at Stout, 1980); *As I Remember Fordham: Selections from the Sesquicentennial Oral History Project* (New York: Fordham University, 1991); and *Diamond Days: An Oral History of the University of Texas at El Paso* (El Paso: University of Texas at El Paso, 1991).

47. Beverly Blois, et al., *Northern Virginia Community College: An Oral History, 1965–1985* (Annandale, Va.: Northern Virginia Community College, 1987).

48. Charles T. Morrissey, "Oral History on Campus: Recording Changes in Higher Education," *Dartmouth College Library Bulletin* 11 (April 1971): 75–76.

49. John Rothstein, "Oral History: A Student's View," *Journal of the New England Association of Oral History* 2 (1988–89): 38–44.

50. Baum, "Looking at Oral History," 2.

Chapter 8

1. The public history uses of oral history are discussed in chapter 1. For the use of oral history in video documentaries, see chapter 5.

2. Laurie Mercier and Madeline Buckendorf, *Using Oral History in Community History Projects* (Los Angeles: Oral History Association, 1992), i.

3. Charles Hardy, "The Urban Archives' 'Discovering Community History Project,'" *Oral History Association Newsletter* 15 (Winter 1981): 4–5.

4. Thelma Russell, "The Humanities Belong to All of Us: A Voice from Public Housing," *Humanities* (Newsletter of the D.C. Community Humanities Council) 6 (Summer 1993): 1–2. "In Search of Common Ground Video to Premiere at Public Humanities Award Program," *Humanities* 6 (Fall 1993): 1, 3.

5. Knox Mellon, "Oral History, Public History, and Historic Preservation: California Birds of a Feather," *Oral History Review* 9 (1981): 85–95.

6. Dan K. Utley, "From the Ground Up: Oral History and Historical Archeol-

ogy," *Sound Historian: Journal of the Texas Oral History Association* 1 (Fall 1993): 18–28.

7. Hardy, " 'Discovering Community History Project,' " 4; Michelle Palmer, Marianne Esolen, Susan Rose, Andrea Fishman, and Jill Bartoli, " 'I Haven't Anything to Say': Reflections of Self and Community in Collecting Oral Histories," *International Annual of Oral History, 1990: Subjectivity and Multiculturalism in Oral History* (Westport, Conn.: Greenwood Press, 1992), 175.

8. Joe Doyle, "Community History in a Community That Doesn't Want It," *Public History: The Newsletter of New York University's Program in Public History* 1 (1984): 6–9.

9. Jerry Carrier, ed., "Goin' North: Tales of the Great Migration," *Philadelphia Inquirer*, 4 February 1985.

10. Mercier and Buckendorf, *Using Oral History*, 16–19, 30–31.

11. Laurie Mercier, Mary Murphy, Linda Peavy, Diane Sands, and Ursula Smith, *Molders and Shapers: Montana Women as Community Builders: An Oral History Sampler and Guide* (Helena: Montana Historical Society Office, 1987), 9–19.

12. George McDaniels, "Folklife Festivals: History as Entertainment and Education," in *Public History: An Introduction*, ed. Barbara J. Howe and Emory L. Kemp (Malabar, Fla.: Krieger, 1986), 277–91.

13. Fernando Columbus, *The Life of the Admiral Christopher Columbus* (New Brunswick, N.J.: Rutgers University Press, 1959), 10.

14. See Ellen Robinson Epstein and Rona Mendelsohn, *Record and Remember: Tracing Your Roots through Oral History* (New York: Monarch, 1978), 2, 16; Robert Bowden, "Recording Your Family Roots," *St. Petersburg Times*, 24 February 1985.

15. Linda Shopes, "Using Oral History for a Family History Project," in *Oral History: An Interdisciplinary Anthology*, ed. David K. Dunaway and Willa K. Baum (Nashville: American Association for State and Local History, 1984), 240, 245.

16. Corinne Azen Krause, *Grandmothers, Mothers, and Daughters: Oral Histories of Three Generations of Ethnic American Women* (Boston: Twayne, 1991). See also Tamara Hareven, "The Search for Generational Memory," in Dunaway and Baum, *Oral History*, 248–63.

17. William P. Fletcher, *Recording Your Family History: A Guide to Preserving Oral History with Videotape, Audiotape, Suggested Topics and Questions, Interview Techniques* (New York: Dodd, Mead, 1986); Shopes, "Using Oral History," 239.

18. Ingrid Winther Scobie, "Family and Community History through Oral History," *The Public Historian* 1 (Summer 1979): 38–39; Carl Ryant, "Oral History and the Family: A Tool for the Documentation and Interpretation of Family History," *Annual of the New England Oral History Association* 2 (1989–90): 30–37.

19. Henry Fairlie, review, *New Republic* 204 (28 March 1988): 20; Robert N. Butler, "The Life Review: An Interpretation of Reminiscence in the Aged," in *New Thoughts on Old Age*, ed. Robert Kastenbaum (New York: Springer, 1964), 265–80.

20. Patrick B. Mullen, *Listening to Old Voices: Folklore, Life Stories, and the*

Elderly (Urbana: University of Illinois Press, 1992), 7, 11; Henry Glassie, *Passing the Time in Ballymenone* (Philadelphia: University of Pennsylvania Press, 1982), 63.

21. Denise Flaim, "Oral History Preserves the Past for Future," *Kenosha* (Wisc.) *News*, 7 June 1993.

22. Tracy Kidder, *Old Friends* (Boston: Houghton Mifflin, 1993); Marie Arana-Ward, "Tracy Kidder," *Washington Post Book World* (5 September 1993): 10.

23. American Association of Retired People, *Reminiscence: Researching Back, Moving Forward* (Washington, D.C.: American Association of Retired People, 1990); "Oral History and the Elderly in Minnesota," *Oral History Association Newsletter* 24 (Winter 1991): 3.

24. Marat Moore, "Oral History: An Organizing Tool and a Healing Art for Labor Union Women," *Oral History Association Newsletter* 26 (Fall 1992): 1–2.

25. "Oral History Used to Enhance Care for AIDS Victims," *Oral History Association Newsletter* 24 (Fall 1993): 1.

26. " 'Voices' Preserving Minnesota History," *Oral History Association Newsletter* 21 (Fall 1987): 7.

27. James B. Lane, "Oral History and Industrial Heritage Museums," *Journal of American History* 80 (September 1993): 607–18; Emory L. Kemp, "A Perspective on Our Industrial Past through Industrial Archeology," in Howe and Kemp, *Public History*, 188.

28. Carol Dreyfus and Thomas Connors, "Oral History and American Advertising: How the 'Pepsi Generation' Came Alive," *International Journal of Oral History* 6 (November 1985): 191–97.

29. David Lance, *An Archive Approach to Oral History* (London: Imperial War Museum and International Association of Sound Archives, 1978), 55–57.

30. David Dunaway, "Radio and the Public Use of Oral History," in Dunaway and Baum, *Oral History*, 333, 336, 342.

31. "Black Workers' History Airing on Radio," *Oral History Association Newsletter* 19 (Spring 1985): 1.

32. Walter Liniger, "The Original Down Home Blues Show," *Oral History Association Newsletter* 22 (Spring 1988): 1–2.

33. Lance, *An Archive Approach to Oral History*, 53.

34. Dunaway, "Radio and the Public Use of Oral History," 337, 339.

35. Kathryn Nasstrom, "Performing *Like a Family*," *Oral History Association Newsletter* 23 (Spring 1989): 3.

36. "Urban Oral Histories Dramatized," *Oral History Association Newsletter* 15 (Summer 1981): 4.

37. Edward M. Miggins, "Communities of Memory," *Oral History Association Newsletter* 26 (Spring 1992): 1, 3.

38. Joe Kinner, "Computer Technology and Oral History," *OHMAR Newsletter* 15 (Summer 1992): 5.

39. Roy Rosenzweig, "Why Read a History Book on a Computer? Putting *Who Built America?* on CD-ROM," *History Microcomputer Review* (Fall 1993): 1–2, 6, 11; Thomas J. DeLoughry, "History Post-Print," *Chronicle of Higher Education* 40 (12 January 1994): A19–20; Roy Rosenzweig and Steve Brier, "Historians and Hypertext: Is It More Than Hype?" *Perspectives* 32 (March 1994): 3–6.

40. William Schneider and Daniel Grahek, *Project Jukebox: Where Oral History and Technology Come Together* (Anchorage: Center for Information Technology, University of Alaska Anchorage, 1992), 1–9; Gretchen L. Lake, "Project Jukebox: An Innovative Way to Access and Preserve Oral History Records," *Provenance* (forthcoming).

41. See Charles T. Morrissey, "The Santayana Watch," *Organization of American Historians Newsletter* 20 (February 1992): 8.

Bibliography

This selective bibliography deals with various aspects of oral history primarily in the United States. A worldwide bibliography would be voluminous given the steady increase in the diverse use and interpretation of oral history in Europe, Canada, Africa, South America, and Asia. Readers interested in non-U.S. sources can profitably consult Robert Perks, *Oral History: An Annotated Bibliography* (London: British Library, 1990). Although the following bibliography excludes journal articles, many citations to oral history articles can be found in the Notes and References. Readers should also consult *Oral History Review*, *Oral History Association Newsletter*, *International Annual of Oral History*, and the annual oral history section in the *Journal of American History*.

Oral History Bibliographies

Havlice, Patricia Pate. *Oral History: A Reference Guide and Annotated Bibliography.* Jefferson, N.C.: McFarland, 1985.

Perks, Robert. *Oral History: An Annotated Bibliography.* London: British Library, 1990.

Trask, David F., and Robert W. Pomeroy III, eds. *The Craft of Public History: An Annotated Select Bibliography.* Westport, Conn.: Greenwood Press, 1983.

Handbooks and Explanations of Methodology

Allen, Barbara, and William Lynwood Montell. *From Memory to History: Using Oral Sources in Local Historical Research.* Jackson: University Press of Mississippi, 1991.

Baum, Willa K. *Oral History for the Local Historical Society.* Nashville: American Association for State and Local History, 1987.

———. *Transcribing and Editing Oral History.* Nashville: American Association for State and Local History, 1977.

Bennett, James. *Oral History and Delinquency: The Rhetoric of Criminology*. Chicago: University of Chicago Press, 1981.

Butler, Robert N. *Why Survive? Being Old in America*. New York: Harper and Row, 1975.

Caudill, Orley B. *The Spoken Word: A Manual for Oral Historians*. Hattiesburg, Miss.: Caudill, 1975.

Charlton, Thomas L. *Oral History for Texans*. Austin: Texas Historical Commission, 1985.

Courtwight, David T., Herman Joseph, and Don Des Jarlais. *Addicts Who Survived: An Oral History of Narcotic Use in America, 1923–1965*. Knoxville: University of Tennessee Press, 1989.

Davis, Cullom, Kathryn Black, and Kay MacLean. *Oral History: From Tape to Type*. Chicago: American Library Association, 1977.

Deering, Mary Jo, and Barbara Pomeroy. *Transcribing without Tears: A Guide to Transcribing and Editing Oral History Interviews*. Washington, D.C.: George Washington University Library, 1976.

Dexter, Lewis Anthony. *Elite and Specialized Interviewing*. Evanston, Ill.: Northwestern University Press, 1970.

Dixon, Janice T., and Dora D. Flack. *Preserving Your Past: A Painless Guide to Writing Your Biography and Family History*. Garden City, N.Y.: Doubleday, 1977.

Dunaway, David K., and Willa K. Baum, eds. *Oral History: An Interdisciplinary Anthology*. Nashville: American Association for State and Local History, 1984.

Epstein, Ellen Robinson, and Rona Mendelsohn. *Record and Remember: Tracing Your Roots through Oral History*. New York: Monarch, 1978.

Everett, Stephen E. *Oral History: Techniques and Procedures*. Washington, D.C.: Center of Military History, 1992.

Fletcher, William P. *Recording Your Family History: A Guide to Preserving Oral History with Videotape, Audio Tape, Suggested Topics and Questions, Interview Techniques*. New York: Dodd, Mead, 1986.

Frisch, Michael. *A Shared Authority: Essays on the Craft and Meaning of Oral History and Public History*. Albany: State University of New York Press, 1990.

Gluck, Sherna Berger, and Daphne Patai, eds. *Women's Words: The Feminist Practice of Oral History*. New York: Routledge, 1991.

Grele, Ronald J., ed. *Envelopes of Sound: The Art of Oral History*. New York: Praeger, 1991.

Harris, Ramon I. *The Practice of Oral History: A Handbook*. Glen Rock, N.J.: Microfilming Corp. of America, 1975.

Henige, David. *Oral Historiography*. New York: Longman, 1982.

Hilton, Suzanne. *Who Do You Think You Are? Digging for Your Family Roots*. Philadelphia: Westminster Press, 1976.

Hoffman, Alice M., and Howard S. Hoffman. *Archives of Memory: A Soldier Recalls World War II*. Lexington: University Press of Kentucky, 1990.

Howe, Barbara J., and Emory L. Kemp, eds. *Public History: An Introduction*. Malabar, Fla.: Krieger, 1986.

Hubbard, Blair, Heather Huyck, and David Nathanson. *Collecting, Using, and Preserving Oral History in the National Park Service*. Harpers Ferry, W.V.: National Park Serivce, 1984.

Ives, Edward D. *An Oral Historian's Work* (videotape). Blue Hills Falls, Maine: Northeast Historic Film 1988.

———. *The Tape-Recorded Interview: A Manual for Field Workers in Folklore and Oral History*. Knoxville: University of Tennessee Press, 1980.

Jackson, Bruce. *Fieldwork*. Urbana: University of Illinois Press, 1987.

Jenkins, Sara. *Past Present: Recording Life Stories of Older People*. Washington, D.C.: National Council on Aging, 1978.

Kornbluh, Joyce M., Brady Mikusko, and Debra Bernhardt. *Working Womenroots: An Oral History Primer*. Ann Arbor, Mich.: Wayne State University, Institute of Labor and Industrial Relations, 1980.

Lance, David. *An Archive Approach to Oral History*. London: Imperial War Museum and International Association of Sound Archives, 1978.

Lichtman, Allen J. *Your Family History: How to Use Oral History, Family Archives, and Public Documents to Discover Your Heritage*. New York: Vintage, 1978.

McMahan, Eva M. *Elite Oral History Discourse: A Study of Cooperation and Coherence*. Tuscaloosa: University of Alabama Press, 1989.

McWilliams, Jerry. *The Preservation and Restoration of Sound Recordings*. Nashville: American Association for State and Local History, 1979.

Moss, William W. *Oral History Program Manual*. New York: Praeger, 1974.

Neuenschwander, John N. *Oral History and the Law*. Denton, Tex.: Oral History Association, 1985; rev. ed., Albuquerque, N.M.: Oral History Association, 1993.

Oral History Association. *Evaluation Guidelines*. Los Angeles: Oral History Association, 1992.

Portelli, Alessandro. *The Death of Luigi Trastulli and Other Stories: Form and Meaning in Oral History*. Albany: State University of New York Press, 1991.

Rosenbluth, Vera. *Keeping Family Stories Alive: A Creative Guide to Taping Family Life and Lore*. Point Roberts, Wash.: Hartley and Marks, 1990.

Schneider, William, and Daniel Grahek. *Project Jukebox: Where Oral History and Technology Come Together*. Anchorage: University of Alaska Anchorage, Center for Information Technology, 1992.

Stave, Bruce M. *The Making of Urban History: Historiography through Oral History*. Beverly Hills, Calif.: Sage Publications, 1977.

Stielow, Frederick J. *The Management of Oral History Sound Archives*. Westport, Conn.: Greenwood Press, 1986.

Stricklin, David, and Rebecca Sharpless, eds. *The Past Meets the Present: Essays on Oral History*. Lanham, Md.: University Press of America, 1988.

Thelin, David, ed. *Memory and American History*. Bloomington: Indiana University Press, 1990.

Thompson, Paul. *The Voice of the Past: Oral History*. New York: Oxford University Press, 1988.

Vansina, Jan. *Oral Tradition: A Study in Historical Methodology*. Chicago: Aldine, 1965.

Ward, Alan. *A Manual of Sound Archive Administration*. Brookfield, Vt.: Gower, 1990.

Whistler, Nancy. *Oral History Workshop Guide*. Denver: Denver Public Library, 1979.

Zimmerman, William. *How to Tape Instant Oral Biographies*. New York: Guanrionex Press, 1982.

Videotaping

Fletcher, William P. *Recording Your Family History: A Guide to Preserving Oral History with Videotape, Audio Tape, Suggested Topics and Questions, Interview Techniques*. New York: Dodd, Mead, 1986.

Fuller, Barry, et al. *Single-Camera Video Production*. Englewood Cliffs, N.J.: Prentice-Hall, 1982.

Jolly, Brad. *Videotaping Local History*. Nashville: American Association for State and Local History, 1982.

Schorzman, Terri A., ed. *A Practical Introduction to Videohistory: The Smithsonian Institution and Alfred P. Sloan Foundation Experiment*. Malabar, Fla.: Krieger, 1993.

Winston, Brian, and Julia Keydel. *Working with Video: A Comprehensive Guide to the World of Video Production*. London: Mobius International, 1986.

Oral History for Teachers and Students

Brown, Cynthia Stokes. *Like It Was: A Complete Guide to Writing Oral History*. New York: Teachers and Writers Collaborative, 1988.

Flynn, Robert. *When I Was Just Your Age*. Denton: University of North Texas Press, 1992.

Gardner, Joel R. "Using Oral History and Folklore in the Classroom." Special issue of *New Jersey Folklore Society Review* 11 (Spring-Fall 1990).

Hoopes, James. *Oral History: An Introduction for Students*. Chapel Hill: University of North Carolina Press, 1979.

Lanman, Barry A., and George L. Mehaffy. *Oral History in the Secondary School Classroom*. Los Angeles: Oral History Association, 1988.

Mehaffy, George L., Thad Sitton, and O. L. Davis, Jr. *Oral History in the Classroom.* "How to Do It" series 2, no. 8. Washington, D.C.: National Council for the Social Studies, 1979.

Neuenschwander, John A. *Oral History as a Teaching Approach.* Washington, D.C.: National Education Association, 1976.

Oxford, Rebecca. *Language Learning Strategies: Conversation Skills through Oral Histories.* New York: HarperCollins, 1989.

Sitton, Thad, George J. Mehaffy, and O. L. Davis, Jr. *Oral History for Teachers (and Others).* Austin: University of Texas Press, 1983.

Stone, Frank A. *Using Oral History in Educational Studies.* New York: I. N. Thut World Education Center, 1989.

Wigginton, Eliot. *Sometimes a Shining Moment: The Foxfire Experience.* Garden City, N.Y.: Doubleday, 1985.

Wood, Pamela. *You and Aunt Arie: A Guide to Cultural Journalism.* Washington, D.C.: IDEAS, 1975.

Oral History Collection Catalogs

Albert F. Simpson Historical Research Center. *USAF Oral History Catalog.* Washington, D.C.: Office of Air Force History, 1977.

Allen, Susan E., and Terry L. Birdwhistell. *The Frontier Nursing Service Oral History Project: An Annotated Guide.* Lexington: University of Kentucky, 1987.

Anderson, Terry H. *A Guide to the Oral History Collection of Texas A&M University.* College Station: Texas A&M University, 1988.

Archives of American Art. *The Card Catalog of the Oral History Collections of the Archives of American Art.* Wilmington, Del.: Scholarly Resources, 1984.

Barnard, Roy S. *Oral History.* Carlisle Barracks, Penn.: U.S. Army Military History Research Collection, 1976.

Bertrando, Betsy. *History Comes Alive: Catalog of Oral History Holdings in San Luis Obispo County.* San Luis Obispo, Calif.: San Luis Obispo Oral History Organization, 1980.

Bibliographical Center of the Institute of Contemporary Jewry. *Oral History of Contemporary Jewry: An Annotated Catalogue.* New York: Garland, 1990.

Bloom, Jonathan, and Paul Buhle, eds. *Guide to the Oral History of the American Left.* New York: New York University Libraries, 1984.

Borneman, Patricia. *Directory to Montana Oral History Resources.* Helena: Montana Oral History Association, 1985.

Brown, Jeffrey P., Andrew O. Wiget, and Colleen M. O'Neil, eds. *Oral History Collections Catalog for New Mexico.* Las Cruces: New Mexico State University, 1989.

Buckendorf, Madeline, and Elizabeth P. Jacox. *Directory of Oral History Resources in Idaho*. Boise: Idaho State Historical Society, 1982.

Catalogue of Memoirs of the William E. Wiener Oral History Library. New York: American Jewish Committee, 1978.

Champagne, Anthony, Cynthia Harrison, and Adam Land, eds. *A Directory of Oral History Interviews Related to the Federal Courts*. Washington, D.C.: Federal Judicial Center, 1992.

Chepesiuk, Ron, ed. *A Guide to the Manuscript and Oral History Collections in the Winthrop College Archives and Special Collections*. Rock Hill, S.C.: Winthrop College, 1978.

Collection Catalog of the Oral History Program. Reno: University of Nevada, 1987.

Cook, Patsy A. *Directory of Oral History Programs in the United States*. New York: Microfilming Corp. of America, 1982.

Ethnic Studies Oral History Project. *Catalog of the ESOHP Collection, 1976–1984*. Honolulu: University of Hawaii at Manoa, 1984.

Forrest C. Pogue Oral History Institute. *Voices from the Past: A Catalog of Oral History Interviews from the Land between the Lakes*. Murray, Ky.: Murray State University, 1982.

Frank, Benis M. *Marine Corps Oral History Collection Catalog*. Washington, D.C.: History and Museums Division, U.S. Marine Corps, 1989.

Goff, Lila Johnson, and James E. Fogerty, eds. *The Oral History Collections of the Minnesota Historical Society*. St. Paul: Minnesota Historical Society Press, 1984.

Heintze, James R. *Scholars' Guide to Washington, D.C. Audio Resources: Sound Recordings in the Arts, Humanities, and Social, Physical, and Life Sciences*. Washington, D.C.: Smithsonian Institute Press, 1985.

Hill, Ruth Edmonds, and Patricia Miller King, eds. *Guide to the Transcripts of the Black Women Oral History Project Sponsored by the Arthur and Elizabeth Schlesinger Library of the History of Women in America*. Westport, Conn.: Meckler, 1990.

Historical Materials in the Lyndon Baines Johnson Library. Austin, Tex.: Lyndon Baines Johnson Library, 1988.

Humphreys, Hubert. *Louisiana Oral History Collections: A Directory*. Shreveport: Louisiana State University at Shreveport, 1980.

Jacob, Kathryn Allamong, ed. *Guide to Research Collections of Former United States Senators, 1789–1982*. Washington, D.C.: Government Printing Office, 1983.

Jimenez, Rebecca Sharpless, Jane Frances Healey, and Harriet Hull Fadal. *Baylor University Institute for Oral History: A Guide to the Collection, 1970–1985*. Waco, Tex.: Baylor University, 1985.

Johnson, Coburn R., and Karen A. Hatcher, eds. *People Will Talk: Oral History Collection of the Mansfield Library, University of Montana*. Missoula: University of Montana, 1987.

Julin, Suzanne. *Index to the American Indian Research Project.* Pierre: South Dakota Oral History Center, 1979.

Kayanti, Vimala, ed. *The UCLA Oral History Program: Catalog of the Collection.* Los Angeles: University of California at Los Angeles, 1992.

Kendrick, Alice M., and Helen M. Knubel, eds. *The Oral History Collection of the American Lutheran Church, Association of Evangelical Lutheran Churches and Lutheran Church in America.* New York: Lutheran Council in the USA, 1987.

Key, Betty McKeever, and Larry E. Sullivan, eds. *Oral History in Maryland: A Directory.* Baltimore: Maryland Historical Society, 1981.

Lunt, C. Richard K., ed. *The Maine Folklife Index.* Orono: University of Maine, 1982.

Mason, Elizabeth B., and Louis M. Starr, eds. *The Oral History Collection of Columbia University.* New York: Oral History Research Office, 1979.

Meckler, Alan M., and Ruth McMullin, eds. *Oral History Collections.* New York: R. R. Bowker, 1975.

Miller, Cynthia Pease. *A Guide to Research Collections of Former Members of the United States House of Representatives, 1789–1987.* Washington, D.C.: Government Printing Office, 1988.

Nowicke, Carole Elizabeth, David K. Allison, and Peter S. Buchanan, eds. *Index of Oral Histories Relating to Naval Research and Development.* Bethesda, Md.: David W. Taylor Naval Ship Research and Development Center, 1985.

Oral History Collection of the Federation of Jewish Philanthropies. New York: Federation of Jewish Philanthropies, 1985.

Oral History Guide: A Bibliographic Listing of the Memoirs in the Micropublished Collections. Glen Rock, N.J.: Microfilming Corp. of America, 1976–83.

Palmer, Joseph W. *A Directory of Oral History and Audio Visual Local History Resources in Public Libraries of New York State.* Buffalo: State University of New York Buffalo, 1985.

———. *Oral History in Public Libraries.* Urbana: University of Illinois Graduate School of Library and Information Service, 1984.

Palmer, Michele. *Catalog of Interviews: Connecticut Workers and a Half Century of Technological Change, 1930–1980, Oral History Project.* Storrs: Center for Oral History at the University of Connecticut, 1983.

Riess, Suzanne B., and Willa K. Baum, eds. *Catalogue of the Regional Oral History Office, 1954–1979.* Berkeley: University of California at Berkeley, 1980.

Ringelheim, Joan Miriam. *A Catalogue of Audio and Video Recollections of Holocaust Testimony.* Westport, Conn.: Greenwood Press, 1992.

Rune, Ann. *Oral History Index: Washington State Oral/Aural History Program, 1974–1977.* Olympia: State of Washington, Division of Archives and Records Management, 1977.

Shumway, Gary L., ed. *Oral History in the United States: A Directory.* New York: Oral History Association, 1971.

Smith, Allen. *Directory of Oral History Collections.* Phoenix: Oryx, 1988.

Stephenson, Shirley E., ed. *Oral History Collection*. Fullerton: California State University at Fullerton, 1985.

Todd, Joe L., ed. *Native American Interviews*. Oklahoma City: Oklahoma Historical Society, 1987.

——, ed. *Catalogue of Oral Histories*. Oklahoma City: Oklahoma Historical Society, 1984.

University of North Texas, *Oral History Program 25th Anniversary Catalog: 1964–1989*. Denton: University of North Texas, 1990.

University of Vermont Library. *Folklore and Oral History Catalogue*. Burlington: University of Vermont, 1991.

Wasserman, Ellen S. *Oral History Index: An International Directory of Oral History Interviews*. Westport, Conn.: Meckler, 1990.

Whealan, Ronald E., ed. *Historical Materials in the John Fitzgerald Kennedy Library*. Boston: John Fitzgerald Kennedy Library, 1990.

Wilkins, Cary C., ed. *The Guide to Kentucky Oral History Collections*. Frankfort: Kentucky Oral History Commission, 1991.

Wrigley, Kathryn. *Directory of Illinois Oral History Resources*. Springfield: Sangamon State University, 1981.

Oral History in Family and Community Studies

Brown, Robert F. *The New Englanders*. Worcester, Mass.: Commonwealth Press, 1980.

Coles, Robert. *The Old Ones of New Mexico*. Albuquerque: University of New Mexico Press, 1973.

Egerton, John. *Generations: An American Family*. Lexington: University Press of Kentucky, 1983.

Ellison, Elaine Krasnow. *Voices from Marshall Street: Jewish Life in a Philadelphia Neighborhood, 1920–1960*. Philadelphia: Camino Books, 1993.

Fee, Elizabeth, Linda Shopes, and Linda Zeidman. *The Baltimore Book: New Views on Local History*. Philadelphia: Temple University Press, 1991.

Ginns, Patsy Moore. *Snowbird Gravy and Dishpan Pie: Mountain People Recall*. Chapel Hill: University of North Carolina Press, 1982.

Glassie, Henry H. *Passing the Time in Ballymenone: Culture and History of an Ulster Community*. Philadelphia: University of Pennsylvania Press, 1982.

Goldberg, Linda S., ed. *Here on This Hill: Conversations with Vermont Neighbors*. Middlebury: Vermont Folklife Center, 1991.

Green, Howard. *Family and Community Life*. Trenton: New Jersey Historical Commission, 1990.

Hall, Jacquelyn Dowd, James Leloudis, Robert Korstad, Mary Murphy, Lu Ann

Jones, and Christopher B. Daly. *Like a Family: The Making of a Southern Cotton Mill World*. Chapel Hill: University of North Carolina Press, 1987.

Hammer, Andrea, ed. *Praising the Bridge That Brought Me Over: One Hundred Years at Indian Head*. Indian Head, Md.: Charles County Community College, 1990.

Kisseloff, Jeff. *You Must Remember This: An Oral History of Manhattan from the 1890s to World War II*. New York: Schocken Books, 1989.

Kuhn, Cliff, Harlon E. Joye, and E. Bernard West. *Living Atlanta: An Oral History of the City, 1914–1948*. Athens: University of Georgia Press, 1990.

Mercier, Laurie, and Madeline Buckendorf. *Using Oral History in Community History Projects*. Los Angeles: Oral History Association, 1992.

Montell, William Lynwood. *Don't Go up Kettle Creek: Verbal Legacy of the Upper Cumberland*. Knoxville: University of Tennessee Press, 1983.

———. *The Saga of Coe Ridge: A Study in Oral History*. Knoxville: University of Tennessee Press, 1970.

Naske, Claus M. *Alaska Statehood: The Memory of the Battle and the Evaluation of the Present by Those Who Lived It: An Oral History of the Remaining Actors in the Alaska Statehood Movement*. Fairbanks: Alaska Statehood Commission, 1981.

Oblinger, Carl. *Interviewing the People of Pennsylvania: A Conceptual Guide to Oral History*. Harrisburg: Pennsylvania Historical and Museum Commission, 1978.

Sitton, Thad. *Texas High Sheriffs*. Austin: Texas Monthly Press, 1988.

Strickland, Ron., ed. *Whistlepunks and Geoducks: Oral Histories from the Pacific Northwest*. New York: Paragon House, 1990.

Warren, Mame. *Then Again . . . Annapolis, 1900–1965*. Annapolis, Md.: Time Exposures Ltd., 1990.

Wolcott, Reed. *Rose Hill*. New York: Harper and Row, 1976.

Ethnic Oral History

Benmayor, Rina. *Stories to Live By: Continuity and Change in Three Generations of Puerto Rican Women*. New York: City University of New York, 1987.

Cash, Joseph H., and Herbert T. Hoover. *To Be an Indian: An Oral History*. New York: Holt, Rinehart & Winston, 1971.

Cowan, Neil M. *Our Parents' Lives: The Americanization of Eastern European Jews*. New York: Basic Books, 1989.

Davis, Marilyn P. *Mexican Voices/American Dreams: An Oral History of Mexican Immigration to the United States*. New York: Holt, 1990.

Gillenkirk, Jeff. *Bitter Melon: Stories from the Last Rural Chinese Town in America*. Seattle: University of Washington Press, 1987.

Hansen, Arthur A., ed. *Japanese-American World War II Evacuation Oral History Project*. Westport, Conn.: Meckler, 1991.

Kann, Kenneth L. *Comrades and Chicken Farmers: The Story of a California Jewish Community*. Ithaca, N.Y.: Cornell University Press, 1993.

Lee, Joann Faung Jean. *Asian-Americans: Oral Histories of First- to Fourth-Generation Americans from China, the Philippines, Japan, India, the Pacific Islands, Vietnam, and Cambodia*. New York: W. W. Norton, 1992.

Leviatin, David. *Following the Trail: Jewish Working-Class Radicals in America*. New Haven, Conn.: Yale University Press, 1989.

Martin, Patricia P. *Images and Conversations: Mexican Americans Recall a Southwestern Past*. Tucson: University of Arizona Press, 1983.

McCunn, Ruthanne Lum. *Chinese-American Portraits: Personal Histories 1828–1988*. San Francisco: Chronicle Books, 1988.

Mormino, Gary R., and George E. Pozzetta. *The Immigrant World of Ybor City: Italians and Their Latin Neighbors in Tampa City, 1885–1985*. Urbana: University of Illinois Press, 1987.

Morrison, Joan, and Charlotte Fox Zabusky. *American Mosaic: The Immigrant Experience in the Words of Those Who Lived It*. New York: E. P. Dutton, 1980.

Namias, June. *First Generation: In the Words of Twentieth-Century American Immigrants*. Boston: Beacon Press, 1978.

Perdue, Theda, ed. *Nations Remembered: An Oral History of Five Civilized Tribes, 1865–1907*. Westport, Conn.: Greenwood Press, 1980.

Rothschild, Sylvia. *A Special Legacy: An Oral History of Soviet Jewish Emigrés in the United States*. New York: Simon and Schuster, 1985.

Stave, Bruce M., and John F. Sutherland, with Aldo Salerno. *From the Old Country: An Oral History of European Migration to America*. New York: Twayne, 1994.

Tamura, Linda. *The Hood River Issei: An Oral History of Japanese Settlers in Oregon's Hood River Valley*. Urbana: University of Illinois Press, 1993.

Vecoli, Rudolph, ed. *Voices from Ellis Island: An Oral History of American Immigration: A Project of the Statue of Liberty-Ellis Island Foundation*. Frederick, Md.: University Publications of America, 1990.

Wright, Giles, ed. *Looking Back: Eleven Life Histories*. Trenton: New Jersey Historical Commission, 1986.

African-American History and Oral History

Blauner, Bob, ed. *Black Lives, White Lives: Three Decades of Race Relations in America*. Berkeley: University of California Press, 1989.

Botkin, B. A., ed. *Lay My Burden Down: A Folk History of Slavery*. Chicago: University of Chicago Press, 1945.

Bullock, Paul, ed. *Watts: The Aftermath: An Inside View of the Ghetto, by the People of Watts*. New York: Grove Press, 1969.

Ellsworth, Scott. *Death in a Promised Land: The Tulsa Race Riot of 1921.* Baton Rouge: Louisiana State University Press, 1982.

Etter-Lewis, Gwendolyn. *My Soul Is My Own: Oral Narratives of African-American Women in the Professions.* New York: Routledge, 1993.

Fry, Gladys-Marie. *Night Riders in Black Folk History.* Knoxville: University of Tennessee Press, 1975.

Gwaltney, John Langston. *Drylongso: A Self-Portrait of Black America.* New York: New Press, 1993.

Hamburger, Robert. *Our Portion of Hell: Fayette County, Tennessee: An Oral History of the Struggle for Civil Rights.* New York: Link Books, 1973.

Hampton, Henry, Steve Fayer, and Sarah Flynn. *Voices of Freedom: An Oral History of the Civil Rights Movement from the 1950s through the 1980s.* New York: Bantam Books, 1990.

Hill, Ruth Edmonds, ed. *The Black Women Oral History Project: From the Arthur and Elizabeth Schlesinger Library on the History of Women in America.* 10 vols. Westport, Conn.: Meckler, 1991.

Holway, John. *Voices from the Great Black Baseball Leagues.* New York: Dodd, Mead, 1975.

Hurmence, Belinda, ed. *Before Freedom, When I Just Can Remember: Twenty-Seven Oral Histories of Former South Carolina Slaves.* Winston-Salem, N.C.: J. F. Blair, 1989.

Moon, Elaine Latzman. *Untold Tales, Unsung Heroes: An Oral History of Detroit's African-American Community, 1918–1967.* Detroit: Wayne State University Press, 1994.

Raines, Howell. *My Soul Is Rested: Movement Days in the Deep South Remembered.* New York: Putnam, 1977.

Rawick, George P., ed. *The American Slave: A Composite Autobiography.* 19 vols. of WPA interviews. Westport, Conn.: Greenwood Press, 1972–73.

Rogers, Kim Lacy. *Righteous Lives: Narratives of the New Orleans Civil Rights Movement.* New York: New York University Press, 1993.

Rosengarten, Theodore. *All God's Dangers: The Life of Nate Shaw.* New York: Alfred A. Knopf, 1974.

Terkel, Studs. *Race: How Blacks and Whites Think and Feel about the American Obsession.* New York: New Press, 1992.

Oral History and Women's Studies

Adelman, Marcy, ed. *Long Time Passing: Lives of Older Lesbians.* Boston: Alyson Press, 1986.

Alexander, Maxine, ed. *Speaking for Ourselves: Women of the South.* New York: Pantheon, 1984.

Casey, Kathleen. *I Answer with My Life: Life Histories of Women Teachers Working for Social Change.* New York: Routledge, 1993.

Coles, Robert, and Jane Hallowell Coles. *Women of Crisis: Lives of Struggle and Hope.* New York: Delacorte, 1978.

Ewen, Elizabeth. *Immigrant Women in the Land of Dollars: Life and Culture on the Lower East Side, 1890–1925.* New York: Monthly Review Press, 1985.

Gallagher, Dorothy. *Hannah's Daughters: Six Generations of an American Family, 1876–1976.* New York: Thomas Cromwell, 1976.

Glenn, Evelyn Nakano. *Issei, Nisei, War Bride: Three Generations of Japanese-American Women in Domestic Service.* Philadelphia: Temple University Press, 1986.

Gluck, Sherna B. *Rosie the Riveter Revisited: Women, the War, and Social Change.* Boston: Twayne, 1987.

———. *From Parlor to Prison: Five American Suffragists Talk about Their Lives: An Oral History.* New York: Vintage, 1976.

Gluck, Sherna Berger, and Daphne Patai, eds. *Women's Words: The Feminist Practice of Oral History.* New York: Routledge, 1991.

Hungry Wolf, Beverley. *The Ways of My Grandmothers.* New York: William Morrow, 1980.

Jones-Eddy, Julie. *Homesteading Women: An Oral History of Colorado, 1890–1950.* New York: Twayne, 1992.

Kahn, Kathy. *Hillbilly Women.* Garden City, N.Y.: Doubleday, 1973.

Kennedy, Elizabeth Lapovsky. *Boots of Leather, Slippers of Gold: The History of a Lesbian Community.* New York: Routledge, 1993.

Kramer, Sydelle, and Jenny Masur, eds. *Jewish Grandmothers.* Boston: Beacon Press, 1976.

Krause, Corinne Azen. *Grandmothers, Mothers, and Daughters: Oral Histories of Three Generations of Ethnic American Women.* Boston: Twayne, 1991.

Manning, Diane. *Hill Country Teacher: Oral Histories from the One-Room School and Beyond.* Boston: Twayne, 1990.

Mercier, Laurie, Mary Murphy, Linda Peavy, Diane Sands, and Ursula Smith. *Molders and Shapers: Montana Women as Community Builders: An Oral History Sampler and Guide.* Helena: Montana Historical Society Oral History Office, 1987.

Personal Narratives Group. *Interpreting Women's Lives: Feminist Theory and Personal Narratives.* Bloomington: Indiana University Press, 1989.

Rothschild, Mary Logan, and Pamela C. Hronek. *Doing What the Day Brought: An Oral History of Arizona Women.* Tucson: University of Arizona Press, 1992.

Smith, Anne. *Women Remember: An Oral History.* New York: Routledge, 1989.

Rousseau, Ann Marie. *Shopping Bag Ladies: Homeless Women Talk about Their Lives.* New York: Pilgrim Press, 1981.

Oral History of Workers

Brecher, Jeremy, Jerry Lombardi, and Jan Stackhouse. *Brass Valley: The Story of Working People's Lives and Struggles in an American Industrial Region.* Philadelphia: Temple University Press, 1982.

Dunar, Andrew J., and Dennis McBride. *Building Hoover Dam: An Oral History of the Great Depression.* New York: Twayne, 1993.

Erlich, Mark, and David Goldberg. *With Our Hands: The Story of Carpenters in Massachusetts.* Philadelphia: Temple University Press, 1986.

Evans, George Ewart. *Tools of Their Trade: An Oral History of Men at Work, c. 1900.* New York: Taplinger, 1970.

Friedlander, Peter. *The Emergence of a UAW Local, 1936–1939: A Study in Class and Culture.* Pittsburgh: University of Pittsburgh Press, 1975.

Hareven, Tamara K., and Randolph Langenbach. *Amoskeag: Life and Work in an American Factory City.* New York: Pantheon, 1978.

Kodama-Nishimoto, Michi, Warren S. Nishimoto, and Cynthia A. Oshiro. *Hanahana: An Oral History Anthology of Hawaii's Working People.* Honolulu: University of Hawaii at Manoa, 1984.

Korth, Philip A., and Margaret R. Beegle. *I Remember Like Today: The Auto-Lite Strike of 1934.* East Lansing: Michigan State University Press, 1988.

Lynd, Alice, and Staughton Lynd. *Rank and File: Personal Histories by Working-Class Organizers.* Boston: Beacon Press, 1973.

Maurer, Harry. *Not Working: An Oral History of the Unemployed.* New York: Holt, Rinehart and Winston, 1979.

Rogovin, Milton. *Portraits in Steel: Photographs by Milton Rogovin, Interviews by Michael Frisch.* Ithaca, N.Y.: Cornell University Press, 1993.

Rubin, Lillian Breslow. *Worlds of Pain: Life in the Working-Class Family.* New York: Basic Books, 1976.

Safier, Gwendolyn. *Contemporary American Leaders in Nursing: An Oral History.* New York: McGraw-Hill, 1977.

Santino, Jack. *Miles of Smiles, Years of Struggle: Stories of Black Pullman Porters.* Urbana: University of Illinois Press, 1989.

Terkel, Studs. *Working: People Talk about What They Do All Day and How They Feel about What They Do.* New York: Pantheon, 1974.

Oral History and the Professions

Abelove, Henry, Betsy Blackmar, Peter Dimock, and Jonathan Schneer, eds. *Visions of History: Interviews with E. P. Thompson, Eric Hobsbawm, Sheila Rowbotham, Linda Gordon, Natalie Zemon Davis, William Appleman Williams, Staughton Lynd, David Montgomery, Herbert Gutman, Vincent Harding, John Womack,*

C. L. R. James, and Mose Lewin by MARHO, the Radical Historians Organization. New York: Pantheon, 1983.

Baer, Michael A., Malcolm E. Jewell, and Lee Sigelman, eds. *Political Science in America: Oral Histories of a Discipline.* Lexington: University Press of Kentucky, 1991.

Benison, Saul. *Tom Rivers: Reflections on a Life in Medicine and Science: An Oral History Memoir.* Cambridge: MIT Press, 1967.

Braden, Maria. *She Said What? Interviews with Women Newspaper Columnists.* Lexington: University Press of Kentucky, 1993.

Brown, Kenneth A. *Inventors at Work: Interviews with 16 Notable American Inventors.* Redmond, Wash.: Tempus Books of Microsoft Press, 1988.

Cook, John W., and Heinrich Klotz. *Conversations with Architects.* New York: Praeger, 1973.

Garrity, John A. *Interpreting American History: Conversations with Historians.* 2 vols. New York: Macmillan, 1970.

Lightman, Alan, and Roberta Brawer. *Origins: The Life and Worlds of Modern Cosmologists.* Cambridge: Harvard University Press, 1990.

Lyle, Guy R. *The Librarian Speaking: Interviews with University Librarians.* Athens: University of Georgia Press, 1970.

Morantz, Regina, Cynthia Stodola Pomerleau, and Carol Hansen Fenichel. *In Her Own Words: Oral Histories of Women Physicians.* Westport, Conn.: Greenwood Press, 1982.

Oral Histories of Arts, Entertainment, and Sport

Balliett, Whitney. *American Musicians: 56 Portraits in Jazz.* New York: Oxford University Press, 1986.

Barkow, Al. *Gettin' to the Dance Floor: An Oral History of American Golf.* New York: Atheneum, 1986.

Cooper-Clark, Diana. *Interviews with Contemporary Novelists.* New York: St. Martin's Press, 1986.

Cummings, Paul. *Artists in Their Own Words: Interviews.* New York: St. Martin's Press, 1979.

Cunnningham, Kitty, and Michael Ballard. *Conversations with a Dancer.* New York: St. Martin's Press, 1980.

Dance, Helen Oakley. *Stormy Monday: The T-Bone Walker Story.* Baton Rouge: Louisiana State University Press, 1986.

Davis, Francis. *In the Moment: Jazz in the 1980s.* New York: Oxford University Press, 1986.

Dunaway, David King. *How Can I Keep from Singing? Pete Seeger.* New York: McGraw-Hill, 1981.

Gitler, Ira. *Swing to Bop: An Oral History of the Transition to Jazz in the 1940s*. New York: Oxford University Press, 1985.

Holway, John B. *Black Diamonds: Life in the Negro Leagues from the Men Who Lived It*. Westport, Conn.: Meckler, 1989.

Perlis, Vivian. *Charles Ives Remembered: An Oral History*. New Haven, Conn.: Yale University Press, 1974.

Ritter, Lawrence S. *The Glory of Their Times: The Story of the Early Days of Baseball, Told by the Men Who Played It*. New York: Macmillan, 1966.

Sarris, Andrew, ed. *Hollywood Voices: Interviews with Film Directors*. Indianapolis: Bobbs-Merrill, 1968.

Schafer, William J., and Richard B. Allen. *Brass Bands and New Orleans Jazz*. Baton Rouge: Louisiana State University Press, 1977.

Shaw, Arnold. *Honkers and Shouters: The Golden Years of Rhythm and Blues*. New York: Collier/Macmillan, 1978.

Smith, Joe. *Off the Record: An Oral History of Pop Music*. New York: Warner Books, 1988.

Steen, Mike. *Hollywood Speaks: An Oral History*. New York: G. P. Putnam's Sons, 1974.

Suid, Lawrence. *Guts and Glory: Great American War Movies*. Reading, Mass.: Addison-Wesley, 1978.

Oral Histories of the Great Depression

Appel, Benjamin. *The People Talk: American Voices from the Great Depression*. New York: Simon and Schuster, 1982.

Banks, Ann. *First-Person America*. New York: Alfred A. Knopf, 1980.

Couch, W. T., ed. *These Are Our Lives*. Chapel Hill: University of North Carolina Press, 1939.

Daniels, Roger, ed. *Eleanor Roosevelt: Oral Histories from the Collections of the Franklin D. Roosevelt Library*. New York: K. G. Saur, 1993.

Terkel, Studs. *Hard Times: An Oral History of the Great Depression*. New York: Pantheon, 1970.

Terrill, Tom E., and Jerrold D. Hirsch. *Such as Us: Southern Voices of the Thirties*. Chapel Hill: University of North Carolina Press, 1978.

Williams, T. Harry. *Huey Long*. New York: Alfred A. Knopf, 1969.

Oral Histories of the Second World War

Adams, Judith Porter. *Peacework: Oral Histories of Women Peace Activists*. Boston: Twayne, 1991.

Drez, Ronald J. *Voices of D-Day: The Story of the Allied Invasion, Told by Those Who Were There.* Baton Rouge: Louisiana State University Press, 1994.

Fox, Stephen. *The Unknown Internment: An Oral History of the Relocation of Italian-Americans during World War II.* Boston: Twayne, 1990.

Gerassi, John. *The Premature Antifascists: North American Volunteers in the Spanish Civil War, 1936–1939: An Oral History.* New York: Praeger, 1986.

Gluck, Sherna B. *Rosie the Riveter Revisited: Women, the War, and Social Change.* Boston: Twayne, 1987.

Hoffman, Alice M., and Howard S. Hoffman. *Archives of Memory: A Soldier Recalls World War II.* Lexington: University Press of Kentucky, 1990.

La Forte, Robert S., and Ronald E. Marcello. *Building the Death Railway: The Ordeal of American POWs in Burma, 1942–1945.* Wilmington, Del.: Scholarly Resources, 1993.

———. *Remembering Pearl Harbor: Eyewitness Accounts by U.S. Military Men and Women.* New York: Bantam, 1991.

Lanzmann, Claude. *Shoah: An Oral History of the Holocaust.* New York: Pantheon, 1985.

Lewin, Rhoda G., ed. *Witnesses to the Holocaust: An Oral History.* Boston: Twayne, 1990.

Mason, John T. *The Atlantic War Remembered: An Oral History Collection.* Annapolis, Md.: Naval Institute Press, 1990.

Motley, Mary Penick, ed. *The Invisible Soldier: The Experience of the Black Soldier, World War II.* Detroit: Wayne State University Press, 1975.

Onorato, Michael P. *Forgotten Heroes: Japan's Imprisonment of American Civilians in the Philippines, 1942–1945: An Oral History.* Westport, Conn.: Greenwood Press, 1990.

Satterfield, Archie. *The Home Front: An Oral History of the War Years in America, 1941–1945.* New York: Playboy Press, 1981.

Stannard, Richard M. *Infantry: An Oral History of a World War II American Infantry Battalion.* New York: Twayne, 1993.

Stillwell, Paul. *The Golden Thirteen: Recollections of the First Black Naval Officers.* Annapolis, Md.: Naval Institute Press, 1993.

Terkel, Studs. *"The Good War": An Oral History of World War Two.* New York: Pantheon, 1984.

Woolridge, E. T., ed. *Carrier Warfare in the Pacific: An Oral History Collection.* Washington, D.C.: Smithsonian Institution Press, 1993.

Oral Histories of the 1960s

Fraser, Ronald, et al. *1968: A Student Generation in Revolt: An International Oral History.* New York: Pantheon, 1988.

Joseph, Peter. *Good Times: An Oral History of America in the Nineteen Sixties.* New York: Charterhouse, 1973.

Kessler, Lauren. *After All These Years: Sixties Ideals in a Different World.* New York: Thunder's Mouth Press, 1990.

Makower, Joel. *Woodstock: The Oral History.* New York: Doubleday, 1989.

Morrison, Joan, and Robert K. Morrison. *From Camelot to Kent State: The Sixties Experience in the Words of Those Who Lived It.* New York: Times Books, 1987.

Strober, Gerald S., and Deborah Hart Strober, eds. *Let Us Begin Anew: An Oral History of the Kennedy Presidency.* New York: HarperCollins, 1993.

Terkel, Studs. *Division Street, America.* New York: Pantheon, 1967.

Oral Histories of the Vietnam War

Baker, Mark. *Nam: The Vietnam War in the Words of the Men and Women Who Fought There.* New York: William Morrow, 1981.

Gioglio, Gerald P. *Days of Decision: An Oral History of Conscientious Objectors in the Military during the Vietnam War.* Trenton, N.J.: Broken Rifle Press, 1988.

Lehrack, Otto J. *No Shining Armor: The Marines at War in Vietnam: An Oral History.* Lawrence: University Press of Kansas, 1992.

Marshall, Kathryn. *In the Combat Zone: An Oral History of American Women in Vietnam, 1966–1975.* Boston: Little, Brown, 1987.

Norman, Elizabeth M. *Women at War: The Story of Fifty Military Nurses Who Served in Vietnam.* Philadelphia: University of Pennsylvania Press, 1990.

Santoli, Al. *Leading the Way: How Vietnam Veterans Rebuilt the U.S. Military: An Oral History.* New York: Ballantine, 1993.

———. *Everything We Had: An Oral History of the Vietnam War by Thirty-Three American Soldiers Who Fought It.* New York: Random House, 1981.

Terry, Wallace. *Bloods: An Oral History of the Vietnam War by Black Veterans.* New York: Random House, 1984.

Tollefson, Jane W. *The Strength Not to Fight: An Oral History of Conscientious Objectors of the Vietnam War.* Boston: Little, Brown, 1993.

Walker, Keith. *A Piece of My Heart: The Stories of 26 American Women Who Served in Vietnam.* Nocato, Calif.: Presidio Press, 1986.

Willenson, Kim. *The Bad War: An Oral History of the Vietnam War.* New York: New American Library, 1987.

Index

The Author

As associate historian in the Senate Historical Office, Donald A. Ritchie conducts an oral history program with former Senate staff. A graduate of the City College of New York, he received his Ph.D. in history from the University of Maryland. He edits the Twayne Oral History Series and has spoken at many oral history conferences and workshops, from Florida to Alaska. His books include *James M. Landis: Dean of the Regulators* (1980), *Press Gallery: Congress and the Washington Correspondents* (1991), and a high school textbook, *History of a Free Nation* (1993). Active in various professional associations, he chaired the Organization of American Historians' committee on research and access to historical documentation, as well as the oral history committee that established the "Pioneers in Public History" interview series for *The Public Historian*. A past president of the Oral History Association and of Oral History in the Mid-Atlantic Region (OHMAR), he has also served on the council of the American Historical Association and the board of the Society for History in the Federal Government. In 1984 he received OHMAR's Forrest C. Pogue Award for significant contributions to the field of oral history.